DIDCOT ENGINEMAN

DIDCOT ENGINEMAN

BERNARD BARLOW

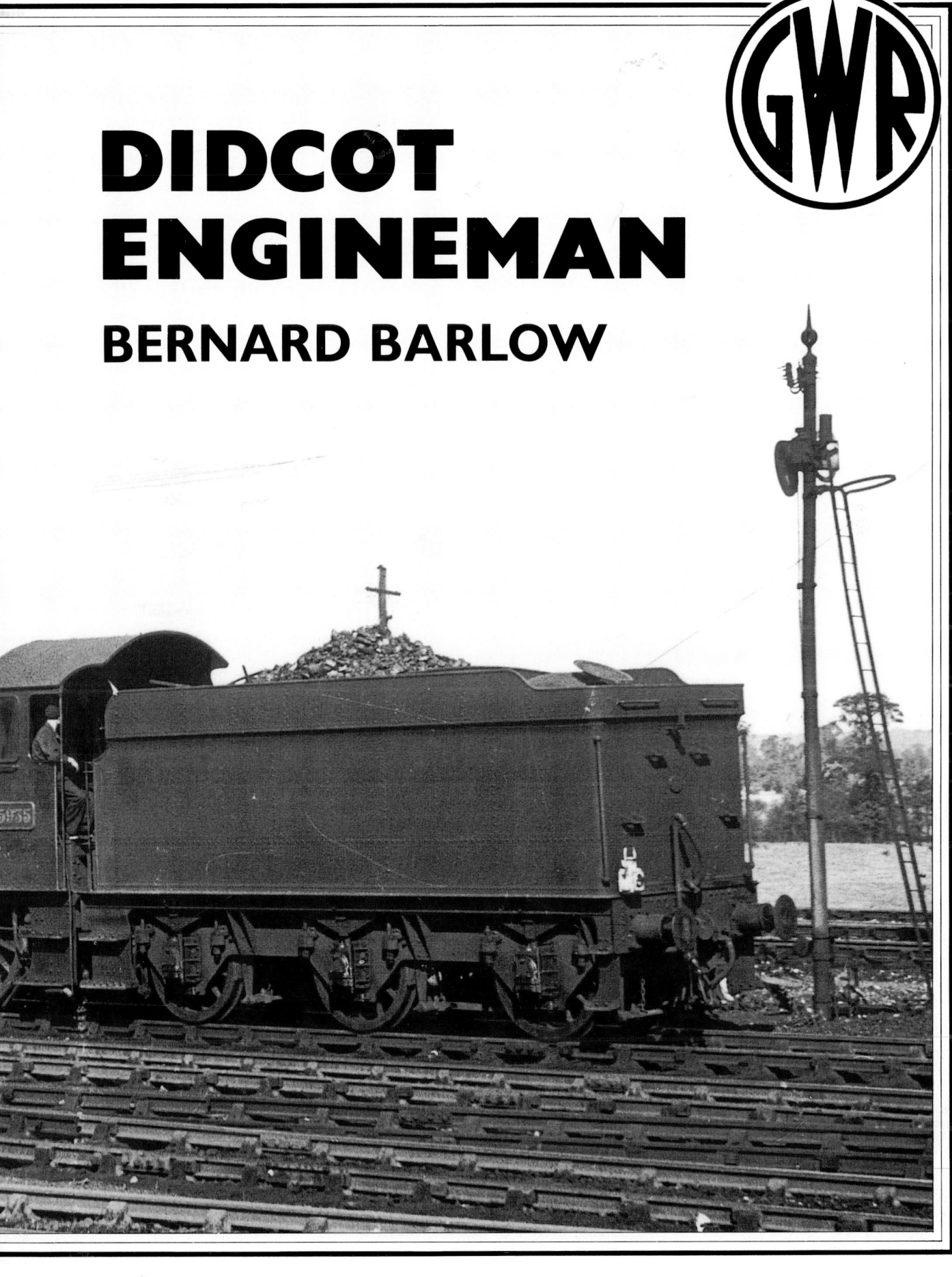

© Wild Swan Publications Ltd. and Bernard Barlow 1994
ISBN 1 874103 20 8

DEDICATION
I dedicate this book to my wife Winifred,
who spent many lonely hours while
I was on irregular shift work.

Half title page: No. 3841 leaving Moreton Cutting on an up freight, with No. 6984 speeding in the opposite direction at the head of a Class 'A' passenger train on the down relief in the early 1950s.
R. H. G. Simpson

Title page: No. 5935 *Norton Hall* waiting at the shed signal at Didcot on 12th October 1949.   *H. C. Casserley*

Designed by Paul Karau
Printed by Amadeus Press Ltd., Huddersfield

Published by
WILD SWAN PUBLICATIONS LTD.
1–3 Hagbourne Road, Didcot, Oxon. OX11 8DP

The boarded crossing in the middle of this view still leads from the subway to Didcot shed. We used it at the beginning and end of every duty. *National Railway Museum*

PREFACE

During my forty years on the railway, I never minded going to work. Despite booking on at any time throughout the day or night in all weather conditions, I always looked forward to my next turn of duty. I felt happy on the footplate, and working steam engines with other locomen bred a certain attitude, a closeness and loyalty to each other. The comradeship that developed among us played a big part in my life and has left me with many warm memories which I have drawn on to compile this book.

Although it is certainly not my intention to present a view through rose-coloured glasses, I don't mind admitting this is a 'fair wind' picture, but I hope it is no less truthful for that. I have not dwelt on the politics and unpleasantness we had to contend with, as raking up injustices after all these years would serve little purpose. We learned to live with it and some things are best forgotten.

What we got out of the life was largely down to our approach and outlook. I always regarded myself as a railway servant, an attitude which is rare today and only emphasises the passage of time. I was proud to be part of it all and derived enormous satisfaction from the teamwork in handling a steam engine, whether firing or driving, and the enginemen I admired and respected had similar attitudes and never complained.

In recording something of my life on the footplate, I hope that I have provided a useful record for future generations, but above all it is my sincere wish that this volume will serve as a small tribute to the dedicated service of all enginemen, loco fitters, signalmen, guards, shunters, shed labourers, etc, who kept the railway going under all conditions, but particularly through the difficult war years.

I have been conscious that memory can play tricks but, aided by other Didcot enginemen, I have done my best to present an accurate and reliable account. However, as so many years have since passed, I hope readers will forgive any errors.

Bernard Barlow

Father and Mother with my younger brothers, Douglas (left), Frederick (right), myself (behind) and Jill, the family pet, at the rear of 119 Wessex Road in 1936.

The east end of Wessex Road where many railwaymen resided. The horse and cart in the distance of this c.1936 view belonged to Krushon, the local fruit and vegetable merchant. *Cty. Donald Farmborough*

CONTENTS

Chapter 1 BOYHOOD DREAMS	1
Chapter 2 LAD PORTER	9
Chapter 3 OLD OAK COMMON	19
Chapter 4 DIDCOT SHED	39
Chapter 5 EARLY TURNS	55
Chapter 6 RAPID PROMOTIONS	65
Chapter 7 OVER THE BRANCH	127
Chapter 8 POSTWAR SERVICE	143
Chapter 9 THE MOMENT OF TRUTH	219
Chapter 10 FADING PRIDE	225
Appendices	
1 Track plan of Didcot station	240
2 Track plan of Didcot Ordnance Depot	246
3 Engine and Enginemen's Turns	249
4 Allocation of Locomotives — Didcot 1939-56	258

The Broadway, Didcot, in the early 1930s.

Collection Paul Karau

CHAPTER ONE

BOYHOOD DREAMS

AMONGST the many hundreds of boys in the 1930s who wanted to be an engine driver when they grew up, perhaps only a few ever realised their ambition. I was one of the fortunate ones.

The Barlows had been agricultural workers and shepherds on the Berkshire Downs, familiar figures at West Ilsley sheep fairs, where they would often test their skills in boxing tournaments to win money. The more sober-minded members of the family turned to lay-preaching at the local chapels.

My father, at the end of this line of rural workers, changed direction completely when he lied about his age and joined the Royal Navy in the First World War. After being demobbed, he joined the Great Western Railway to become an engine cleaner at Didcot, a decision which was to have a great bearing on my future.

I was born in Dorchester on Thames in 1922, brought into the world by my Granny Jerome, a qualified midwife for the area. Her son Dick became my favourite uncle and a great influence in my young life. He was one of a family of hurdle makers, and was usually to be found working across the river in the woodlands of Little Wittenham, a small, quiet village dominated by the ancient and famous Wittenham Clumps. When I was a small lad I remember both Father and Uncle Dick carrying me shoulder-high so that I could peer into the hawthorn hedges near Little Wittenham church, which in those days were full of nesting birds such as the greenfinch, bullfinch, linnet, thrush and blackbird. This fostered a lifelong interest in nature and wildlife.

During the school holidays, when I stayed with my grandmother, she gave Uncle Dick 1/6d to buy me a fishing rod in Wallingford. On a

This picture of 2943, passing through Didcot with a down express in April 1933, fills me with emotion. It shows the footpath on the right where, as a schoolboy, I spent many happy hours engine spotting. It was known as the cinder path – happy days! Later I discovered it was part of the official walking route from the loco shed and station to Foxhall Junction and the Ordnance Depot, but we seldom used it when relieving trains.   *Dr. Ian C. Allen*

lovely summer's day I went to Little Wittenham to try it out from the bridge by Day's Lock. I loved leaning over the bridge and looking into the water, mesmerised by the swirling water-weed and tiny insects, or dragonflies hovering by the water lilies. That day an elderly chap there took an interest when he spotted a fish, and using my new rod, he baited and hooked a large pike, but in its struggles to get away it broke the rod and left me with some awkward explaining to do!

We lived in a thatched cottage in St. Martin's Lane, not far from Bowditch's farm. At harvest time when threshing tackle was due, everyone was up and on the lookout by 6.00 a.m. The fear of fire was inbred into country folk and my Granny Jerome was only too aware of the risk of stray sparks landing on her roof while the traction engine chugged down the lane. I could only have been five or six years old, yet I can still remember standing outside the cottage on a chilly autumn morning before it was light, holding onto my grandmother's hand, while we waited for the procession to arrive. We could hear the chug of the exhaust long before it came in sight, then, when it drew closer, the rattle of the drawbars. As it passed, the ground vibrated whilst the huge wheels crushed the loose surface of the lane only inches from where I stood. I could feel the tremble through the soles of my feet. It was an unforgettable sight, with sparks floating down from the exhaust as the engine towed the threshing machine and elevator towards the farm, leaving behind it the smell of burning coal. I was hooked!

While we were in Dorchester, my two brothers were born, Frederick, four years younger than me, and Douglas, six years younger, both destined to share the family's involvement with the railway. My father was cycling seven miles each way between Dorchester and Didcot shed, and working long shifts. However, with three young sons, he became eligible for a council house, and promotion to a locomotive fireman put him in the wage bracket to be a reliable tenant of the Wallingford Rural District Council at 119 Wessex Road, Didcot. This became my home, only ten minutes walk to the station, and with my bedroom facing the railway.

As I lay in bed with the window open, I could hear the express trains approaching Didcot, a soft distant sound at first, which gradually

Looking south from the Broadway along St. Peter's Road to Wessex Road in 1931. My bedroom window at No. 119 is circled.
Packer's Studio, cty. Brian Lingham

Rymans Lane (opposite Didcot cinema) as it was in my boyhood. This was my route to Manor School. *Cty. Brian Lingham*

Five of the boys in this group, taken at Manor School c.1930, were destined for the footplate. They are: *Back row, 1st and 3rd from the left*, Gerald and Bill Warr (fireman and driver), *5th* Sam Essex (driver), *7th* Percy Talbot (driver), and *7th in the front row* myself.

increased as they approached the station, where the rhythmic sound of clashing metal resounded as the wheels crossed the junction pointwork. Their approach was often heralded by a long piercing shriek on the whistle or sometimes short sharp blasts or a 'pop-pop' to draw the signalman's attention. The sound of the racing train faded into the distance, then all was silent — until the next one.

My mind was filled with magical ideas of the far away places they were going to, and naturally it wasn't long before my thoughts turned to a career on the footplate.

I was sent to Manor School, and most nights, before going home, I would spend time watching the trains go by from the lineside path which led from Foxhall bridge down to the station. I didn't like being shut up indoors and spent as much time as possible outside. I used to go around with Charlie Wilcox, Phil Smart and Alfie Burton, and as a regular gang we spent much of our time playing in the copse (the Eastern Plantation), or

The top end of Foxhall Road.
Cty. Brian Lingham

Foxhall Road as it was when I raced from school to watch the 'Cheltenham Flyer' pass under Foxhall bridge. In later years, the double bend was straightened out.
Collection Donald Farmborough

The new Didcot Senior School science lab and science teacher, Mr. Worthy. The door on the left was being held open by the headmaster, Mr. Minhinnick, predictably nicknamed 'Minnie' by the pupils.
Cty. W. I. Robinson

in the GWR meadows where the company's horses were given holidays. From the stream there we used to catch sticklebacks, redthroats, crayfish and the occasional newt, but we weren't really allowed in the company meadows and my father always knew when we'd trespassed. "How did you know?", I'd ask, and he would reply "That doesn't matter, you are not to go there again." We also fished in the provender pond, or in the 'strips' beyond the sewage works where we would find plovers' and snipes' nests. We also used to cycle out to the Thames at Sutton Courtenay.

We were all interested in the railway and often watched what was going on. If we were near the line we could hear when a train was coming from the sounds of the track. In hot weather, when the joints closed up, the rails warbled and sometimes pinged as trains approached. We saw coaches slipped while playing in the station area and watched goods trains being banked off the West Curve when we were near Foxhall bridge. Alternatively, we might watch some shunting from the footpath alongside the down main. For a time, at least, the joys of fishing and bird-nesting gave way to the excitement of the railway world. As I became familiar with the various procedures, I could recognise the sounds of what was happening while I was laying in bed at night. Intermingled with the express trains was the noise of local shunting engines marshalling trains in the goods yard, sometimes with safety valves blowing, but always with the accompaniment of clashing buffers, from the duller clang of the first one of a rake, continuing up the scale to a higher pitched ping of the last one, like someone running fingers up the ivories of a piano keyboard. The sound of a goods train assisted by a banker off the West Curve towards Foxhall Junction was unmistakeable. The driver of the train engine gave a 'cock-a-doodle-do-do' ('crow' + 1) on the whistle when the signal came off and the banker in the rear replied 'cock-a-doodle-do, cock-a-doodle-do-do-do' (2 'crows' + 2). Then from my bedroom window I could hear the heaving blasts of exhaust as the two engines began to move the 700-800 tons of freight off the curve.

Only very rarely would we buy a penny platform ticket to sit and watch from the platform, and I was ten years old before I travelled by train, and that was to the Oxford Radcliffe Infirmary with the complications of a trapped nerve which resulted from a broken arm set on the kitchen table.

When I was eleven, I went to the new Didcot Senior School, which later became Didcot Girls School. Educationally, I was a late developer, floating in the intermediate stream. Although I wasn't much good at maths, I enjoyed school and liked natural history and English, though my favourite subjects were sport and gardening. The school was very strict and I remember my form master sending me off to the head, who gave me the cane for getting my cash sums wrong. I got them right afterwards! On another occasion,

BERKSHIRE EDUCATION COMMITTEE.

DIDCOT SENIOR SCHOOL.

SCHOOL REPORT.

For School Year ending Summer 1935.

Name of Pupil **Bernard Barlow** Age 13.3 Average Age of Form 13.1
Form 2B No. of Pupils in Form 40 Position 1

Subject.	Max. Marks 100.	Observations.
English—Composition	87	Good. DR
„ Grammar, Literature, Poetry	61	Good. RC. Keen and intelligent. OhT
„ Vocabulary, Dictation, Penmanship	64	
Arithmetic—Mental	72	Good. DR
„ Mechanical (Rules)		
„ Reasoning (Problems)	35	Works hard. RC.
History	64	
Geography	75	V.Good. CMA
Music and Singing	39	Fairly good. S.M.A.
French		
General Knowledge		Very pleasing results. OhT
Science: for—Physics, Hygiene, Biology (Boys) [38, 24, 21]	83	Good. J.K.L.
Domestic Science: for—Hygiene, Biology (Girls)		
Art and Mechanical Drawing (Boys) [42, 30]	72	Good work; very fussy
Art and Handwork (Girls)		
Woodwork (Boys)	70	Quite satisfactory. H.S.M.
Needlework (Girls)		
Commercial—Shorthand, Book-keeping		
Total Marks	722	Maximum 1100
Average %	65·6	

Conduct: Not readily amenable to Discipline.   Attendance: Perfect.

General Remarks:— Has done good work and deserves his advance in Form. He must exercise greater self-discipline, so that constant supervision is not necessary.   W.R. Dev Robinson. Form Master

He has done well to get the 1st position: Well done. But we should be much happier about him if his conduct report was better: he requires too much supervision for behaviour.   K.B.Richards. Headmaster

The interest and sympathy of Parents is welcomed in all matters appertaining to the education of their children.
The Headmaster is particularly anxious to confer with parents of School-leavers with reference to employment.
This Report should be retained for purposes of reference, especially for School-leavers.

as a punishment, I was given a bent table fork and had to dig up 200 daisy roots from the quadrangle lawn, where I was on exhibition to all the other children. If we were caught running in the corridor, we had to stand outside the headmaster's door and wait to be caned. The headmaster, who incidentally came from Exeter, was a good man and a bit of a psychologist. He could certainly instill discipline and respect, and I can still see him testing the flex of the cane before using it.

At 4 o'clock each afternoon, I rushed out of school and made straight for Foxhall bridge to

Didcot Senior School, seen from the entrance in Glyn Avenue.

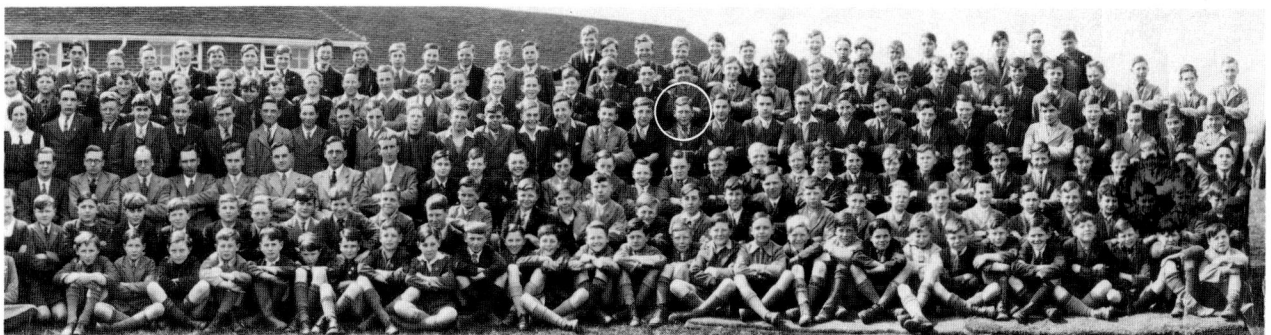
I am circled in this group of pupils at Didcot Senior School in 1936, the year I left.

I also feature in this view of Mr. Holman's woodwork class.

A gardening class.

One of the open corridors on the edge of the quadrangle.

Photos cty. W. I. Robinson

I was 11 years old when this picture of the 'Cheltenham Flyer' was taken speeding through Didcot at 4.15 p.m. one afternoon in April 1933. I might even have been standing on Foxhall bridge, which can just be seen in the background. The 28XX on the down relief was probably only moving slowly towards Foxhall Junction, where it would have been switched across to the down main after the 'Flyer' had gone.
Dr. Ian Allen

wait for the 'Cheltenham Flyer' to pass by. As I leaned over the bridge, my ambition to become an engine driver intensified as the great train drew nearer. All the signals came off at precisely 4.15 p.m. Back along the line, in the distance, there was the first hint of steam, then the rumble, a metallic sound as though the rails were singing, and at last she came into view, finally engulfing me in her acrid smoke as she thundered under the bridge.

When I was thirteen, Rector Wills offered me a part-time job carrying out various daily chores. There were twenty-four pairs of shoes to clean and polish, chickens to feed and eggs to collect, wood to chop for the fire, and I always had to make sure there was a clean bucket of water for the closet in the garden. The Rector's shoes had to be particularly clean, as his soles could be seen while he was praying. I worked from 7.00 till 8.00 in the morning and another hour after school each day for six shillings a week, 4/6d of which I gave to my mother.

When I left school in 1936, the Rector offered me ten shillings a week to continue with him, but I fancied a change and got an errand boy's job with Calaghan's fish and chip shop while waiting for a position on the railway.

CHAPTER TWO
LAD PORTER

A number of other boys from my school joined the railway to become porters, signalmen, fitters, etc., some of us being given preference if our fathers were already employed by the Great Western. This 'father and son' tradition was a benefit to the railway company, as young boys, like myself, were not completely raw recruits, but already had some basic idea of the work and discipline involved, together with a great desire to learn the trade as thoroughly as possible. This all helped to produce the right sort of employee.

There were, of course, inter-family jealousies and rivalries which sometimes resulted in unexpected transfers to other depots, or promotion being a little slow! But in spite of this, most youngsters were given tremendous support by the older professionals, who were only too glad to help by imparting some of their hard-won knowledge.

My father never encouraged me towards the footplate and even though my friend Charlie Wilcox joined the Great Western as a cleaner, I was told that I'd be better off in the traffic department. In September 1936 I became a lad-porter at Oxford station, my first taste of the responsibilities of being a full-time 'working man' beginning at about 3.30 a.m. one Monday morning! My mother had great difficulty in waking me up – I had never been expected to get up quite so early before, and a few years later she had even greater difficulty with my younger brother Frederick when he joined the railway. Mother would stand over him until he dressed before she left the bedroom, but as soon as she

Oxford station up side forecourt as I knew it. In the early mornings we queued along the side of the building, from approximately the car on the left to the Camp Coffee advert (near the 'Way In'). We took passengers' luggage from cars and taxis onto the platform, and attracted by the tips, even some guards joined us. This picture was taken in October 1935. *National Railway Museum*

9

Oxford station, looking north in 1925. The small wooden hut on the right, at the south end of the main buildings, was the porters room where I stayed between arriving off the paper train at 5.00 a.m. and starting work at 6.00 a.m. All the enamel adverts were taken down when the station was repainted in 1926, but otherwise the scene was unchanged in my time.

R. Greiffenhagen, cty. Brian Wright

had gone, he would fall back into bed again, complete with clothes!

After a quick breakfast, but still half asleep, I dawdled to Didcot station at 4.15 a.m., in plenty of time to catch the 4.40 newspaper train to Oxford, where I was due to start my duties at 6.00 a.m.

I soon settled into the routine and found that with an hour to wait at Oxford before I began work, there was the opportunity of having a cat-nap in the somewhat dingy porters cabin at the end of the up platform. In later years, the ability to relax anywhere and have naps like those was to prove a great advantage in relieving stress and tiredness.

At 6.00 a.m. Oxford station suddenly awoke, with parcels traffic to handle and the steady arrival of passengers for London. The busiest periods, however, were the beginning and end of term, when students swelled the number of passengers.

I recall the ritual of 'kwilling' (queueing) when all the porters stood outside the station, waiting for the arrival of taxis or private cars with luggage to be carried on to the waiting train.

One morning, I was edging my way up the line of porters, gradually moving towards the head of the queue as each took a client. A senior porter, who was stirring up trouble, urged me to jump the queue, and, like an innocent lamb, I stepped out to open the door of a taxi out of turn. Carrying his luggage, I led the passenger to a first class corner seat, back to the engine, then held out my hand and received a half-crown tip. Feeling rich and successful, I pocketed the money and raced back to the queue, but my triumph was shortlived. Much to my surprise, I suddenly felt a thump around both ears from the senior porter whose place in the queue I had stolen. I was told to hand over my half-crown, as it was considered part of a porter's wages! It was a hard lesson, but it taught me something of the discipline that was to last throughout my railway career.

However, there was always a chance to make up my 'losses' when the next train arrived. With passengers beckoning for a porter, there was

A closer view of the entrance to the booking office where I queued as a lad porter. *National Railway Museum*

The up side buildings and platform at Oxford in 1935. *National Railway Museum*

The down side buildings. *National Railway Museum*

usually a collective rush to the first-class compartments where all the wealthy travellers would be found. Here, tips varied from a few pence to a ten shilling note, but sixpence was the usual amount I received, and it was not long before the sum of the tips equalled a weekly wage, which was about ten shillings. Some porters at the larger stations made even double their wages in tips, but something about this system niggled me in later life, when I compared it with the 'wages only' lot of the enginemen.

In February 1937 I was transferred to Pangbourne, where I continued to serve as a lad porter for a few more months. It was here that I first enjoyed the friendly manner in which the older railwaymen cared for a young lad, sparkling with enthusiasm. Although I was very self-assured, I needed guidance from a more experienced steady person.

I worked in the parcels office with senior lad porter Harold Pearman and porter Freddie Day, and helped goods porter Harry Smith loading and sheeting wagons in the goods yard. My other duties included cleaning the lavatories, sweeping the platform, cleaning and lighting the gas lamps and collecting tickets. Of course I didn't know who anyone was when I first got there, and when I challenged one gentleman for a ticket he produced a director's medallion!

To fit in with the timetable, I had a lunch break of an hour and three-quarters, which I spent inside Pangbourne signal box, where I got to know the signalmen through delivering train notes and correspondence.

We had to walk alongside the down main line to reach this nerve centre which nestled in the chalk cutting. As I negotiated the long flight of steps to the box, I could hear cow-bells ringing, levers being clamped into the frame and the noise of the telephone. Above all this was the sound of cheerful whistling. When I opened the door, there was Edgar Wheeler, a duster over his shoulder, gazing out of the window at the panorama of lines, awaiting the appearance of an up express train which was soon to appear around the slight curve in the cutting. His smile, almost hidden under his moustache, and the friendly greeting he gave me, said it all.

It was a colourful scene with red, blue, yellow, black and white levers and shining brass block instruments; even the linoleum on the floor was highly polished, and the iron stove glistened with its coating of black lead. The oil lamps hung down from the ceiling like those seen in the

EDGAR WHEELER

Pangbourne signal box features in the distance of this view, showing how handsome and dignified the station used to be. I used to clean the glasses of the gas lamps and light them with a long lamplighter's torch. *L & GRP*

Didcot Telegraph Office was on the west end of the up main/down relief platform, on the left of this picture looking towards London in 1935. Like the rest of the station, it was a wooden building, but during the war years it was bricked along each side as an air raid precaution.
Collection Donald Farmborough

saloon bar of a Western film — in fact everything glistened.

I soon learned that each bell had a different tone, so that the signalmen would know on which track the train was approaching. When all the bells were sounding it made no musical sense to me, but it certainly did to Edgar. To my delight, he would sit on the window-ledge and tell me which bell to answer and which lever to pull, how to accept a train when the 'call attention' bell rang, and the correct order in which to pull the levers. I soon learned how to work the box, but always under his guidance.

I recall that when the electrically operated signals came in, some signalmen injured themselves when they forgot that the levers no longer required a powerful lunge to move them. This problem was overcome by reducing the height of the levers concerned so that only one hand was necessary to operate them.

Edgar was another railway personality who left a great impression on my fertile mind. As my skills grew, my personality was also maturing under men such as him.

My next transfer was to the Didcot Telegraph Office as a telegraphist messenger in the summer of 1937. The Chief Clerk, Jack Griffin, was a

Bernard Barlow at 16 years old.

very amiable man, and the other clerks, Peter Arnold and Jimmy Jeremy, were very good to me, perhaps because I could write legibly and spell quite well!

There was a strict routine which had to be carried out every day and this included the morning time-check from Greenwich. At 11 o'clock, when all staff at the depots were on duty, all watches and clocks had to be synchronised. One dash, two dots, two dashes and one dot — the morse message 'TIME' — came over the telegraph.

'Be brief', we were always told, and in many cases this involved set code words for certain railway procedures. Very important train messages were 'TAS's and 'MT's giving the departure time of a train, followed by a 'G' for 'Go', whilst vehicles on the rear of a passenger train from a particular station would be preceded by the word 'COW'. When vehicles were conveyed at the front of a train, the code was 'CLOTH' followed by its time of departure from Didcot. Accuracy and concentration were vital, and I found this work very rewarding.

The important item of equipment we used in the Telegraph Office in those days was the 'needle'. Two half-inch bone pins in a hanging position protruded from a metal drum. A needle was attached to the centre which had little wings, possibly made of paper. When the handle underneath was operated, the electric contact caused the needle to tip to one side or the other of the two pins, making the 'dot' or 'dash'.

Another vital instrument was the 'sounder' or Morse code key, housed in a small hooded box connected to several stations. The keys were marked 'PT' for Paddington, 'RG' for Reading, 'DD' for Didcot, and 'SW' for Swindon.

It was during my time in the Telegraph Office that I became interested in a transfer to the Locomotive Department as most of my mates had been successful in being accepted as engine cleaners, with the prospect of a career on the footplate. They used to rib me about having a nice clean messenger's job and wanted to know why I didn't join the ranks of real men.

Working on Didcot station, I was closer to steam, some of the engines stopping on the down relief right opposite the office. One of my duties was to scrub the office floor, so I often approached the crews for a bucket of hot water from their coal watering pipe. They were a friendly lot and often invited me on the footplate.

By this time, my boyhood interest in steam engines was becoming stronger, and I could see that the image of the loco crews was far more masculine than office work. The activity on the footplate also looked compatible with my restless nature and it was an outside job. I had 'ants in my pants' and needed action, I could not be caged in, and, besides, the wages were higher.

In response to my application for a transfer to the Locomotive Department, I was offered a vacancy at Old Oak Common — the only depot accepting recruits at the time — and found myself faced with the first ordeal at the Great Western HQ at Park House, Swindon, where I attended a medical for acceptance on the footplate. I was anxious and fearful. Perhaps they would find something wrong with me, or I would fail the oral tests. There was a half-mile to walk to the dingy three-storey Victorian building, and on top of that, it was a cold, grey winter's morning. By the time I reached the front door, the half-mile felt like ten.

My first test was for 'distant vision' in a long room, then I had to pick out certain colours of wool in a box of mixed skeins. So far, so good. My vision was 20/20. I was also able to answer questions from the Black (Rule) Book, and take down some simple dictation, but worse was to come.

"Strip to the waist and take off your shoes."
"Open wide — let me check your teeth . . ."
"Show me your hands . . ."
"Now for your ears. Can you hear me, boy?"

With hardly a pause in between, I had to say 'A-aah" with a cold spoon on my tongue, and then came the command "Drop your trousers, hurry boy, hurry . . . " There was no time to feel nervous as I turned around, bent down and touched my toes, legs wide open, and had the necessary checks for hernia, varicose veins and flat feet!

Next I was told to cross my legs, and when he rapped my knee, the reflex almost hit the examiner in the face. He was obviously satisfied, and to my relief seemed to be human at last, when he said to me in a new and kindly voice, "That wasn't too bad, was it, my son?"

He never did say the magic word 'Pass', but merely gave me a note for the Administrator at Headquarters. I was now passed fit and ready to join an elite band of locomen. The rest was up to me.

CHAPTER THREE

OLD OAK COMMON

ON a cold wet Monday morning in February 1938 I walked out of Ladbrook Grove station, to be greeted by Vic Hughes, my landlord, who was standing outside the station entrance. He soon recognised me, a fresh-faced country boy, with a heavy suitcase. We had never met, but my father had asked him to take me in, and, although we were two complete strangers, we seemed to have something in common. I can only guess that it was being of a railway family. Anyway, he greeted me by taking my case onto his shoulder and saying, with a rich London accent, "You must be Bernard Barlow". From the very beginning he made me feel at ease, knowing I had never been far from home.

He was of average height, slim body, but very strong muscular physique, as all locomotive firemen were. Vic had been a cleaner with my father at Didcot and now he was a senior Old Oak fireman approaching 40 years of age. He was one of many who, like my father, were allowed to do less demanding firing duties because of their advancing years. Not until 1942 did either of them become drivers.

Walking down Ladbrook Grove towards my lodgings was an experience I have never forgotten.

A sunlit arrival at Paddington. I hadn't been to Paddington before, but it wasn't like this when I got off the train on that miserable morning in February 1938. My father, who saw me off at Didcot station, explained that when I arrived at Paddington I had to look back for the stairs up to Platform 13. At the ticket office at the top of the steps, I asked for Ladbrook Grove and made my way there on the Metropolitan Railway.
C. R. L. Coles

I was used to the fresh air and peace of the Berkshire Downs but now I was surrounded by nothing but buildings, strange smells, Victorian streets full of hustle and bustle, with Londoners pushing and rushing all over the place. What a contrast to the small community I had just left behind. Vic knew how I felt and I was anxious to come to terms with these surroundings.

Arriving at 19 Barlby Gardens, a small terraced house, just off the Grove before passing over the GWR main line, gave me a sense of comfort for it was a quiet location, with green poplar trees, reminding me of home. Vic introduced me to his wife, who shook my hand and smiled. I felt uncertain of myself but she was very pleasant to me. We agreed I should pay one pound per week as they knew my wages were only 19s 5d, 19s 11d, 19s 5d, and £1 5s 0d per week in that sequence.

Vic wanted to know all about me, and I soon got lost in conversation, an exercise to gather an idea of my likes and weaknesses. Sitting in his chair, with the Ekco radio behind, I remember him smoking a pipe supported by his right hand. He spoke through strong yellowed teeth clenched around the stem. Only to press the tobacco further down the barrel, blow his nose, laugh or emphasise something by pointing it at you like a gun, would the pipe leave his mouth. He was a most amiable man who I soon grew to trust, but I was aware of being only the lodger and always tried to show respect and take no liberties.

I had been given that Monday off for travelling, and had to report to Old Oak Common the next day. Vic kindly showed me the way to the huge locomotive shed, the route I was shown being the one I was to follow; under no circumstances was I to take short cuts. It was a three-quarters of an hour walk.

Vic's wife, known to me always as Mrs. Hughes, was a short, gentle woman, a typical family centre pin. Vic always addressed her as 'Mum', but I never did. They had two children still at school, Ivy, who was fourteen, and Richard who was twelve.

Being a healthy 16 year old, I was always ready to eat, and fortunately I was with a family who were familiar with the irregular hours of a railwayman. My meals were always provided to fit in with my shifts, 6.00 a.m.–2.00 p.m., 2.00 p.m.–10.00 p.m. or 8.00 p.m.–5.00 a.m. I missed the fresh food I had enjoyed at home with vegetables straight from our garden, but I soon adapted to baked beans, etc. Fast food had now arrived and the tin opener was used more than the vegetable knife.

Slowly I accepted my surroundings without letting anyone know how I really felt. My bedroom window overlooked the gasometer west of Ladbrook Grove Bridge and I still remember the smell of gas, mixed with a cocktail of pollution from coal-fired houses and car fumes. Oh how I pined inwardly for the fresh air and the green countryside I had left behind.

That first Monday was also my first night in a strange bed, and the alarm clock — a large German make, I recall — was set for 4.30 a.m. Vic had loaned me his valued timepiece — it had to be reliable — and stood it inside the china handbasin to increase the sound. The loud ticks echoed and sent me into a hypnotic sleep. When the alarm sounded at 4.30 a.m. it was deafening. Startled, I was unable to find the plunger in the darkness of the unfamiliar room. Crawling out of bed, dazed and feeling for the clock, I stumbled. The basin, clock, and small table all crashed to the floor. Finding the clock next to the chamber pot underneath the bed, I stifled it with my pillow until I could turn on the light. I turned the dreaded thing off. Peace at last! From now on, alarm clocks were to herald my duty and always to be obeyed. No longer did I have my mother to rely on for calling me if I overslept. I was on my own.

The great day had arrived; I had my lunch packed in a satchel, containing a small jar of tea leaves mixed with condensed milk and sugar, usually soft cheese triangles wrapped in silver foil

19 Barlby Gardens (second house from the right) with Mrs. Hughes in the doorway. We learned that the bowl on top of the Belisha beacon was glass, after accidentally knocking into the post when sky-larking. It just fell off and smashed into fragments!
Reproduced by kind permission of Ordnance Survey

Looking towards Paddington from Scrubbs Lane bridge. Barlby Gardens was opposite the right-hand gasholder. Sometimes I walked home along the trackside with one of the Old Oak Common 'table men' who also lived at Barlby Gardens. This was all very unofficial and we had to climb over the backyard wall, but it was quicker.
C. S. Perrier, cty. David Jenkinson

(these were difficult to open with dirty, oily hands!), four slices of bread, an apple or banana, and sometimes a slice of cake (seldom homemade).

Starting out on my first day, dressed in my father's smart overalls, I closed the front door quietly behind me and, filled with anxiety, set out on the route Vic had shown me the day before, but now I was alone in strange surroundings. London is a huge place and loneliness soon crept up on me, shivers ran down my spine, and my legs felt wobbly. It was a cold damp morning. With satchel swinging on my shoulder, the walk took me along Dalgarno Gardens to Scrubs Lane. I happily quickened my footsteps as the chill of the morning brought me round from the sleepy feeling I had. Turning into Scrubs Lane, the early morning Londoners were hastening to work, milk floats rattling over the uneven street, trolley buses laden with passengers, their heads buried in newspapers, even at 5.30 a.m., bicycles weaving in and out of motor traffic. Haste! Haste! The tempo was fast and now I was being carried along with this strange way of living.

Leaving Scrubs Lane by way of a gate in the Canal Bridge, I descended the footsteps onto the Grand Union Canal bank, which ran parallel to the main railway line. Apprehensively, I followed

Looking north over the bridge carrying Scrubbs Lane across the main line. The arrow points to the steps leading down to the canal. *Reproduced by kind permission of Ordnance Survey*

the lonely path, with the canal on my right, brick wall on my left, and the early morning mist rising off the water. I was expecting the worst, as undesirables frequented this Dickensian area and felt relieved when I finally came to another gate in the wall which led to a footbridge across the up engine and carriage line from Old Oak Common to Paddington. Head held high, my stride quickened as I overcame the feeling of panic – soon I would be safe among railwaymen again.

Walking across the footbridge from the canal towards Old Oak Common shed, the sight of the

The scene that confronted me, looking west from the footbridge on my first day, the awe-inspiring Old Oak Common carriage sidings. The right-hand line leading from the engine shed was occupied by a couple of engines waiting for the road.
The Hulton Deutsch Collection

OLD OAK COMMON

various engines coming off shed filled me with excitement. All in full steam with safety valves blowing and grey smoke drifting from their chimneys, there were 'Kings', 'Castles' and 0–6–0 tanks for shunting at Acton Yard or hauling coaches up and down the carriage line to Paddington. Early morning was a busy time and, as I surveyed the scene, I felt really proud that I was now to be a part of it all. It never occurred to me that I would be doing anything else as I descended the steps from the bridge opposite Old Oak Common Signal Box. Following the path between the main line and carriage sidings, I reached the coal stage bank, with passenger locomotives on the south side and goods locomotives on the north. My imagination ran riot as I passed by locos coming off the up Fishguard sleeper and

The footbridge over the engine and carriage lines on my approach to Old Oak shed from the canal. The picture on the left shows the view from the footbridge towards Paddington.
Reproduced by kind permission of Ordnance Survey and B. Y. Williams

many other overnight trains. Old Oak Common covered a huge area. Suddenly I felt lost, and a feeling of doubt crossed my mind; had I done the right thing?

I found my way to the cloakroom, which was a dingy room containing wooden washing troughs and rows of coat pegs, and was soon questioned by my new workmates, who asked my name and where I came from. I was christened and thereafter known by my mates as 'Didcot'.

It was soon clear to me that the senior cleaners were leaders who never had to be crossed — you had to comply. The tough and mouthy ones romped about with a swagger, showing off their power to a raw recruit like myself. Anyway, soon I was befriended by two cleaners who had quiet manners and helped me over the mysteries of initiation into the ranks. During assembly in front of the stores, I was given my paybill number 771, and issued with a small, square brass plate, stamped 'GWR' and bearing that number. This was my official pass, licence or number plate, which I collected when booking on duty and handed in to the time clerk when booking off at the end of the shift. The chargeman cleaner put me with Ginger Jeremy who was to be my skipper.

To my amazement, there were 104 cleaners at Old Oak in those days. They were split up into gangs of four, each with its own No. 1 or skipper. No. 4 was known as the 'Joey', the raw recruit who had to do the most unpopular tasks, as well as fetching and carrying. The skipper was the one we never argued with — if we didn't carry out his instructions we were soon in trouble. We were even expected to do his work when he was skiving off. Being the 'Joey' in the gang, I had the dirtiest jobs of all, and my smart overalls, which had been my father's, were soon covered in grease.

During my first week I was measured for clothing by the storekeeper, but it was some time before I received my official clothing issue, two pairs of overalls consisting of jacket and trousers. Not until I had completed twelve firing duties would I be eligible for a serge overcoat, jacket and cap.

At the start of each shift the engine cleaners would assemble in gangs of four outside the stores, waiting for the chargeman cleaner to tell us which locos to clean. Different classes of locos were allotted different times; for example, we were allowed four hours for a 'King' or 'Castle' class,

three hours for a 'Hall' or '28XX', two hours for a '68XX' or '63XX', and just one hour for an 0–6–0 tank, so a combination was arranged to make up the day's work. In a 48-hour week, eighteen different locos could have been cleaned by any one gang of four.

When we were allocated a loco, the 'Joey' was sent to fetch the cleaning materials, often 3–4lb of cotton waste (from mill spoils) and 1lb of waste soaked in a light oil for the paintwork. The amount issued varied according to the size of the loco. This was divided between members of the gang, and when the oily waste ran out, we never dared ask for more. We scrounged from other locomotives which had been in service, looking for any disused waste left on the footplates.

The goods engine side of Old Oak coaling stage and water tower; passenger engines were coaled on the opposite side. The building in the right background housed the workshops whilst the sidings on the right were used to hold the supplies brought in on the Rogerstone coal train. The 'tanky' was on shed pilot duty which included shunting coal wagons onto the coal stage. *C. R. L. Coles*

I often dipped my waste into the bogie well of a 'King' or 'Castle' where oil collected from the crossheads and oil wells on top of the slipper bars. We were really pleased to find any old newspapers to use as cleaning material. We were also issued with a ladle of brick dust paste emptied onto a sheet of brown paper. This was a moist paste ideal for burnishing brass and copper.

Having collected our allotment, we proceeded to find our loco in the huge shed. On arrival, the skipper usually looked round to assess the task before tossing pennies, or our brass tally discs, on the 'heads you win, tails you lose' principle, which might let you off a particularly nasty job!

The loco was divided into four sections; the upper part above the footplate, including the boiler, was divided into two sides, driver's and fireman's, and included the inside motion. The other was everything outside below the footplate, including the wheels and tender, again divided into two sides.

The No. 2 and No. 3 followed the skipper in tossing up for their choice, leaving the 'Joey' with the dirtiest parts to clean. On top of that, if the skipper said "You can do my part as well", and cleared off, the poor 'Joey' had to do the lot. We knew it was no use kicking, because if we objected too strongly, things were made very difficult for us.

We started by wiping the grime and grease from the paintwork first and followed with the oily waste, usually smeared on in the shape of an S, before a final polish with clean waste. If the lining on an engine was really grimy, we used to clean it with brick dust paste, which was primarily used for the safety valve rose, the copper top to the chimney, the brass name and number plates and the brass beading on the splashers. Brick dust paste was also used to scour the buffers and front valve and cylinder covers of the four-cylinder engines and often we'd divide them into quarters, which looked very effective.

There was satisfaction in making a loco look really presentable and there was not only a lot of competition between the gangs, but rivalry between the two cleaners who did the boiler of the same engine. Very often, one cleaner, being more efficient and hard-working, could make his side look a lot better than the other, to the extent that the copper on the chimney and the brass on the safety valve covering were noticeably cleaner on one half!

In those days, drivers and firemen took an interest in the cleaners, and the question of discipline arose many times. On one occasion, I remember a driver who came up in rather a belligerent mood and said, "Who's supposed to be cleaning the valve gear underneath?" One of the cleaners replied, "I am, but you'll have to wait until I've finished cleaning the top." The driver made it quite clear that he wouldn't wait, but the lad refused to come down, saying, "I'm going to clean the top part first. Bugger off!" Not surprisingly, the driver reported this flagrant disobedience to the chargeman engine cleaner, and the lad was hauled up in front of the shed foreman. However, even in those days, the lad had a trade union representative who got him off the charge of being insubordinate to a driver! The unions were getting a very strong hand and this was my first experience of their effect. I witnessed the incident and had no doubt that the lad should have been disciplined.

Chargeman Coles was the most feared, for although he was fair in his dealings with us, we were never allowed to cut corners. He would closely inspect every part, and if he found any oil, grease or dirty patches when he gently stroked a finger along the paintwork, or tested underneath the footplate by rubbing with a clean cloth, it was remedied immediately. He was a small man who seemed hard, cold and emotionless. Humourless behind his steel-rimmed glasses, his eyesight had failed him for footplate duties, but he was sharp-eyed enough to spot areas that we had not cleaned properly. He was a disciplinarian, respected for what he was, but I am sure he kept a lot to himself. He kept a watch on us youngsters, and turned a blind eye when he caught us wrestling with each other. On one occasion he stood in the shadows, viewing a friendly tussle between two

The stores counter where we drew supplies. The names of the cleaners were displayed on the noticeboard on the right. There were 104 names and Bernard Barlow was the last one!

R. C. Riley

skippers. As we each became aware of his presence, one by one we idly strolled away. It was enough to know that he was watching — he didn't need to say anything.

To clean under locomotives, we stood in a pit between the rails, with our head and shoulders between the frames and valve gear. There were all sorts of unpleasant things to be found under a loco — from the fur of a fox to the mangled remains of a pheasant; I even remember finding part of a greyhound — all quite traumatic to a young 16-year old.

Before working on a loco and especially before going underneath, it was the skipper's responsibility to put a 'NOT TO BE MOVED' red warning board on one of the lamp brackets, but even with that in position, it could be an unnerving experience underneath, for you were never quite sure whether it might move. I was often anxious underneath and alert to any movement around the engine. I found some of the parts between the frames very difficult to get to, especially underneath the webs, as we called them — the large castings on the axle which balanced the big ends. I feared that a loco would be moved and I might

Sunlight penetrating the gloomy interior of one of the Old Oak Common roundhouses. It was immensely satisfying to be a small part of all this, but to a country boy like myself it could seem like being caged inside a Victorian prison at times.

C. R. L. Coles

The first passenger side table (one of four). The chief fitters and boilersmiths office can be seen behind the 50XX without tender. This is where many years later I made enquiries about 5029 after it had failed on a Rugby Special, as recalled in Chapter 9. The large lever on the timber boarding was used to move the table manually when the electric motor drive failed. The upright handle operated a large bolt which locked the table to each road. *C. R. L. Coles*

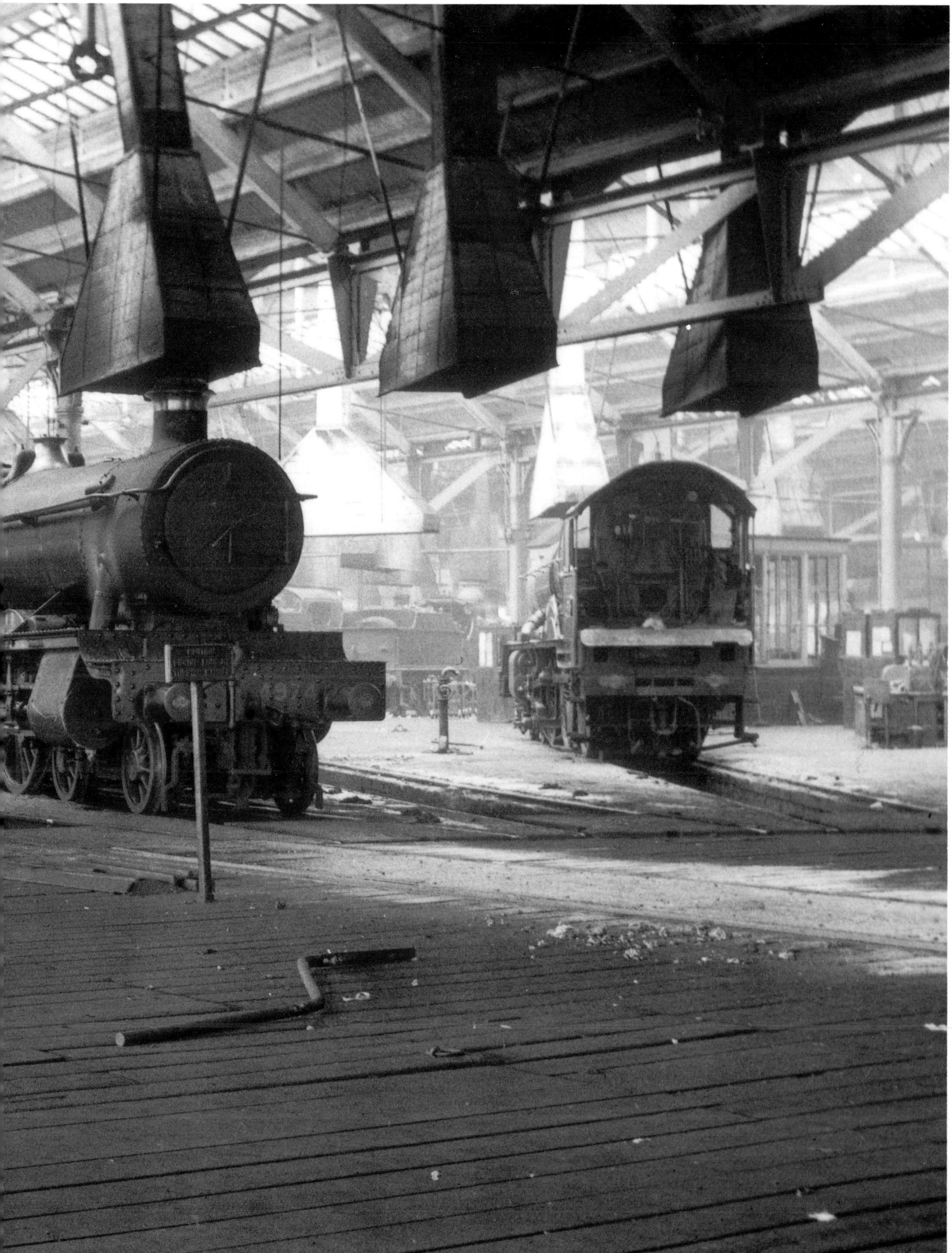

end up crushed against the inside — and accidents like that did happen. A well-known driver at Didcot was crushed and killed in exactly this manner.

The reason for the concoction of loose tea leaves, mixed with condensed milk, provided by my landlady, soon became apparent. Each skipper in a gang had a tea can, and in turn each cleaner a brew, so we had four tea breaks, each occupying a very welcome ten minutes. The tea time was spent in the cab of a loco, preferably a 'King' or 'Castle', which was in steam and stabled inside the shed close to the one we were cleaning. One of us would sit in the driver's seat, one on the fireman's, and the other two on the upturned bucket and fireman's shovel. Many happy tea breaks were experienced in this manner. A comradeship developed between us, the future footplate crews. We asked each other questions on the locomotive's various controls, and even imitated the driver by 'nicking up' the reverser, and the fireman by using the shovel. If we knew who the crew were, we would sometimes half prepare the loco. These tea breaks remain some of my fondest memories, and they certainly fed my appetite for footplate life.

The staff canteen was used by some cleaners, but the place never appealed to me or my immediate colleagues, particularly when it was dominated by some rough, tough lads who were badly in need of discipline when eating food. I had no stomach for their antics and preferred to sit peacefully in a loco cab with my choice of mates. Perhaps I had been subjected to a strict upbringing? I had known food taken away from a weaker cleaner by a burly hulk because he fancied what the lad had. This showing off by the bully caused hilarity with others, but I found it unsavoury.

Pleasant meal breaks were also often spent with my mates in the St. John Ambulance Association. Having been encouraged to join, I soon developed a keen interest and really enjoyed it. On a cold winter's day we would sit in the repair shop around a brazier made from an oil drum perforated with a coal pick and stood on two metal brake blocks. Coal was plentiful and the heat radiated to keep us cosy as we sat round it in a circle on makeshift seats holding our First Aid manuals. Each in turn asked a question and it was surprising how we improved our knowledge this way without tutors or specialists to teach us. All our skills were self-taught. Meal breaks like this were sheer delight, with a wonderful atmosphere rich with the warmth of friendship and a shared common interest. That year, 1938-39, I won an award for outstanding performance for a junior. My efforts had been rewarded, and my interest in First Aid was maintained throughout my railway career, as I successfully passed First Aid exams every year.

There were no sinks, baths or showers at the shed, the washroom simply consisting of crude wooden troughs, with hot and cold water sprinklers, often covered with slime and running into foul-smelling drains. I preferred to wash in a bucket outside. There were no lockers to hang clothes, just open racks for personal belongings. When I got back to my lodgings each night, I took off my oily boots and overalls and placed them outside, behind the wash house door. I had a strip wash and changed into cleaner clothes. By the weekend my overalls became very oily, but having two pairs allowed the used ones to be soaked for 48 hours in strong soda water in a bucket, to dissolve the oil and grease. Then I scrubbed them with a large scrubbing brush on a corrugated metal board. Sometimes Vic and I would do each other's. It was a job that at least provided a welcome opportunity to clean my hands and nails at the same time. No matter how much effort we put in to personal hygiene, it was impossible to remove all the black oily grease from the skin completely. The bath at Vic's house was covered with a wooden top and used as a table during the week. Only at weekends did the top come off and we all took turns to enjoy a weekly soak.

I was always glad to see my father, who regularly arrived on No. 5934 *Kneller Hall* off the 8.42 a.m. Didcot–Paddington. Knowing I was having a lean time, he often gave me 2/6d to help pay the landlady when I had a short week, and perhaps might bring a clean, smartly-pressed set of overalls from my mother. I would change on the engine and leave the dirty ones with him. I kept a keen eye on every loco that came in to turn, but, when spotting *Kneller Hall*, I soon went missing, risking a dressing down by my chargeman. I never did get caught as we usually kept out of sight of the Locomotive Superintendent's office where 5934 always stayed for a while. Knowing this dodge, I took advantage of chatting to Father on the blind side of the footplate. Working

1930s London as I saw it. *Albert Sweet, cty. Douglas Croker*

together, we would take water, shovel coal forward, sweep up the footplate and clean the oil cans. Anything to look busy.

Feeling rich, with cash in my pocket, I bade Father and his mate farewell. The following week our next-door neighbour, Reg Sewell, would be the fireman on 5934, and so the ritual continued until my father was demoted to a lower link because of loss of seasonal work. However, the Didcot crews seldom missed bringing me the odd shilling and even clean clothes. I never did let my gang know what I was absent for.

There were days when I found myself with five shillings in hand, allowing me the luxury of going to the City. My previous service entitled me to a privilege ticket which was made out to The Bank. Costing 3d, it was used as a 'Rover', and I was able to visit any underground station. This was a good perk which I used for visiting museums, the Houses of Parliament, Westminster Abbey, St. Paul's Cathedral, Hyde Park, Kensington Gardens, all the usual tourist haunts. My weekends alternated between these trips and visits home to Didcot.

When I was out with my mates on one visit home, they said my brogue was cockney — to them I had become a Londoner. Such was the influence of surroundings at Old Oak.

I soon developed a routine, which helped me cope with life in London, but I never truly settled, a brave front was the best I could manage, forced to accept that the future had been set.

While we were cleaning a loco towards the end of our allotted time, the crew would arrive to prepare it for service. We were only too pleased to help and very often the cleaner would do the oiling underneath for the driver to save him going 'inside'. These drivers could usually be identified by their very clean overalls! The fireman's job could be very hot in the summer when temper-

Paddington station in the 1930s with 4049 *Princess Maud* in No. 3 platform and No. 2913 *Saint Andrew* in No. 1 platform. Squealing wheel flanges were a familiar sound here as arriving trains entered the curved platforms. *George Stickler*

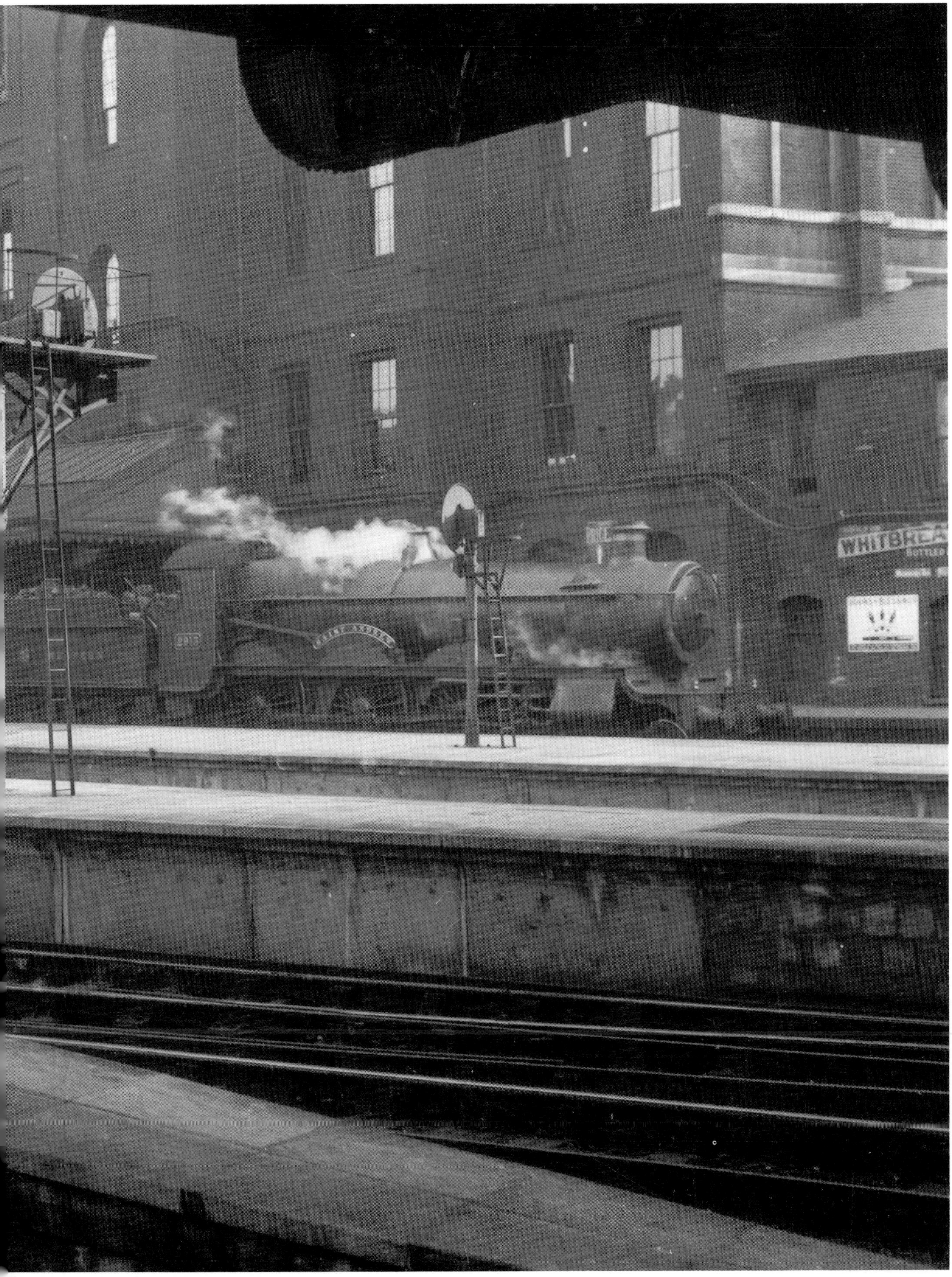
PRICE
WHITBREA
BOTTLED

Looking west over Subway Junction c.1930.
G. N. Southerden

Looking west from Lordhills bridge towards Subway Junctiom. The track in the left foreground was the No. 1 up engine and carriage line, with the down main alongside. The train in the foreground was waiting on the No. 2 up engine and carriage line and the carriages behind were occupying three of the four dead-end sidings here. The up main and up relief lines were out of sight behind the coaches whilst the track alongside the Metropolitan served as the down engine and carriage line.
L. E. Copeland

atures inside the shed were in the nineties. Some would strip to the waist to build up the fire, and could be seen really working hard, with rivulets of sweat running down their bodies over the black coal dust which had settled on their skin when breaking up coal and trimming the tender. We might help breaking up the coal and sweeping the footplate and at the end of the six-day week our favourite drivers and firemen would often reward us with a pack of five Woodbines or Player's Weights.

It wasn't long before the management realised they had a young telegraphist as an engine cleaner who would be useful in the office. The chief running clerk asked if I would be prepared to work the two shifts, 6.00 a.m. – 2.00 p.m. and 2.00 p.m. – 10.00 p.m., assisting with general office duties. Not really knowing what was

The 'Cornish Riviera', one of the more prestigious trains, leaving Paddington in 1935.　　　　　　*H. L. Boston*

A final look west over the Old Oak carriage sidings and the approach to the engine shed on the right. *National Railway Museum*

involved, I reluctantly accepted, reluctant because I didn't really want to leave the comradeship that I had built up with the engine cleaners I had been working with. However, my time in the booking-on and booking-off office gave me an insight into how the whole business worked and a different angle on things.

I had the job of filing the drivers' daily records in numerical order and got to know the names of some of the drivers stationed at Old Oak. I also took telephone messages, including details from Cardiff area control advising us of what coal wagons were in the train which we called the 'Roggy' (Rogerstone), with coal for Old Oak Common. These wagons were from different South Wales collieries, the names of which were quite unfamiliar and difficult to spell. The controllers used to think we were quick at writing down these names, but the trick was to note the number of wagons and use your own shorthand code for the place names, the spellings of which could be looked up later without any panic. The message could then be transcribed properly and correctly onto another pad. These details went to central office who dealt with booking or recording these coal wagons.

I was a high-spirited lad and well remember being kept in check. On one occasion when one of the clerks was doing a crossword in the *Daily Telegraph*, I happened to come up with the answer to a clue that was puzzling him. I still remember it — 'a sweet you can eat as well as gold'. "Nougat", I said to him, "Ha, ha, ha, it takes a little lad like me to tell you." I got a well deserved smack around the ear which left my head ringing. I had been a cheeky little devil and it did me no harm. We both laughed it off.

I thought a lot of the staff in that office, particularly Horace Huckle, the chief clerk. He was a tall, thin man with longish unkempt hair and flat feet. He was a chain smoker as well, and, although his appearance was far from prepossessing, his knowledge was outstanding. It was his job to roster all the crews to cover the complex train diagramming, and he was depended on by the management to arrange cover for the alterations brought about by seasonal timetable changes. He knew the timetables and engine requirements in detail. His was no easy task, particularly for the Bank Holidays or Christmas services when some of the trains ran in four or five different parts. He started at 9.00 a.m. in the morning but often worked through the night to accomplish his task.

My duties in the time office alternated with engine cleaning and by now I was getting to know some of the drivers.

Brief moments of excitement fired my determination, like meeting Francis Street, a top link engineman at the pinnacle of his career. I was cleaning 5026 when he asked me if I would retrieve a big end cork which slipped from his fingers while he was oiling one of the outside little ends of this 'Castle' class loco. As I had been watching him closely for some time while cleaning the little end, I noticed the cork bounce on the floor and fall into the pit. The gloomy interior of the shed at Old Oak was not the best place to find a lost cork, but, without replying to his request, I quickly jumped into the dark pit under the loco and found it. His face said it all — a grin, followed by "Thank you, my son. You have excellent eyesight and will make a good engineman one day." An engineman who had driven 'The Cheltenham Flyer' telling me I would be successful made my day. He then asked me to oil the underneath, the inside big ends, valve gear, oil boxes and inside little ends — a privilege indeed. All the time he was outside patiently making sure I did not miss anything. It was an honour to be under the instructions of a top link engineman who'd actually driven 'The Cheltenham Flyer' that I had watched so many times as a schoolboy leaning over Foxhall bridge. Brief though this encounter was, the experience always remained with me.

Considerably heartened by his remark, and proud to be at last amongst the 'Kings', 'Castles', 'Halls' and 'Granges', I immersed myself in cleaning duties, swinging like a monkey from the handrails of the locos, 'toeing' my way along each tender, gripping the top with my left arm whilst cleaning the tank with my right. This left me with tennis elbow, which I still suffer from today. We had no ladders or scaffolding to help, but had to rely on our natural agility to spring up or twist our bodies in awkward positions in order to crawl underneath the locos.

Our overalls soon became a mass of oil and grease, the palms of our hands developed callouses, our nails split, and the skin around our knuckeles became discoloured and ingrained with the grime of oil and coal.

I developed a friendly relationship with the staff officer, and one day, when delivering a telegram to his office, he asked me if I'd like to transfer back to Didcot as they needed cleaners there for the summer service. I offered him a packet of Craven A cigarettes if he could arrange this for me. After he'd made a quick telephone call to Swindon HQ, I was told to report to Didcot at 8.00 a.m. next Monday. I was sad to leave my friends but very glad to be going home.

A down express passing Westbourne Park in 1936. I travelled back to Didcot on the 11.15 p.m. slip. *H. L. Boston*

Didcot station, looking towards Bristol in the mid-1930s, showing the location of the engine shed to the north of the platforms. The three coaches and van left on No. 2 running road were later shunted over to the Newbury bay which just features on the extreme left.
L & GRP

The forecourt of Didcot station in the early 1930s. The main part of the building on the right was the station master's house.
Packer Studio

CHAPTER FOUR
DIDCOT SHED

A mid-1930s view of the shed approaches viewed from Platform 7. *National Railway Museum*

MY return to Didcot loco shed for the summer of 1939 was really a bit of an anticlimax. Compared to Old Oak Common, the shed was tiny and the tempo of work slow. For more than a year I had been used to a bigger, faster and livelier place. On top of that, I had not been expected!

I convinced the shed foreman that I had been sent by the staff clerk at Old Oak Common, and after he had made a 'phone call, which I overheard, he appeared satisfied that everything was in order, but there seemed to be a strained atmosphere which I would learn all about later.

Being sixteen years old and the youngest cleaner, I was given callboy duties and assisted the storekeeper. Of the fourteen cleaners, the three most junior worked the 6 a.m. – 2 p.m., 2 p.m. – 10 p.m. and 10 p.m. – 6 a.m. shifts in the stores. This was good training for me as I was learning about all the tools of the trade and meeting all the crews as they came in for their requirements. All that was necessary to keep a loco in service was issued at the stores, including the regular kit carried on each engine, which comprised fire-irons, which were usually chained and padlocked on the engine, firing shovel, coal pick, bucket, spanners, hand brush, spare boiler gauge glasses, detonators, gauge lamp, flare lamp, barrell feeder, flat feeder, pep pipe, and two headlamps. Apart from the coal pick and the bucket, this equipment was locked in the tool boxes along with the oil jugs, and the keys handed in with the lamps at the end of the shift. The keys had labels with engine numbers attached and were hung over the lid catch on top of one of the headlamps. The fireman collected the lamps and keys from the stores on his way to the engine and was responsible for checking that all the tools were on board when he got there. He also had to check if any of the detonators were out of date (over five years old). They were colour coded for each year in rotation, black, white, red, blue and green. They also had to be checked for signs of rust or damaged clips and replaced if necessary.

The driver drew cotton waste and oil. There were four different types of oil, heavy duty for the valves and pistons; a lighter one for the various oil wells on the loco such as the big ends,

39

knuckle joints and axleboxes; paraffin and a heavier burning oil for headlamps and flare lamp. These were all pumped from overhead storage tanks in the stores.

It was also my job to fill and trim the headlamps which were returned by the firemen as the locos came on shed. We had a rack of 100 headlamps in the stores and as each pair was handed in I had to take out the oil wells and fill them, wipe off any spilt oil with cotton waste and, after refitting the carrier, turn up the wick and pinch off any crust which had formed. Sometimes if the wick was a bit frayed, it was necessary to cut some of it away with scissors; this was to avoid a smoky flame. It was also essential to clean and polish the optic and reflector of each lamp to provide a good light, and lift the flap on the top of the chimney to make sure it was clear of any soot. Finally, I had to examine the red shade carried in the sleeve on the door of the lamp and make sure that was also clean — all useful experience for the future.

Most locos were prepared during the 6 a.m. – 2 p.m. shift which was always the busiest. During the night shift, 10 p.m. – 6 a.m., I had chance to use the large bin of cotton waste for a cat-nap prior to the callboy duties which, starting around midnight, took up most of the shift. I had to cycle out to crews within a mile radius of Didcot, although men living outside the area were seldom late. I was issued with a bicycle, a sou'wester hat and cape, and a pair of leggings as the crews on my list had to be called in all weathers, one hour prior to their booking-on time. Sometimes I had to borrow the storekeeper's watch.

The furthest call was East Hagbourne, a dark journey at 2.00 a.m. on a wet windy night, especially if the oil lamp on the front of the cycle blew out. Of course I was not used to all

Didcot shed stores, showing the window in the far end where locomen booked on and off. At one time the storeman had acted as timekeeper, booking train crews on and off duty, but during my time there he was purely rresponsible for the control and issue of equipment and materials. The large tanks held (from left to right) lubricating oil, cylinder oil, paraffin and cleaning oil. Fire-irons were stowed underneath, beyond the ambulance cabinet. The wooden cabinet on the right held various fitters requirements, whilst the cotton waste bin was behind the drum-shaped stove. *National Railway Museum*

this, but callboy duties gave me the courage to face the loneliness of long dark nights. A deep snowfall meant walking and pushing the bike. On one particularly severe night a silver frost left everything coated in ice, and when the bike went one way and I went the other, I had to abandon it and continue on foot.

Under these conditions a callboy's life was miserable, chasing time and never giving up. I have to admit it bred determination in me and a solid training for punctuality which, after all, was the key to running a reliable railway. I had to make sure I was on time at each house. Some of the men were already up and only a tap on the door was needed, but others who had been 'on the beer' the night before were more difficult to arouse! Throwing up a handful of gravel at their bedroom window, or tapping it with the clothes-line prop was then necessary.

Men like these usually blamed the callboy if they were late for duty, saying they hadn't been called, and there was often a dispute when I got back to the shed at 6 a.m., but mainly the crews were very kind, offering cups of tea or even sharing their breakfast if the weather was cold.

I remember calling on one senior driver who had been a bachelor all his life. I was calling him for his last turn of duty, and he was waiting for

The interior of Didcot shed before completion in 1932. The offices and other rooms which led off the wall on the left were as follows: shed foreman (external annexe added c.1941), running foreman, booking-on office, lobby, stores, enginemen's cabin, chief fitter and boilersmith, fitters and boiler washout staff mess, chargeman engine cleaner, shed staff, cleaners, lavatories. *National Railway Museum*

me with a cup of tea. Here was I, just beginning my career, and his was about to end. It was an emotional moment as I asked him if he had any regrets, and he told me that he had missed out by never getting married — the footplate had been his bride. I felt that he was about to face a sad and lonely retirement. As I was leaving, I could see tears flooding his eyes as he put his hand on my shoulder and said, "Well, lad, you must carry on where I leave off." With a lump in my throat, I was lost for words and gave him a rather croaky farewell. As I continued my rounds, the rain-filled dawn seemed symbolic of that parting.

After only a few months in the stores, I was on engine cleaning duties again. On Tuesdays to Fridays we worked from 9.30 p.m. to 6 a.m. but, as Sundays attracted extra pay, the Monday morning duty started at one minute past midnight

Pride of Didcot, *Kneller Hall*, in front of the shed on No. 1 road in the late 1930s.

Engineman Jack Hacker in the cab of No. 5934.
P. Smart

No. 1925 fitted with a 'fish fryer' spark arrester for use in the Ordnance Depot. No. 2007 was used on the Lambourn branch.
L. W. Perkins

and lasted until 8 a.m.! The alternating shifts were 6 a.m.–2 p.m. and 8 a.m.–4.30 p.m. On the night shift the senior cleaner earned extra money by doing four hours firedropping or tube cleaning.

Cleaning practice at Didcot varied little from Old Oak although the discipline was a little stricter because the chargeman cleaner, Ernie Didcock, had only twelve cleaners at most to supervise. However, he was very fair and had no problems with us, and I was pleased to be working in the cleaner, more modern building at Didcot, well ventilated with smoke hoods over each of its four straight roads.

The early morning passenger locos were given special treatment at Didcot. In particular I remember No. 5934 *Kneller Hall* which, being the only 'Hall' class at Didcot, was given special treatment. She was turned out spotless inside and out to work the 8.42 a.m. Didcot–Paddington and we took great pride in knowing that heads would turn when she went on shed at Old Oak. Some drivers would even stop the loco outside the superintendent's office!

Some of the Didcot locos were away from the depot for days, eventually returning in a very dirty state. This gave us extra work as nothing had been done to them. Having worked on the Lambourn branch, the little saddle tank, No. 2007, came back each week during the summer covered with masses of dead flies collected along the Lambourn Valley. They covered the brake gear and motion and caused an awful stench under the smokebox.

On the 6 a.m. – 2 p.m. shift the senior cleaner was permitted to cook breakfast for the whole shift in the cleaners' mess room or 'cabin'. This was the last room along the inside of the engine shed, next to the lavatories. Here we had a wooden table, two bench seats and a large tortoiseshell stove 3ft high which was kept going on coal taken from the nearest loco. A very large frying pan fitted perfectly on the top of the stove which had previously been stoked up until it glowed. The smell of all the eggs, bacon, sausages and fried bread drifted across the loco shed, cruelly taunting our senses until 8.45 a.m. when we wiped the worst of the oily grime from our hands with cotton waste soaked in paraffin and, in our oily overalls, eagerly lined the seat of a wooden bench to enjoy a truly mouthwatering treat. These banquets have left me with some of my fondest memories – I only wish I could re-live them.

Like the other sheds in the London Division, Didcot was in the charge of a locomotive chief foreman who was directly answerable to the London Divisional Superintendent. In my time there was an allocation of some thirty locos and about sixty footplate crews. As far as I can remember, there were two loco foremen, a staff clerk, two support clerks, three storemen, a foreman fitter, boilersmith, two fitters, two fitter's mates, two boiler-washers, three fire-droppers, an ash loader, three coalmen, three fire-lighters, a shed cleaner, a chargeman engine cleaner, and twelve cleaners — a staff of around 170.

During my time as cleaner I soon picked up the way the shed was worked. Crews bringing engines on shed at the end of a duty left them 'up the bank' on the ash road, buffered up (but not coupled) to the loco in front. If the 'bank' was full, returning engines were left in 'the field'. Before leaving the engine, the crew would lock the tools away, chain and padlock the fire-irons, and drop the keys and headlamps into the stores. The driver made out his ticket and handed it to the clerk and both men checked the board or duty sheet for their next turn.

Locomotives were moved through disposals by the shed crew who worked 10 p.m. — 6 a.m., 6 a.m. — 2 p.m. and 2 p.m. — 10 p.m. At the start of the wartime arrangements, an assisting shed crew had worked 11 p.m. — 7 a.m. only, but when extra men and engines arrived for the war effort this was increased to three shifts of 7 a.m. — 3 p.m. and 3 p.m. — 11 p.m. so that there was always a crew on duty for any emergency. These men also prepared engines and generally 'mucked in' as required. They were 'medical men' — drivers and elderly firemen confined to the shed perhaps, for instance, for failing the eyesight test. Otherwise there might be a passed fireman who was available for driving.

The new shed at Didcot shortly after completion. The room in the base of the coal stage served as a messroom. Firelighters were also kept there, thrown in from a van stabled directly outside the door. As part of the air-raid precautions, an ash shelter was built c.1941 over the two tracks on the left of this picture to contain the light from fires or glowing ash thrown out during disposal.

National Railway Museum

DIDCOT SHED

Didcot shed on a cold day in February 1937. In really cold spells, small 'frost fires' were maintained in the pits inside the shed, at the south end of each road, to keep the building frost-free.

However, there were times when a younger fireman carried out these duties. With low steam pressure, commonly 40 lbs or less, handling these engines called for care and skill. When there was insufficient steam to create vacuum for the brake, the reservoir was drained, leaving only the handbrake. Stopping a 120-ton engine like this was no easy task, and handling the regulator in these conditions could be nerve-racking. With really low steam it was a case of closing the cylinder cocks to conserve any steam, then, leaving the regulator wide open, moving the reverser backwards and forwards several times to get any movement. Any points to be changed were handled by a mate on the ground immediately after the wheels had cleared the blades, at the same time the reverser would be wound or thrown back, then with valves moaning like an unwilling animal gasping its last breath, the loco would gently come to a stand and slowly reverse direction to creep down into the shed. Providing the momentum was kept, a loco could be kept moving even when there was no steam registering on the clock and, with any luck, using the reverser to stop it, the handbrake was only necessary to secure it when it had been stabled. Sometimes when we took a gamble and lost, locos had to be rescued from awkward places where they might have become stranded. The '30XX' ROD engines used to move even when it seemed there was no pressure left.

It was more serious if a loco could not be stopped, as happened one dark night in the 1940s when my colleague Ralph Huggins and a young Welsh fireman were moving an LNER loco from under the coal stage. The shed firelighter had filled the boiler right up so that he had an easy night, but the gauge frame was higher than a Western engine and he didn't realize he'd overfilled it. When the crew moved the engine, the regulator lifted the water into the cylinders and the loco 'hydraulicked'. They couldn't stop the loco by closing the regulator and the large engine slowly gathered speed, spewing a shower of sooty water from the chimney. They both panicked and jumped off, to watch the loco disappear off towards the turntable. When they

DIDCOT 1928 STAFF	(31 engines)
Foremen: Loco shed	1
Running	2
Foreman's Clerk	1
Clerks	2
Engine Drivers	55
Engine Firemen	55
Chargeman Engine Cleaner	1
Engine Cleaners	20
Ash Filler	1
Boiler Washers	3
Coalmen	3
Fire Droppers	4
Fire Lighters	3
Shed Labourer	1
Stores Issuers	3
Tube Cleaners	2
Shop Grades (fitters/smiths, etc.)	15
Total	172

No. 3375 *Sir Watkin Wynn* on No. 3 road and an unidentified 22XX on No. 4 road on 28th June 1936. *Collection Peter Winding*

No. 3448 *Kingfisher* at Didcot in 1936, the engine on which I nearly lost my signet ring, as recalled in Chapter 7. *H. C. Casserley*

DIDCOT SHED

got there, out of breath, they found the engine over the stop blocks buried head first in the soft ground.

It was pulled back onto the track with a '28XX' but, having suffered the runaway hulk speeding across its deck, the old boarded undergirder turntable (similar to the one at Reading) never revolved easily again and it was impossible to balance a loco on it properly. It was clear that the frame had been damaged and it was soon replaced by a new overgirder one which proved a real blessing and far easier to handle.

Engines left 'up the bank' first received attention from the two firedroppers who carried out disposal, cleaning the smokebox, firebox and ashpan, using their own tools which were kept propped up against the ash shelter provided during the Second World War. These were usually chained and padlocked to it.

The shed crew then moved the loco under the coal stage for filling by the coalman. While this was going on, the crew would often slip into the messroom under the water tower to avoid the dust. Then, when this was done, the engine continued along the down road and onto the turntable if necessary. It was then positioned inside the shed if possible or left in 'the field' until it could take its place in the correct sequence.

Working from duty sheets, a good shed crew were able to organise the whole shed without fuss, stabling engines in correct sequence for departure. The night shift was the busiest and the shed was most full during the latter part of the day. Sometimes, to save turning, they would swap individual engines of the same class that might already be facing the correct way for the next duty, all, of course, working closely with the shed foreman. It was a complex task requiring familiarity with workings and considerable concentration. Bill Champ, an 'accommodation man', was brilliant at keeping tally of the shed. Of course, locos were in and out all the time but generally the shed was arranged so that No. 1 road, nearest the offices, was clear by the time the fitters booked on, so that engines could be moved in or out of the workshop. In fact, being alongside the messrooms, No. 1 road was rarely used for preparation but held locos for fitters' repairs or washouts. Engines working off No. 1 road were therefore left at the front, perhaps just under cover, but mostly outside. This was a sore point with crews who had to prepare their engines without any shelter from the wet, cold and windy conditions which often prevailed in the small hours. The 4.00 a.m. light engine for Newbury, the engines for the two Winchesters, the 4.30 a.m. passenger pilot and the 2.25 a.m. Thatcham were usually put on this road.

No. 2 road was a dead-end siding used for washouts although engines for some of the mid-afternoon jobs might well be put on top of one of the washouts, and more washouts put in after they had left.

Nos. 3 and 4 roads were furthest from the accommodation and used for the preparation of the vast majority of turns.

'The field' was really used for shunting or temporary stabling of locos, particularly if an

We haven't been able to find any pictures of the old boarded turntable, but this was the replacement after the argument with the LNER 2–8–0 ROD locomotive. For quite a while during the war, 3419 was stabled 'over the table', on one of the radiating sidings, for carriage warming, as mentioned on page 61.
Roye England

No. 1334 in the field in 1931. When I was a young fireman I had an unexpected fast run to Oxford when driver Harry Walker and myself were told to take over this engine one Sunday evening after it had returned from the 3 p.m. passenger to Lambourn. We took a fast passenger train to Oxford in 13 minutes! This train may have been run for passengers stranded at Didcot, but I can't be sure now — only the run sticks in my mind!

Collection Peter Winding

engine needed to complete an earlier part of a sequence in the shed was late back. Only after its return could the others be properly stabled in front of it.

For some years before the war, much of the end of these sidings was covered with a huge coal reserve, infested with rats, over 6 and 7 roads. This came in handy in the early war years during the interruption of supplies, and I spent many a shift helping to load it into 10-ton wagons for the coal stage. We placed a large metal shovelling plate at the base of the 9ft high coal heaps, which gave something for the shovel to slide on. Swinging it up into a wagon, through the side door, we had to make sure we loaded the far corners first so the further points of the vehicle were full before closing the door. Only then was the rest of the wagon filled by shovelling the coal even higher over the sides. Because of the time it had been stored in the open, this coal had deteriorated and gave off poor heat.

No. 8 road was used for long-term cripples, loaded ash wagons, box vans with firelighters, sheeted sand wagons or loaded coal wagons if the siding south of the coal stage was full.

The assistant shed crew, 7 a.m. – 3 p.m., tended to 'shunt the bank' after breakfast using any convenient engine which had come in with surplus fire (before the war, the 6.00 a.m. to 2.00 p.m. early turn shift shunted the bank). This involved collecting loaded ashes from the ash road and putting them into No. 8 road. Empty loco coal wagons were then collected from the foot of the coal stage ramp, where there was a combined hand and pedal-operated catch point, and put into the ash road for filling. Loaded coal wagons were collected from the siding immediately south of the coal stage and propelled right up the ramp to the far side of the coal stage, so they could be gravitated back along the siding as required by the coalmen.

The sidings behind the shed were used for engines waiting to go 'to factory', often due at Swindon for a general overhaul. Surplus coal in the tender or bunker had to be shovelled out, either onto another locomotive, or for the nearby stationary boiler — another back-breaking job. Only enough had to be left for the journey to Swindon. These engines were left there with labels on the gauge frame and handrail reading 'Works Manager Swindon'. Sometimes, if they were serviceable, they would work a train to Swindon, but otherwise, when scheduled for a factory appointment, the rods were removed and they were sent with a rider on board on a down freight to Swindon, marshalled next to the brake van. Locos from other depots were often sent to Didcot on their way 'to factory'; they were either left on top of 'the field' or on the short sidings 'over the table'.

The fire-droppers had one of the most unpleasant tasks, cleaning out hot fireboxes. Breaking up clinker formed on the firebars using a 12ft long iron bar weighing half a hundredweight, or using the 'Britannia', an even heavier 12ft iron-handled rake, were not jobs for weaklings. The large lumps of clinker and the larger residual ash were taken out through the firehole doors with a 10-12ft long-handled shovel, the effective handling of which was a skill in itself, especially when everything was so hot.

After cleaning out the firebox, the smokebox had to be emptied using a shovel and a small rake which looked something like a hoe. Often the ashes cascaded out over the front footplate when the smokebox door was opened and the blast pipe was all but buried. Shovelling this all out, while inhaling the fumes drifting through the tubes from the firebox, was a lousy job and more often than not the wind blew the fine dust back into your face. However, the worst part of the job was emptying the ashpan from beneath the engine. Rather than risk red-hot ashes landing down your neck while crawling beneath the ashpan, after opening the dampers it was usual to enter the pit from under the tender and to begin raking out the hot ashes. Sometimes the cinders in the ashpan were on fire, just to add to the hazardous ash which came out in clouds of fine dust like talcum powder spreading everywhere as the long rake was pushed, then pulled back towards the unfortunate fire-dropper. After crawling out of the pit he would shake himself like a bird having a dust-bath. Watching the clouds of dust being shaken off was a sight — we never really knew whether to laugh or sympathise, though we all generally had a light-hearted attitude.

The bank was feared by many men, because of the sheer hard graft. At times the pit and side areas were completely covered with ashes and clinker which accumulated from the continual servicing when there was a heavy demand for locos to cope with traffic requirements. The ashes were loaded into empty coal wagons by one man, Ted Betteridge, who was very skilled with a shovel. He would load 10 tons of ashes a day and was allowed to leave work as soon as he'd reached this target. Starting at daylight during the summer months, he would finish by midday. It didn't surprise any of us that he wasn't included in an official work study that was once carried out! He was an exception and an artist with a shovel. If he was off sick or on holiday, little was achieved until he was back.

Once loaded, the hot ashes would occasionally ignite, causing concern until doused with the coal watering pipe of the nearest loco. Ted apart, the coalman's duty was the most arduous, coaling the locos as they came in for servicing. As already mentioned, loco coal was delivered to the higher level of the coal stage in wagons pushed up the steeply graded bank. The siding ran through the structure and extended far enough beyond it to hold about five wagons, each laden with 10-20 tons of coal. These vehicles were braked securely on the gentle gradient which allowed them to be

Loaded loco coal wagons on the stop blocks beyond the coal stage. They were pushed up the siding by the shed pilot, then as each wagon was required, it was gravitated through the building by the coalmen.
National Railway Museum

gravitated through the building as required. They were unloaded into the fifteen 10 cwt tubs which were rolled across the wrought iron floor of the coal stage and discharged into the locos below from two tipping ramps. These tubs were kept filled in readiness, and, when each loco came alongside, the coalman would push them flap first onto the counter-balanced ramp, release the flap catch and, following the usual warning given by tapping the iron floor (or the water overflow pipe which ran through the stage from the overhead tank) with a coal pick, he would tip the coal into the bunker or tender below. There was often a scramble below to get under cover to avoid being showered in coal dust. Spillage from overfilling was commonplace but inevitably there were mishaps and at busy times it was not unknown for the coalman to tip one of the tubs after the engine had been moved!

On one dark night I recall an argument between the shed fireman and the coalman, Jack Sargent. The fireman wanted extra coal on an engine at a time when the coalman was very busy and the situation flared into a row. The driver waiting below after the coal had been tipped could no doubt hear the raised voices and moved off, leaving them to it. The fireman ran down the coal stage steps still shouting and in the heat of the moment the coalman jumped off the stage, thinking the engine was still underneath. Incredibly after landing safely some 15ft or so below, amongst the spilt coal, he got up unhurt and continued the chase. The fireman escaped.

The most common incidents involved runaway wagons on the steep bank of the coal stage siding. The brakes on these wagons were pinned down using a brake stick which was something like a square section cricket bat. If the brakes of the loaded wagons weren't pinned down quite hard enough, they would silently creep away. By the time the coalmen noticed what was happening it was often too late to arrest their momentum and the poor coalmen would find themselves straining on the brake stick while the wagon slowly gathered speed. It was usually a losing battle and the catch points at the bottom of the bank would derail the wagons which inevitably ended up embedded axle deep in the soft ground.

Some of the coal from the Welsh mines arrived in huge lumps the size of a man's body. Such lumps might fracture as they landed in a tender but they had to be broken up prior to tipping into the bunker of a tank engine. Struggling to break up an oversize lump through the small bunker hatch while travelling along was sheer hell for any fireman.

A mixture of characters worked as coalmen at Didcot over the years; two of those I got to know, Freddie Knapp and 'Tad' Jones, were of the old school of railwaymen, dedicated and giving many years loyal service. Freddie was slightly built with a slender physique but very strong. He was a hard worker and calm in all situations. 'Tad' Jones was a similar build with a tuft of whiskers over his upper lip. These would twitch when things got rough. He walked four miles each way to work and shovelled between 15 and 20 tons of coal a day. They both wore strong boots, and overalls tied around the ankles and wrists, a neckerchief tucked inside their collars, usually a cloth cap and a small towel to wipe or mop up the sweat and wipe away the coal dust from their faces. Their hands became grimy and coarse with callouses and split nails. They seldom wore gloves which were regarded as a sign of weakness — these men were tough.

The coal stage was a hostile place in winter with easterly and northerly winds blowing through the huge openings and whipping up the coal dust. Sometimes the wagons arrived frozen and the coal had to be broken loose with iron bars. It was also a lonely place to work on night shift when some 25-30 locos were coaled.

Their 'cabin' or messroom in the base of the structure was a dismal place where they washed in a bucket of warm water stood on the floor. It was filled from the injector waste water pipe (heated by opening the steam valve) of whatever engine happened to be standing outside at the time. I still remember the aroma of soap as I walked into that cabin as the coalmen were cleaning up prior to going off duty. The hot soapy water sloshed everywhere as they washed their black faces with cupped hands, and the water in the bucket became increasingly contaminated with coal dust, leaving a thick scum clinging round the inside. Stripped to the waist, careful attention was given to their ears, nose and eyelashes using a flannel. The clean clothes they wore home were kept in a ground-level locker which doubled as a bench seat. A pint of beer at the Prince of Wales or the White Hart was well deserved at the end of a shift.

Often as a cleaner I had the task of loading the sand furnace. A wagon would be stabled alongside and, standing inside it, a pair of us had to swing shovel-loads of wet sand over our heads into the top of the bin. This really was back-breaking and as the day wore on and the wagon emptied, the distance we had to throw the sand increased. Once full, the bin was heated by a coal stove to dry the sand so that it would run freely from the sandboxes on the locos. Sand from the furnace was sieved through a wire mesh to collect any stones and taken to the locos in buckets by the fireman.

When I became a senior cleaner, my duties included tube cleaning. This meant crawling into a hot firebox to clean down the tube plate over the brick arch, scraping solidified ash from the eye of the tubes and cleaning the tube plate with a wire brush. We also cleaned the studs on the inside of the firebox stays and cleared the ashes off the top of the brick arch. Any ash or clinker was forced through the firebox grating into the ash pan. All of the work inside the firebox was awkward, not least trying to get yourself out again afterwards.

We wore face masks when we were inside, and tied our overall trousers around the ankles, and sleeves above the wrist. Unpleasant and physically demanding it certainly was, but on a cold winter's night it was a good warm place to hide!

After this the tubes were 'rodded' from the smokebox using a thin 3/8in diameter rod, 14ft long, with a dart-shaped end. A piece of cloth tied round the end would remove most obstructions but for really stubborn blockages we used a screw-type rod.

When we had finished, the boilersmith would shine an acetylene lamp into the smokebox and check that each tube was clear. Clean tubes aided steam efficiency and I am certain that in later years, because of the unpleasant nature of this task, many tube cleaners didn't carry out the work properly, thus contributing to the apparent decline in efficiency of the steam loco more than any other factor.

The mechanical staff were skilled men with specialist knowledge and experience; they worked under William Miles, a very able chief fitter who'd served as a fitter on a Royal Naval battle cruiser. He was a short, alert person with sharp, twinkling eyes and bushy eyebrows. Although quick-spoken so that he was not the easiest person to follow, he positively brimmed with knowledge. He had such a confident manner that no-one dared challenge him on anything mechanical whether General Manager or fitter. He was the king-pin at Didcot and was respected throughout the London Division by all who knew him. I really admired him and, coming from such a disciplined background, he was a loyal employee who contributed much to the railway.

Working conditions were primitive by today's standards. Everything was covered in grease and oil and the naked flame of a flare lamp was the fitters' only source of light while working underneath a loco. A fitter and his mate worked as a

Bill Miles, chief fitter at Didcot. I really liked him as he was one of the few who knew what he was talking about. *Cty. R. Miles*

An up freight passing over Gatehampton troughs with the levelling tank on the right. The Basildon distant signals were electrically operated, the one just passed slowly returning to 'caution'.
C. R. L. Coles

team, dealing with running repairs of locos in service.

The maintenance routine system was called the MP11 — the title of the instruction manual. Basically, this involved the examination of all parts of each loco on a time or mileage basis. All moving parts, valves, pistons, gear linkage, wheels, etc. were examined every 6,000 or 12,000 miles, whilst parts like the boiler, safety valves, etc., were examined on a time period of three, six or twelve months.

Locos in service also had an 'X' day examination before working a vacuum goods or passenger turn, whilst others on goods or pilot work were examined once a week. This was nearly always carried out when a crew were preparing the engine so that any problems found could also be brought to the attention of the fitters. Otherwise, any faults discovered by drivers out on the road were booked on a repair card at the end of each turn.

We used to help out with boiler wash-outs which were carried out according to the time a loco had been in service, i.e. '60XX' and '50XX' every four days, '59XX', '68XX' and '28XX' seven days, and the smaller 0—6—0s fourteen days. As boilersmith's mate, I had to raise steam in the stationary boiler at the rear of the shed, alongside No. 3 road. This was from an old Dean loco and it bore a plate giving the boiler number 947. It was connected to a system of pipes which carried steam around the shed for wash-out purposes and pumping oil up into the overhead storage tanks in the stores. Steam was piped alongside the wash-out road to the side of each loco. Water was taken from hoses connected to ground-level hydrants. Each hose had a pointed nozzle which was placed inside the oval openings at the top of the firebox.

All boiler plugs and mud-hole doors were removed to help with a thorough washing-out, the mud-hole doors being large enough at the bottom of the boiler to allow shale and fine shingle to be washed out. Often it was necessary to use metal rods to clean out large deposits.

Waiting at the control valve to operate the handle, the boiler-washer would shout 'On' or 'Off' as needed, but with the incessant noise in the engine shed, the message was sometimes misheard and the poor fellow often got a soaking!

As the pay for this was on a piecework basis, with so many hours allowed for each loco, I'm convinced that the work was hurried — the sooner the job was done, the earlier they could finish. I don't think some of the locos had the really thorough wash they needed, in between boiler inspections, and I was later to experience the problems this caused.

Thursday was pay day and just before 2 p.m. a figure would be seen walking down to the shed carrying a case which was also chained to his waist. Shadowed by the chief clerk, they locked themselves in the office and put each employee's wages into a small round tin (about 1in diameter and 1½in deep) with a numbered lid. These tins were more commonplace when sovereigns were in use. Meanwhile, outside the pay office, the dress parade began; the lads, wearing their best outfits, with neatly-combed Brylcreemed hair, formed an orderly queue. At exactly 2 p.m. the window hatch would be lifted, and each of us gave our number to the clerk, who took a small oval-shape copper token with the relevant number on it from a small wooden cabinet and handed it in to the pay clerk. There was just enough room through the small hatch to exchange the token for the pay tin! After prising open the lid (sometimes we had to bang it against the wall first), we emptied the money into our hands and handed back the empty containers which were returned to a wooden box with a sloping half lid, where they remained until the following Thursday.

As a senior cleaner, I was never fortunate enough to assist the fitter who travelled out to Goring to clean and service the Gatehampton water troughs. I often wonder how many of the crews of the crack expresses from the larger depots realised the humble role played by Didcot shed in maintaining the water supply in the famous troughs situated between Pangbourne and Goring some 43 miles from Paddington. Travelling at anything between 40 and 90 mph, locos would pick up water via a scoop beneath the tender. If the tank had got too empty, the axle-box springs could hold the tender a bit high for the scoop to do anything other than top it up a bit, but with ideal conditions the tank could be filled to the extent that it was all too easy to flood the tender. If the scoop wasn't wound up soon enough, water cascaded from the air vents and flooded the footplate with not just water but a sea of muddy coal dust.

There were four feeds spaced along each trough which were fed by gravity from the huge levelling tank by Basildon road bridge. The Didcot boiler-washers would periodically travel to Goring station and walk out to Gatehampton pump house which supplied the 620 yds long troughs. One of the team pushed a rubber 'squeezy' along the troughs. This was a broomlike tool with an indiarubber head specially shaped to fit, It was something like a shrimp net in shape. While he pushed the water out of the way, two of the others, one on each side, swept out the rubbish which had accumulated in the bottom, using wire-headed brooms.

The fourth member of the team acted as look-out to warn of approaching trains by blowing a whistle. While engrossed in carrying out the work it was inevitable that standing clear was left to the last minute which all too often resulted in a fair soaking from the spray of an engine taking water at speed.

The pump-house attendant, Teddy Hewett, travelled each day from Didcot to Goring. He maintained the pumps and treated the water with a lime solution to neutralise it for the benefit of the loco boilers. Teddy was a real character, a true Edwardian in his manner and appearance. Of medium build, he had a thinning hairline, and long sideburns joining a moustache which was stained by smoking. He often held a small pipe in his teeth and wore a red and white neckerchief, gold ear-rings, and a cloth cap which was soiled on the right-hand side of the peak through his habit of frequent adjustment. Sometimes it was over his brow and sometimes on the back of his head.

When off duty, his dress was also Edwardian, with a velvet jacket with pearl buttons over a waistcoat and gold watch chain. His drainpipe

No. 2007 at the back of Didcot shed. In hot weather, water in the saddle tank used to get too warm for the injectors to work properly.
Lens of Sutton

Teddy Hewett. *Cty. J. Hewett*

trousers were often studded with pearl buttons and the black spats over his shoes were polished to a mirrorlike gleam. He was an elegant man who always had a cheerful word for me.

I may not have helped at the troughs but I did once have the pleasure of delivering some firelighters, oil and cotton waste to Newbury, which was an outstation of Didcot MPD. On Monday mornings one of the saddle tanks, 1925 or 2007, was delivered to Newbury by a Didcot crew who returned with the old one for wash-out and servicing. The stores were usually carried on board but on that particular morning they had been forgotten and I obliged.

Eventually I became the most senior cleaner at Didcot and in the early part of 1940 I had my first firing turn. I was very surprised when the booking clerk told me to look at the enginemen's duty roster. There was my name — B. Barlow, engine cleaner — marked in the firemen's column. Fred Jones was the driver and the engine was No. 2783, an 0–6–0 pannier tank with an open cab. Excited, I raced home to tell my father, who gave a broad grin. He knew I had been paired with an excellent driver for my first turn.

CHAPTER FIVE

EARLY TURNS

I booked on duty at 5.30 a.m., but long before this I was dressed and ready. I arrived ten minutes early but Fred was already there waiting for me. We had ten minutes to read notices and five minutes to collect the keys and walk to the engine which had already been prepared by the 4.30 a.m. prep crew. "Well, lad, follow me", he said cheerfully and led the way, walking with a side-to-side gait. Most locomen had this swing to their walk, which I maintain came from keeping their balance at speed on a lively footplate. Fred was a typical Welshman who, like many of his contemporaries, had left the valleys after the First World War or during the Depression. He probably only just scraped through the minimum height requirement for footplatemen, but his slight appearance was deceptive; he could handle an engine with ease. He had a magnetic personality and was full of encouragement. He enjoyed teaching me the secrets of the footplate, his explanations were detailed and straightforward and his patience with a raw recruit seemed endless. No wonder my father had given me such a broad grin when I had told him who my driver was.

Fred showed me round the loco and together we checked the tools and equipment. I had brought a bottle of tea with me which I was told to put on the dish over the firebox to keep warm.

It was now 5.45 a.m. and I was on the footplate peering over the bunker when Fred asked me to take off the handbrake. After giving a short, sharp whistle to warn of the move, Fred opened the regulator and we glided away from the shed and made our way to Didcot Ordnance Depot where we were to spend the shift shunting.

As cleaners, we had never been allowed on the footplate when the engine was in motion, so this was the first time I could feel what it was like to

No. 2783 fitted with a 'busby' spark arrester, the engine I had for my first turn with Fred Jones. This picture shows fireman Bob Clark leaning out of the cab one Sunday in the summer of 1938.
Courtesy Bob Clark

be on a moving locomotive. I was thrilled — at last I was to spend a whole shift where I felt I belonged.

We never received any tuition, we were just expected to know. Fred told me what to do as we went along. "Put the flap up mate", I was told. This was the metal plate which largely covered the firehole and was operated by a chain. As the water level dropped, he put on the injector. "Put some coal on mate", was my next instruction. I picked up the shovel, which was inside the coal hole, with my right hand on the shaft and my back turned to Fred. Poor man! He burst out in his rich Welsh accent, "No man, no, come y'ere, come y'ere." I had picked up the shovel the wrong way round for a GWR loco man, and was soon shown the correct way of handling it.

The restricted space on the footplate of a small tank engine was an experience to remember, and to use a full-length shovel which seemed as long as the width of a footplate was not very easy.

"Keep a sharp look-out mate", Fred told me, his musical voice coming across the cab. I was expected to see that all was clear on my side when we shunted backwards and forwards. Often I was caught off balance after Fred had applied the brakes a bit sharply. To steady myself on one of these occasions I caught hold of the first available support. It was a hot pipe, which scalded my elbow, but not a word to Fred. I learned the hard way.

Fred was no fool, he knew that I was having a few rough edges knocked off, and was deliberately catching me off balance, teaching me how to survive. Having seen Fred perform his shunting duties, pulling the tall reversing lever backwards and forwards was amazing. He was so short, only 5ft 2in, that the reverser handle reached just below his chin. Each movement was done with ease, a skill developed over many years. Never over-exerting himself, he knew just the correct time to alter the reverser, using the movement of the locomotive to assist him, just prior to stopping. I was taking everything in and keeping all Fred's movements in my mind. Watching him and other drivers was to prove very helpful in years to come but the earliest impressions seem to have been those most indelibly implanted in my mind.

The next day it was back to earth again with the usual cleaning duties, but there were other occasional adventures. I had a couple of firing turns to Swindon, the first with Harry Mapson on a '28XX' and another with Percy Steel and an LNER engine. On that trip a gauge glass burst, but as there were two gauge frames on LNER engines, we just carried on using the other one.

Running a special to pick up passengers stranded at Oxford gave me my first opportunity to fire on a passenger train. George Willis was the driver and the engine was 1334. I felt quite lost and realised what a lot I still had to learn.

When we had completed twelve firing turns, we were entitled to a serge jacket, an overcoat and a cap. I had done thirteen when I put in my official application. Then one day when I went to draw my wages at the end of the short three

A 'tanky' cab, similar to 2783. The bent handbrake handle was typical, caused by falling lumps of coal while the bunker was filled from the coaling stage.

Winchester Chesil. My first wages as a fireman (£4 10s 0d including lodging allowance) were collected from the office under the canopy.
D. Thompson

months summer service, I was told to report to Old Oak again on the following Monday morning. This came as a complete surprise. I was a permanent employee so I couldn't understand why I was being moved out while other cleaners recruited on a temporary basis were being kept on.

However, I did as I was told, arranged to go back to the same lodgings, and reported to Old Oak where I was put on time office duties. On the Tuesday morning when I booked on duty, I was told there was something in the stores for me. It was the jacket, cap and coat, which I took back to Barlby Gardens that night with pride.

I think it was the following morning that I had to deliver a telegram to the staff clerk, who looked at me in astonishment as I entered his room. "What the hell are you doing back here?" he exclaimed. As he'd fixed me up with what he regarded as a permanent transfer to Didcot earlier in the year, he was straight on the telephone and giving someone an earful. Within minutes he had arranged a free travel pass, and I was on my way back to my lodgings to re-pack my case and catch the Didcot slip coach on the 11.15 a.m. Paddington to Weston-super-Mare express.

My father made some enquiries and we soon realized that I had been used as a pawn in some internal politics. I was caught up in a web of intrigue. Now I was beginning to realise why I was offered a vacancy at Old Oak rather than Didcot when I first applied for a transfer to the loco department. However, with the outbreak of the Second World War, circumstances changed, the shed foreman was replaced and promotion was quicker.

By this time the effects of the war were beginning to become apparent. The railways were a vital part of the war effort and, with the need for manpower, promotions were quicker. In the autumn of 1940 I moved to Winchester to take up my first post of fireman. There was no telling where vacancies would arise, so I was lucky to get something not too far away and just at the other end of the Didcot, Newbury & Southampton line. I took the place of a fireman from Reading, lodging with George Light, head shunter. He and his mother took in railwaymen. Mrs. Light was a real old-fashioned lady, a warm and motherly sort, stocky, with long hair kept in a bun, and long starched clothes.

She was very friendly and for 10/- a week fed me well; there was always plenty of food. I called her Ma and she even quite voluntarily washed and scrubbed my overalls, so I gave her an extra 2/6d.

On the early shift I booked on at about 6 a.m. The loco, usually a '22XX', had already been prepared by the overnight shedman. The two drivers there were Bob Hester and Tom Keon, but most of my time was spent with Hester who was kind to me. I was keen to learn and before leaving Didcot, one of the senior firemen gave me some firing tuition over a pint in the Marlborough Club.

No. 2289 at Winchester shed. The coal under the wall had to be hand-shovelled into the tender. *E. Branch*

No. 2227 outside Winchester shed on 9th July 1945, just as we used to leave the engine after working the 5.50 p.m. from Didcot to Winchester. Steam coming from the chimney could sometimes mean leaking tubes, but many of the engines were in poor shape during the war years. This picture also shows the absence of cab side windows at this time. *G. L. Hoare*

EARLY TURNS

With only one loco and a small turntable, the tiny shed at Winchester Bar End was a quiet place with a slow tempo, especially when compared with Old Oak! Once again I suppose I found it a bit of an anticlimax, and to my mind the drivers appeared to show off a bit in front of me in a flamboyant manner. Anyway, I wasn't impressed — their engines seemed like toys compared to the 'Kings' and 'Castles' I had cleaned.

Coming off shed on the early turn, we collected the coaches from the adjacent siding and, leaving the station at 7.5 a.m., worked the Reading passenger train to Highclere or Woodhay, where we changed over with a Didcot crew on the 4.30 Didcot freight and worked the southbound goods back to Bar End yard, shunting at each station on the way. If we'd hit any pheasants while working the passenger train, we stopped on the way back to pick them up, and if that sounds like an outside chance, we had as many as seven on one trip.

On arrival back at Bar End yard, there was shunting to do, including running back up the line to Winnall Gas Works and Kingsworthy.

If we were on the late turn we booked on at about 12.15 p.m. to relieve the early crew, and began by turning the engine. We collected an up freight train (12/40 Winchester) from the sidings and rang for permission to leave the yard.

We worked as far as Whitchurch or Litchfield, where we changed footplates with Newbury men and returned to Winchester with the 12.45 p.m. Didcot passenger train. After running round, and sometimes stabling the coaches for the early morning passenger train the next day (this varied with summer or winter timetables), we took over the 4.55 p.m. Southampton passenger train, which Southern men had worked in. This time we worked further north, and changed over with Didcot men, bringing the 5.52 p.m. from Didcot into Winchester. This involved a tricky bit of judgement for a new fireman — running the fire down ready for disposal, yet keeping enough steam to work the train.

On arrival we stabled the coaches in the yard and went on shed and carried out disposal — the only time we as firemen were expected to do this. We left a small fire inside the back of the firebox, under the doors, to save the night man lighting up again.

During this period I recall standing near my lodgings on St. Catherine's Hill, watching the dramatic spectacle of the dock yards at South-

A 32XX arriving at Chesil with a train from Southampton. The signalman came out of his box to collect the single line token from Shawford Junction.   *E. Branch*

ampton being bombed. The heroic residents, like many others, had their determination to carry on strengthened by the Blitz.

After just six weeks I was sent back to Didcot, for good this time. I was put into the pilot link where there were 18 turns — all shunting duties in the local marshalling yards. I was staggered to see the changes that were taking place. A special link had been created for relieving goods trains with 48 turns of duty around the clock, two sets of men booking on every hour.

Within a very short time the 40-50 sets of men at Didcot were increased to something between 90 and 100, and what had been a spacious shed became overcrowded with locos of all descriptions.

On occasions there was a serious shortage of places to berth oncoming locos as they arrived for servicing. The firedropping pit was often full up and the queue so long that crews left their engines outside the shed signal until there was room for them to be brought in. The whole character of the shed changed. Every member of staff had taken pride in the neat and tidy appearance of the site — there had hardly been any ashes to be seen, spilt coal had been picked up, the shed floor kept spotless and the locos regularly cleaned. Now the increased allocation and the urgency of keeping as many locos as possible serviced and available for duty for the demands of increased traffic resulted in a fall in standards of cleanliness and neglect of equipment. The whole area became untidy. The ashpit road was soon blocked with clinker and spent fire ash left in heaps where it was thrown out of each loco. At times the pit between the rails was so full that it was impossible to crawl underneath an engine to rake out the ash pan.

All of this made moving around the site pretty treacherous when we were plunged into darkness during black-outs, when the air raid sirens wailed out from high on top of the provender stores. We were left scrambling around under the intermittent warbling of distant enemy aircraft.

The falling standards in pride and general morale bred a careless attitude which in turn led to a shortage of equipment. The tool boxes on the locomotives were not being locked up and tools were used elsewhere and not replaced. Shortages were made up from other locos, and even the locos themselves were sometimes cannibalised by crews and maintenance staff to keep others in service.

Gathering tools prior to going off shed became such a nightmare that many of us started to hide them away! I kept a coal watering pipe inside the overflow pipe from the water tank over the coal stage. The outlet was below the cabin window which was handy when walking past on my way to the shed. I hid my shovel and handbrush in the stationary boiler at the back of the shed. This obviously contributed to the shortage but it was a great relief not having to search for things and it was everyone for himself at that time.

To arrest the problem, the cabin beneath the coal stage was pressed into service as a tool room, staffed in shifts by three retired drivers who'd been asked to return. They were Joe Beckenham, Arthur Workman and Joe Nicholls. A system was introduced whereby the tools for each engine were collected and returned in a bucket at the beginning and end of each shift. Each bucket contained a flare lamp, gauge frame lamp, spare gauge glass and rubber rings, a gauge frame spanner, 5/8 x 7/8 and 5/8 x 3/4 spanners (for the valve spindle glands of the '22XX' there was also a set pin spanner), a handbrush, coal watering pipe, a cannister of detonators and two red flags. When collecting the bucket, the fireman was also issued with a shovel, coal pick and engine headlamps.

The bucket system was a successful turning point in speeding the release of locos for service. Later on, attempts were made to return to locked tool boxes, but the shortage of equipment was so serious that it became necessary to rob other engines again. The large padlocks were easily broken by turning them upside-down over the top of the securing bracket and giving them a smart clout with the coal pick. I have to confess that I found this necessary on many occasions.

It was all the more frustrating to be handicapped by wartime tool shortages at the very time when there were extra demands on men and machines. It was not at all unusual to be stuck with a fireman's shovel with only half a blade, to have to sweep up with cotton waste, or use one of the engine headlamps to keep an eye on the level of water in the gauge glass.

On top of all this we had to contend with canvas sheets to enclose the cab to prevent any light from the fire showing in the darkness. In the same connection the firehole flaps were removed from all locos and we had to keep the firebox doors closed when running at night. As an aside, this also meant that a generation of new firemen had no experience in handling the flap until several years later.

Another problem at this time was that of locomotives remaining in use for days at a time without servicing. Their fireboxes became full of clinker residue, ashpans were full, preventing the passage of air through the firegrate and boilers sludged up.

When the Blitz started on London, there was such serious congestion that goods trains were held everywhere. I recall nine lined up in the up goods loop at Foxhall Junction. I was detailed to engine mind all these one night until crews could be found, and the next day I was still waiting with them. In fact it was not until 6 p.m. the following evening that any movement of these took place.

Poor coal and dirty fires, and forced steam pressure through rapid demand when a stranded train was eventually required to move, involved much use of the blower, and all the expansion and contraction associated with continual stopping and starting caused tubes to become blocked with ash and suffer leakage around the tubeplates. Engines that became really useless had to be taken to shed for attention. Didcot was often overwhelmed by crippled locos, presenting a scene like a battlefield.

The influx of staff drafted in from all corners of the GWR made Didcot a very cosmopolitan village. Cornishmen, Welshmen and Londoners were among those called away from their families for wartime duties, and a number of Irishmen were brought in as extra staff. They were a tough bunch of fellows, strong, hardened men who did a marvellous job — a real credit to the war effort.

Accommodation for all these staff was provided in sleeping coaches, stabled in the carriage sidings to the south of the shed, and heated by various engines connected via an underground pipe system. However, because of the distance involved, the heating proved inefficient and the sleeping coaches were moved to the back of the shed on No. 5 and No. 6 sidings, and No. 3419 was stabled nearby on one of the sidings radiating from the turntable, or 'stood over the table', as

This railwaymen's hostel was built during the war years to replace the temporary accommodation provided firstly in sleeping coaches and then the prefabricated buildings at the foot of the Newbury bay embankment. The new hostel was initially managed by Mr. and Mrs. Cliffs.
National Railway Museum

Firemen Aubrey Bevan, John Weston and Cyril Moore (standing), and drivers Eddie Faulkes and J. Thursdon (seated) at the new hostel in 1943-4.   *Cty. Johnny Weston*

we called it. It was kept in steam 24 hours a day to provide heating, and the ash from cleaning its fire piled up alongside until you could walk up the slope to get on the footplate! The tender was filled from a nearby hydrant. The refreshment room on the station served as a canteen for the extra staff, but this was a far from ideal situation and eventually a proper hostel was built to the east of the station.

Handling staff of so many origins was no easy task but, whether by luck or design, the shedmaster, Bill Young, was the finest appointment for the post that I ever knew. He was a Welshman, and an ex-footplateman, as all loco foremen were in those days. He was of small stature and walked with a slight limp, punctuated by a side-to-side roll easily recognised from a distance. He wore a trilby hat carefully positioned, just tipped over his forehead, with the brim turned down to shield

A down express entering Didcot. Lower Broadway, on the far side of the allotments, can just be seen running towards Marsh bridge.
Philip Hopkins

his eyes. We only saw him without it if we were being interviewed. He had a jovial countenance and had no problem in coming down to the level of whoever he was dealing with — he could curse and swear with the rest. When travelling by train on official duty he was entitled to first class travel but, if any loco crews were on the train, he preferred to join them, even sitting in on a game of cards.

Soon known as 'Briggam Young' or 'Youngie', he never showed any stress or tension despite his responsibility. He had a friendly good-humoured manner throughout the war years at Didcot; his bark was worse than his bite and his personality such that the staff responded with maximum effort.

I remember his cool manner over a derailment in the Ordnance Depot. Youngie arrived with the breakdown vans and asked where the driver was. Reluctantly, he was told that he'd gone to the canteen for a pint of beer! Youngie's response was awaited with apprehension but he just said "Good idea, I'll go and join him." There was no fuss and no recriminations.

No. 8470, one of the LMS 2—8—0s, leaving Didcot West End signal box with an up freight on 29th March 1947. I liked these but preferred Western types. We had all sorts of engines during the war.
H. C. Casserley

The breakdown crew soon had the loco rerailed and I remember when Youngie was waving from the window of the departing breakdown van, there was a tremendous sigh of relief by us all; we'd feared a rocket because the staff were at fault, but he ruled all the more effectively for his restraint.

By this time I had been a shunting engine fireman for a few months and was learning the different ways of doing my duty with varying requirements and advice from different drivers. Some had no time for inexperienced firemen and enjoyed seeing us get into difficulties, especially if our personalities did not mix. Being on the footplate together was like a marriage between drivers and firemen. If it worked it was wonderful but with any clash in temperament, it could be hell. Sometimes men were paired for several years.

To me it was frustrating to fire to those who I could already see were poor drivers doing things badly or incorrectly. Sometimes my feelings showed and an aggressive driver might drive the engine even harder and make me work all the more. They knew I would kick, but this was a double-sided affair and I knew that my assistance and cooperation would be needed later, and when the occasion arose I could give a gentle reminder that it took both of us to handle a steam locomotive.

Most drivers were a pleasure to work with and skilful enginemen. That they'd learned as firemen was all too apparent if they picked up the shovel and the good ones always gave the fireman an easy trip.

As the war years dragged on, there were shortages of food, and luxuries became scarce. Extra tea ration was supplied by the Ministry of Food for essential wartime occupations such as train crews. Enginemen were issued with supplies of tea, sugar and condensed milk every fourteen days and it was under these circumstances that the copper tea-can was adopted instead of a bottle of tea. The copper tea can originated from the boilersmiths at Old Oak Common and soon became popular. We purchased our own for two shillings and sixpence. Sometimes duties could extend to some thirty hours, so we filled our cans with water wherever we could and took our tea breaks whenever the chance occurred. We soon got to know where all the drinking water taps were all over our patch of the system.

A full tea can with a lid was wiped over with cylinder oil and held in the firebox on the tip of the shovel blade. The water boiled very quickly — almost in seconds — and a matchstick floating in the top of the can prevented a smoky taste to the tea. The hot can was taken off the shovel with a spanner through the handle, and the tea was added before the water went off the boil. The result was nectar and thereafter the tea-can became an essential part of our equipment. I became a sort of tea alcoholic and my taste for the brew still lingers.

CHAPTER SIX
RAPID PROMOTIONS

IT was all shunting work in the lower links, but useful experience in gradually learning how to handle strings of wagons and work under the direction of numerous shunters. I was only in the bottom links for a very short time before being put into the new relief link, but the work we did sorting and forming trains gave me a good general understanding of how traffic was worked and an intimate knowledge of the yards at Didcot and their functions.

The engines for all these jobs were what we called 'tankies'. Those I remember include 907, 1742 (open cab and the finest steamer), 1861, 1925 and 2007 (both 'saddlebacks'), 2076, 2783 (open cab), 2784, 3622, 5710, 5735, 5744 and 7709.

The duties in the lower links were:

THE PILOT LINK (No. 7 LINK at one time)

UP YARD PILOT (3 shifts)
Book on 9.45. Off shed 10 p.m.
The engine for this turn, a 'tankie', was already prepared for us. It stayed out for 24 hours on this duty, which was manned in three 8-hour shifts. It always faced 'downhill' (smokebox towards Swindon) so the driver was on the inside of the curve for the shunters' signals. Because the drivers were 'cripple link' or 'medical' men, the same ones regularly worked the three shifts. At this time they were Frank Cox, Joe Withers and Fred Wells. The 9.45 a.m. turn was the busiest, and the sound of the pilot barking as it struggled with long strings of wagons, and the clanging of all the buffers and couplings, could be heard over Didcot throughout most of the night. Our task was to sort traffic arriving from the North into trains for Winchester, Westbury, etc. We took a meal around 1.00 a.m. after making up the train for the 2.00 a.m. Thatcham. We drew this up out of the yard and left it on the running road, then stood near the shunters cabin on the next track to the running road, between the carriage sidings and the goods yard, for our meal. The blackout was in force at this time, so we worked under blackout sheets which completely enclosed the cab. Although this could be a nuisance, even the open-cabbed panniers became nice cosy places to eat a meat pie or sandwiches, sheltered from the cold night air. We continued sorting for the rest of the shift until we were relieved at 5.45 a.m. The up yard pilot also usually cleared the cripple sidings.

Book on 5.30 for 5.45 a.m. to relieve in up yard
Book on 1.45 for 2.00 p.m. to relieve in up yard
On both of these relief duties we walked to the up yard and took over the engine which was usually standing by

Nos. 1925 and 2007 on 'the bank'. *Collection Peter Winding*

No. 5744 on up yard pilot duty with a shunter's 'chariot' in the centre yard on 12th October 1949. Even with the 'busby', this was a good free-steaming loco. The building in the background housed the relief cabin, shunters cabin, yard inspector and lavatories.

H. C. Casserley

the shunters cabin. The shunters also changed over at the same time. Work on the morning turn included marshalling the 8.25 a.m. Hungerford Fly which had been partly made up by the previous shift. The shunters stopped for breakfast around 8.00 a.m. after pulling this train out of the yard. There was less work on the late shift as fewer trains left the up yard at night. We were officially allowed to take a meal break of about twenty minutes between the third and fifth hour of our duty, but we often had about an hour. We stood on the 'Dardanelles' and had a fry-up on the shovel. On the late shift we usually stopped around 5.00 p.m. after forming the 6.05 p.m. Westbury. If things were not too busy, the shunters would usually slip over to 'The Prince' for a pint. We would start to run the fire down towards the end of the shift and about 9.15 some drivers would also slip off for half an hour in the pub, leaving the fireman to do any movements that might be required. I would also lock up the tools ready for when the driver returned to take the engine on shed.

No. 6 LINK (Ordnance Depot and Centre Yard)

Didcot Central Ordnance Depot was a vast rail-served complex established during the First World War to supply 'anything from a nail to a muleshoe', including blankets, pots and pans, even musical instruments and, of course, munitions. Much of the equipment came in bulk straight from manufacturers, to be stamped with the crow's foot

No. 1925 with 'fish fryer' spark arrester.

marking for identification, before being stored ready for distributing to the various units. Recovered items were also sent there — I remember masses of equipment coming back from France, for instance, after the fall of Dunkirk in 1941.

At this time there were seven tank engines at work there each day, usually panniers, but we also had two 'saddlebacks'. A Mr. Pictor was the Depot Master for the GWR with three inspectors working under him — Lithgo, Boseley and Tosh Burton. All engines working in the depot had to be fitted with 'fish fryers' — a mesh fitting over the chimney as a spark arrester, whilst those fitted

RAPID PROMOTIONS

with a proper 'busby' were used in the magazines if at all possible.

'HUMP' SIDINGS (Ordnance Depot)
Book on 5.30. Off shed 5.45 a.m. (3 shifts)

The engine for this job faced 'uphill' towards London and worked at the six sidings marshalling outgoing trains. They weren't hump sidings at all but were served from a spur which ran into a small copse on a slightly rising gradient, which meant that wagons could be gravitated into the sidings. The pilot here was used to sort traffic from the gulleys, Milton, 'S' shed and the Magazines into trains to be worked away to destinations such as Hanwell Bridge or Banbury, although much of the traffic was taken to Didcot Yard by any of the pilot engines en route to Didcot shed, via Foxhall Junction. Engines working trains away from the depot or transferring traffic to Didcot yard, usually collected them via a connection from the up relief line, although trains and wagon trips sometimes left from the Lower Yard and out via the West Curve. This was a busy duty with a relief crew taking over at 1.30 p.m.

However, the night turn was considerably easier. We booked on at 8.30 p.m. to walk over to the Hump Yard and take over. The walking time allowed from the shed was 45 minutes. As there was no more traffic from the Lower Yard during the night, we had usually finished by about 1.00 a.m. when we had our break in the Hump cabin, an old coach brake van. Afterwards we were kept there as stand-by in case we were needed, so we rested until we took the loco back on shed about 5.45 a.m.

There were times on the loco during a pleasant summer's night that we could enjoy a peaceful solitude and I could hear nightingales warbling their shrill tunes. As the night set in, our blacked-out cab, hidden in the coppice, seemed so distant from the hostilities in Europe.

One night later in the year, my mate, Bob Paxton, suggested I walk back to the locomotive shed to draw our

Inside the Ordnance Depot, looking east towards the offices and 'T in' and 'T out' transfer sheds which feature on the horizon. The tracks in the foreground were from gulleys No. 2 and 1 respectively, whilst the higher level sidings on the right were part of the lower yard. The one nearest the camera was a dead end but the second one led to the Hump sidings. *National Railway Museum*

wages as the pay office would close at 8.00 p.m. and we didn't get relief until 9.15 p.m. Bob had made out a pay slip authorisation for me to present to the pay clerk. Setting off on foot and allowing enough time to arrive before 8.00 p.m., I struggled through the dense coppice in the direction of the track leading out to Foxhall signal box. In the falling darkness I was about to pass through the gate when I was confronted with "Halt! Who goes there?", and a 303 rifle with fixed bayonet pointing at me. "Friend or Foe?". "Friend!" I sharply replied. I was stunned, my whole body locked into a solid freeze. My skin began to quiver, pimples raised instantly on my arms and my mouth dried up. "Advance and be recognised!" was the next command. With legs heavy as lead and trembling, I slowly walked closer. "Oh, it's you" came the reply in a Geordie accent, much to my relief. I quickly stated my business and explained I would be returning shortly.

Having collected the wages, we both had cash to celebrate my charmed life at The Prince of Wales. When it turned out that Bob knew that Bill Waters, the landlord, had some beer, which wasn't always so easy to come by in those days, I realized why he wanted his wages!

On another occasion when I was on the early turn Hump Pilot, during the late summer of 1941, when the dawn was a couple of hours old, I saw a number of black specks slowly approaching from the southern skyline. As they grew larger, I recognised them as aircraft returning from night bombing of Germany. They had dropped their deadly cargo under darkness, to return in daylight. When they were overhead, they were very low and slow, almost

Looking west towards 'E' sheds, with the central REME workshops on the right. The line of vans to the right of shed E5 were in No. 3 gulley, whilst the steam crane to the left was on the line connecting with gulleys 2 and 1. This untidiness was typical of the war years.

hovering. They were Whitley bombers returning to RAF Shippon, Abingdon, some with only one or two engines working and some with large yawning gaps visible in their fusilages, where they had been shot up. I can often remember feeling how lucky I was working on a shunting engine while those airmen had risked deadly horror on flying duties.

LOWER YARD PILOT (Ordnance Depot)
Book on 8.20. Off shed 9.00 a.m.
The engine for this job faced 'downhill' towards Swindon. We came off shed and ran to the West Curve Yard, via the up running line and West Curve Junction, to collect a train which had already been prepared for us to take to the depot. We propelled it out onto the down running line beyond West Curve box and pulled it round the West Curve into the depot where the guards would unlock the gates to let us in. We stopped short of the Lower Yard, ran round the train via the adjacent lines and propelled the train into the sidings.

The lower yard pilot's duty was to shunt incoming traffic which usually arrived as a train from Banbury or trips from Didcot Yard (via West Curve entrance). The wagons had to be sorted for each gulley and put in the sequence for the sheds served by each of the gulley pilots. This duty also involved shunting 'T in' and 'T out' Transfer Sheds alongside the Lower Yard and assisting the

A similar view to page 67, showing some of the WD vans. I remember runner beans and sunflowers being grown at the end of the shed on the left.
National Railway Museum

Looking west towards No. 2 gulley. The track diverging to the left led to No. 1 gulley whilst the elevated line on the extreme left was one of the lower yard sidings.
National Railway Museum

RAPID PROMOTIONS

Hump pilot, collecting wagons from the transfer road and returning them after sorting. The Hump and Lower Yard were connected by up and down running/reception lines. In my time this duty was worked in one shift, the engine running back to shed around 4.30 p.m., often working a trip to West Curve Yard.

'THE GULLEYS' (Ordnance Depot)
Book on 5.30. Off shed 5.45 a.m. (three turns, one for each gulley, manned in two shifts)

The engines for the three 'gulleys' faced 'downhill' towards Swindon and were already prepared for us. We all moved out of the shed yard, usually all coupled together with the Milton pilot. As ever, these things varied, but I have seen as many as seven depot pilots coupled together at the shed signal. We ran over to the depot via the down relief and entered through the Hump sidings. On arrival each of the gulley engines coupled to their trains and picked up their shunters who, for some of the time, rode on the shunters' trolley which was always next to the engine and equipped with shunters' poles, lamps and re-railing ramps for any mishaps.

We propelled the wagons down the middle of the three lines of each gulley, delivering to the sheds on one side on the way down and sorting traffic for collection on the return journey. The under shunter walked ahead and called us over the road crossings whilst the head shunter carried out most of the coupling and braking of the wagons, always working on the driver's side. The vehicles were nearly all box vans, locked and sealed with a wire secured with a galvanised metal tag bearing the crow's foot symbol.

We took sandwiches with us and took our break when we reached the bottom or far end of the gulley, then

A view from the guard's van of a freight on Didcot West Curve travelling towards Foxhall bridge and Foxhall Junction signal box. The signals read to main loop (off), ordnance depot No. 1 sidings, No. 2 sidings, and the platform inside the depot. During the war, this platform was used for workers brought in direct by train from Banbury and Oxford.
Barry Warr

worked back engine first, serving the remaining sheds and picking up any wagons we'd sorted earlier on the other side. No. 3 gulley was a bit shorter but the loco on that job also served the Magazines and had to have a 'busby' spark arrester chimney as fitted to 907, 5710 and 5744. No. 907 was terrible for steaming, a real bitch of an engine, probably mainly because the 'busby' was choked up and never cleaned out properly.

On the way back up the gulley, the shunters usually rode on the engine, the under shunter still seeing us over the crossings while we sounded long warning whistles. There was a canteen not far from the top end of the gulleys (and nearest to No. 3) and many of the drivers and shunters that welcomed a pint would find time to slip over there, particularly if it was known that there was some beer on tap as there was always a shortage. When they knew the canteen was open, these men always made sure there was a shunt in hand before leaving the gulley, usually towards the end of their turn. A return trip usually took the best part of a shift to complete.

When all the traffic had been collected, the shunter would report to the yard inspector and the head shunter would call the train forward towards the entrance gates and back into the lower yard for sorting prior to being put in the Hump sidings.

Throughout the work it was necessary to keep an eye on the amount of water in the tanks by using the three little test water cocks in the cab. When the water only showed from the bottom one, it was necessary to leave the wagons and run back up to the Lower Yard to fill up from the pillar tank there, although the tanks would normally last the return trip.

The normal routine when we finished the work, was to fill the tanks and get some coal forward ready for the next crew, then put the engine on the front of the next raft of wagons for the gulley and sit there waiting for relief around 1.00 p.m.

We were allowed 35 minutes walking time back to the shed to book off, the official route from the depot being out of the main gate past the guard, then along past the copse, up the footpath leading to Foxhall bridge and down to the station on the path on the side of the bank by the down main.

The relief crew carried out the same procedure with another train of wagons from the Lower Yard and also took their meal break when they got to the far end of the gulley.

One dark night, some time after the evacuation of Dunkirk, I was going down one of the gulleys on an extra duty with George East. He was a passenger fireman just made up. The air-raid siren wailed and the sentry on guard rushed up to our loco and told us to take cover as an

No. 2076 with 'busby' spark arrester for work in the magazines.
L. Hanson

George Willis (on the right) loading stock coal at Lydney when he was a cleaner there. He became my driver for a while when I was in the pilot link and always had a sense of humour.
Cty. Bob Willis

RAPID PROMOTIONS

enemy aircraft was in the area. Fear gripped me. We decided to shelter under the loco, but before we could get off, a brilliant flash temporarily blinded me, debris pitter-pattered onto the cab roof, followed by loud explosions in rapid succession — seventeen in all. Then the sound of the plane grew fainter as it made a rapid exit through the night sky. A lonely German bomber had delivered its deadly cargo, but little damage was done. Anyway a hiccup like this was not going to stop us from carrying on with our shunting. During the 'all clear' which sounded for two minutes, the tension just flowed out of my body.

'S' SHED (Ordnance Depot)
Book on 8.45. Off shed 9.30 a.m.

After preparing our engine, we ran light to the depot and, with the shunter guiding us over the road crossings, made several trips propelling rafts of wagons from the Lower Yard to 'S' shed. At one time this was the largest shed

This picture of the line leading down to No. 1 gulley, also features the grounded coach body (seen in the distance beyond the raft of wagons), which served as a mess room, and, alongside it, the ground frame cabin at the neck of the Hump sidings. The building on the right was a packers hut.
National Railway Museum

No. 1861 fitted with 'busby'.
R. H. G. Simpson

Looking west from the down relief platform No. 5, featuring West End signal box and the provender stores. The centre yard was to the right of the Oxford line, which is seen heading away through the middle of this picture. The No. 1 running road from the West Curve yard (where the single LMS wagon was standing) was used by trains from the north which were left there for the centre yard pilot to deal with. The engine bringing the train in would uncouple (approximately where the wagon is pictured) and go on shed. Any goods from Swindon came in via the West Curve and were backed into this road from the north. The centre yard pilot would generally rest on this line, again roughly where the LMS wagon was standing. The second track, above the roof of the corrugated iron lamp shed on the right, the No. 2 running road, was used for traffic to and from the up yard, whilst the line in front of the old timber-built relief cabin on the right was the No. 3 running road. The sidings between No. 1 and 2 running roads were known as the centre yard and those between the No. 2 and No. 3 running roads were the 'Dardanelles' where the up yard pilot sat. The brake van to the right of the No. 3 running road was on the cripple sidings, the roof of the C & W shed appearing to its right in the background.

C. L. Mowat

The view north from West End signal box with the Baltic siding in the foreground, the up and down Oxford branch and centre yard sidings.

RAPID PROMOTIONS

in Europe, each side being provided with a pair of internal sidings. The platforms were served by putting all the loadeds on one road, then pulling out the empties from the platforms and putting the loadeds in. If we made too much smoke inside this enormous shed or sat there with the safety valves blowing, there were soon complaints. At the end of the shift we either worked a trip to Didcot Yard or went back light engine to the shed, sometimes coupled to other pilots, and signed off about 5.00 p.m.

CENTRE YARD PILOT
Book on 1.15. Off shed 2.00 p.m. (3 shifts)

The engine for this duty faced 'downhill' towards Swindon and was prepared by the men on the 1.15 p.m. shift. It stayed out for 24 hours and was manned in three 8-hour shifts. The engine from the previous day usually came back on shed as the first one went out. The centre yard was used to form down trains for the north — it was the donkey of the yards.

Traffic for sorting was left on the West Curve No. 1 road, a reception line alongside the up line from Oxford. Traffic left here came from 'the Depot', all the 'Flies' and northbound trains put off at the West Curve. Traffic for Didcot from the north was taken off at Hinksey and brought in on the 'Flies'. When the up yard was busy, the centre yard was also used to receive trains like the up 'Fly' or Hungerford 'Fly'. The No. 1 road was also used for the reception of down trains which normally arrived on the down northern goods loop on the East Curve, then pulled over the top, beyond the north box, and backed into either the up or West Curve yards.

Trains for the north left from the top end of the West Curve or up yards, engines coming off the shed reaching

No. 907 returning to shed on 12th October 1949. This engine had the reputation of being the worst steaming loco at Didcot, many firemen giving up with it in despair.
H. C. Casserley

them via the down running line to Oxford. Down traffic from the up yard was usually pulled up to start from No. 6 road of the centre yard. This was the up goods line, used for transfer traffic from the centre and up yards.

While shunting the centre yard, we handled a maximum of 20 wagons at a time, which was the exact number that would fit between the signal on the up end of No. 2 road and the entry points to Nos. 3, 4, and 5 sidings.

Towards teatime on the 1.15 p.m. shift, we used to go over to the west yard to pick up sheeted traffic from the provender and shunt traders coal wagons from the provender and cattle pen roads. There was also usually something to collect from the goods shed. Steam coal was left on the Baltic, a long siding adjacent to the down Oxford line, also used for 'hot boxes' or overspill from the other yards. We could be called over to the west yard at any time.

At one time during the war, the sheer volume of traffic required a 24-hour west yard pilot which, manned in three shifts, helped with all the sorting, but while I was in the link the west yard was shunted by the centre yard pilot.

Didcot North Junction, looking towards Oxford, just showing the top end of the up yard. *National Railway Museum*

A closer view of the junction. The USA engines mentioned on page 88 were berthed in the siding beyond the footbridge. *National Railway Museum*

The west yard tended to get used for overflow traffic from the centre yard.

We put all the traffic collected into centre yard No. 2 road, keeping No. 1 road free if possible, and took our meal break on the loco in Dardanelles sidings around 5.30 p.m. before sorting it all out. After 6.00 p.m. No. 1 road of the centre yard was never empty so we were kept on the go the whole time. The Reading, Winchester and Swindon 'Flies' were all put into No. 1 and overflowed onto the West Curve because there was not enough room, and there was a couple of trips from the depot.

Book on 9.15. Relieve at 9.30 p.m.
Book on 5.30. Relieve at 5.45 a.m.
On the night shift we booked on at 9.15 p.m. and had ten minutes to read notices and five minutes to walk over to the centre yard where the pilot would be standing by on the West Curve or the Dardanelles.

We waited until the next shift of shunters arrived at 10.00 p.m. and started by preparing the 11.40 p.m. pools for Oxford. During this shift, the 10.10 p.m. Bristol to Banbury goods arrived on the up relief soon after midnight and left traffic in the Baltic. We were also sometimes called out to bank freights on the West Curve. A regular one was the 8.15 p.m. Banbury to Bristol, a van train, not weighed and consequently usually overloaded. It stopped on the West Curve each night for examination and often got stuck trying to pull away again. Foxhall box would often ring across for us to bank it away. At some point during this shift we also cleared any cripples or 'hot boxes' left from down trains at Foxhall or up trains in the Baltic, taking them to the wagon repair sidings. Our meal break was usually 1.30–2.00 a.m., then after the break we would shunt the 3.45 a.m. Hinksey. The 'Alexandra Docks' class 'F' freight (7.55 p.m. A.D. Jct.) went through around 2.00 a.m. and left traffic which was collected later on the last run of the 'three tripper'.

On the morning shift we booked on at 5.30 a.m., relieving the previous crew at 5.45, again in the Dardanelles. This shift was more of a clearing-up job shunting the Provender, then after the Swindon 'Fly' had called at either the west yard or centre yard, collecting station trucks, shunting the goods shed, and sorting the yard for local traders. Later, after the Reading 'Fly' came into the west yard or centre yard, we might shunt the Cripple sidings or Rich's siding where we delivered the occasional tank wagon for a small oil storage depot there. We broke off about 8.30 – 9.00 a.m. for breakfast which was always a fry-up on the shovel on the Dardanelles while the shunters cooked theirs in the cabin.

No. 5 LINK OR SHED LINK
The drivers were 'light duty' or 'eyesight' men who worked as shedman and assisting shedman. The shedman was responsible for berthing and the assisting man looked after 'the bank'. He was responsible for checking disposals, coaling, etc. and turning. The shedman's duty was covered in three shifts: 6.0 a.m. – 2.0 p.m., 2.0 p.m. – 10.0 p.m., and 10.0 p.m. – 6.0 a.m., whilst the assisting shedman worked 7.0 a.m. – 3.0 p.m., 3.0 p.m. – 11.0 p.m. and 11.0 p.m. – 7.0 a.m. Their firemen booked on at the same time and in practice shared the movements around the shed yard, usually single-manned. (For details of this job see page 44).

My experience broadened rapidly when I was put into a new relief link formed to accommodate the sudden influx of locomen drafted in from other areas to cope with the increasing volume of freight traffic. The arrival of 48 new train crews transformed Didcot loco into a cosmopolitan group. Suddenly there were 150 sets of enginemen and firemen instead of the original fifty. As already mentioned, they were accommodated in sleeping coaches to the rear of the engine shed — a most unpleasant situation, which fortunately only lasted until the necessary railway hostel had been built. A number of the men, however, had found comfortable lodgings locally, and even ended up by marrying a 'Berkshire Beauty', the daughter of their landlord. Indeed, some of these families are still in the neighbourhood today.

It had been agreed that the new link would be non-progressive, i.e. no seniority or promotion. Because the men were unfamiliar with the area, they had to learn the road between Reading and Swindon and were restricted to working along that stretch of the main line. A system was developed whereby two crews booked on duty every hour throughout the day and night, every day, each crew working a 48-hour week in six 8-hour shifts. Three senior Didcot drivers, Bill Jones, Rex Brotherton and Steve Freeman, were appointed relief supervisors to provide 24-hour cover. They were based in a relief cabin established in a former PW hut in Didcot Centre Yard, five minutes walk from the engine shed. They were attached to Reading Relief Control who were in constant touch, advising them of where the relief crews were needed. We were given a time to book on for the week and most of the time served the official eight hours (early or late shifts), often spending long periods in the relief cabin waiting for trains to arrive and passing the time with a game of cards. I spent many happy hours playing solo, three-card brag or cribbage and even carried my own cribbage board for a long while. Some of the messroom table tops incorporated a crib board in the woodwork. Some drivers were card fanatics — any odd minute and out came the cards. It certainly helped to while away some long and lonely hours waiting in a goods loop for the block to clear.

Sometimes we worked very long hours. I remember a 104-hour week, and sometimes we

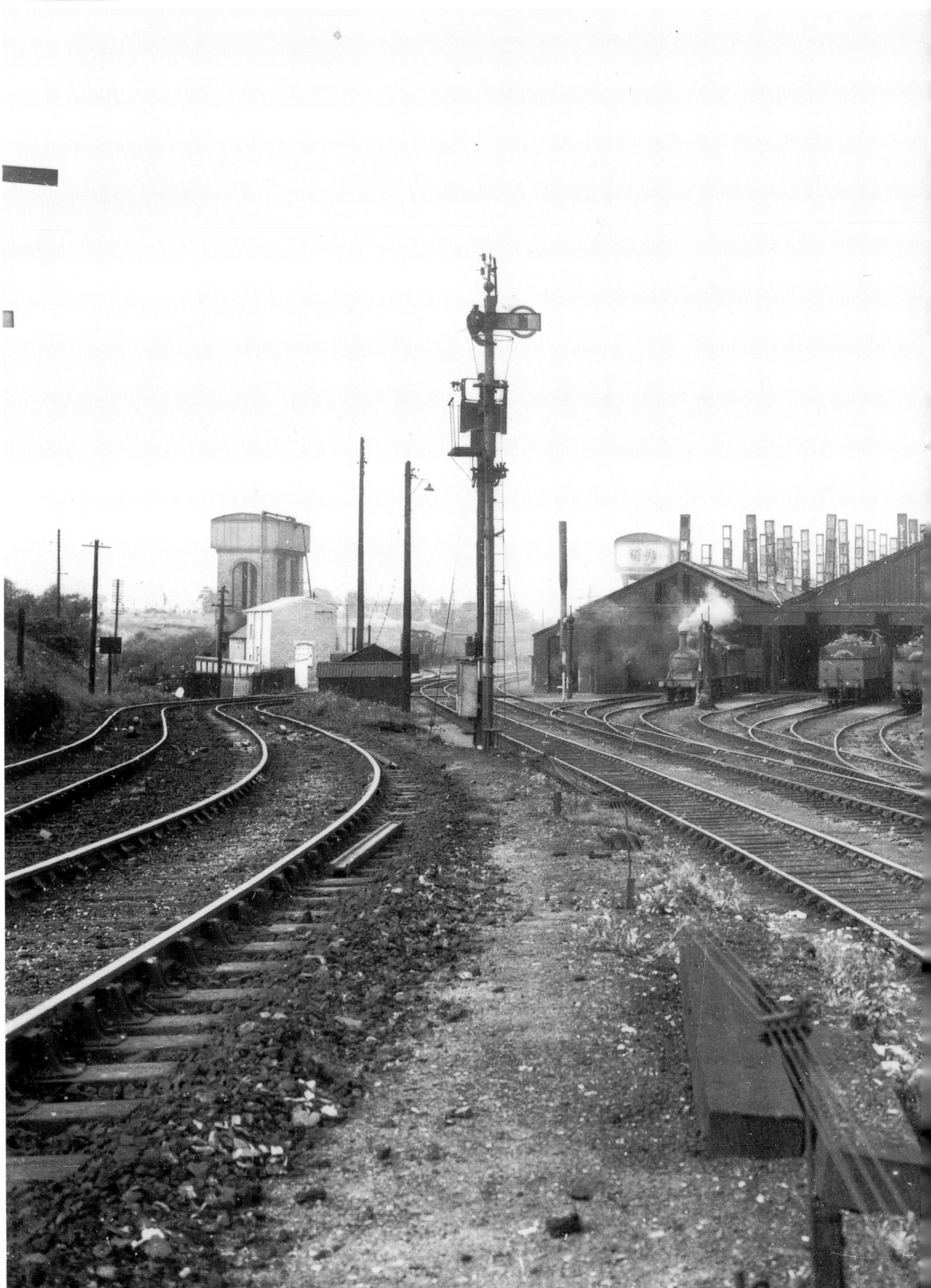

Reading shed in the 1940s. When we were in the relief link during the war, we rarely came on shed here as we usually relieved trains on the road. Even when we had to collect an engine, it was brought up to the shed signal at the West Junction end. One of the LMS 0–6–0s loaned to the GWR can be seen on the left. They were not very popular with any of the crews, and the seats, which hooked over the side of the cab, were usually missing. Our coal watering pipes wouldn't screw on their fittings and they didn't have ATC. The Didcot LDC minutes for October 1945 record 'they have now returned to the LMS', much to our relief!

National Railway Museum

On the relief control work, we rarely ran into Swindon station, but were relieved in the down goods loop alongside Swindon goods yard. We reported to the relief cabin (opposite Swindon Goods Yard signal box) waiting in the crew room for instructions to be given through a hatch in the wall from the adjoining relief supervisor's office. If we worked back, we usually picked up a train from the up goods loop, but if we were near the end of our hours, or weren't required, we walked to the station to catch a passenger train back to Didcot, walking along the side of the track, and, if there was time, calling at the wartime canteen (run by British Restaurants, I believe) behind Swindon East signal box. We crossed to the up side using the boarded crossing at the foot of the ramp in the foreground.

H. C. Casserley

We caught the next available train back to Didcot, but, if there was a large gap in the timetable, we would hitch a lift in the brake van of any passing freight or parcels. If we had a word with the signalman, he would often unofficially stop a freight at a signal just long enough for us to get on! We never rode on the engine. This picture shows 2927 at Swindon with an up express in 1946.

H. C. Casserley

spent long stretches of 24-30 hours on the footplate when the Blitz was at its height.

A complete goods train crew consisted of driver, fireman and guard. To complete the emergency link, it was therefore necessary to promote forty goods guards. Railwaymen inexperienced in train running came from all parts of the GWR system — porters from Paddington, ticket collectors, goods shunters, parcel porters, all thrown into the deep end. True to solid Great Western Railway tradition, they blended in as train crews. In no other area of railway work does the true character of a person emerge. Most of these men proved extremely able, developing a friendly attitude towards the engine crews who they relied upon to help them learn and come to terms with their new situation. I often coupled up the train, helped with shunting movements, pinned down brakes, etc., and in return the guard often made cans of tea or even helped in shovelling coal off the back of the tender. In fact we helped each other; it was a pleasure working with such men.

Most of my time in the relief link was spent with Reg Johns, a newly made driver from Pontypridd. He was a friendly and cheerful Welshman, well-built and stocky, with a great zest for life, content with his pint of beer, game of cards, rugby and male voice choirs in his spare time. He had the sort of warm-hearted personality that attracted people to him, and we evolved a strong respect for each other as our friendship developed.

In the early days of our working partnership I was able to help Reg with my knowledge of the local routes. As a fireman he had been accustomed to small 0-6-0 tank engines in the Welsh valleys and now he had the responsibility of working tender engines on passenger and goods services, with their more complicated exhaust injectors, travelling at up to sixty or seventy miles an hour through unfamiliar territory. It was a bit like going from a rocking-horse to a racehorse!

We grew close, but I was hurt once when he doubted my word. I had been playing cards in the Marlborough Club at Didcot and during a game of Solo I had seen all four suits dealt, but when I started to tell Reg, he just wouldn't believe me and ridiculed my story. I felt cross seeing his utter disbelief, so I didn't even try to finish the story.

One cold winter's night, Reg and I were instructed to relieve the crew of a freight train at Foxhall Junction, on the west curve at Didcot. We set off at a slow walking pace in the blackout, on a particularly dark night, picking our way over the signal wires and point rodding running alongside the track. We never took the authorised route to Foxhall Junction from the relief cabin in the centre yard but crossed the marshalling yard by the West End signal box, then alongside the up relief. Suddenly we heard the air-raid siren on top of the provender stores begin to wail out. In the far distance, searchlights could be seen crisscrossing the blackness of the night sky over Coventry, and the sound of enemy aircraft — a distant drone overhead — mingled with bursting anti-aircraft guns, and the sound of shells exploding like stars in a glowing mass on the horizon.

'Red Alert' meant taking shelter to wait for the 'All Clear', and we hurried to the nearest shelter, only to find it ankle deep in water. When there was a lull in aircraft noise, we made our way towards the train, only to hear the unusual sound of an intermittently blowing safety valve. This puzzled us both.

As we turned the corner at Foxhall, we couldn't see what the engine was, but as we got nearer we could make out the dark silhouette of something Southern. To climb onto the footplate of such an unfamiliar loco was a bit unnerving, particularly in the middle of an air raid. It was *Trevithick*, a 'Remembrance' class 4–6–0 and completely different from standard GWR types. However, we soon discovered the principal parts — how the water injectors worked, and where the dampers, cylinder cocks, and the different sand levers and reverser were.

Although the 'All Clear' siren had been sounded, it was certainly not all clear on the footplate yet. We stowed our gas masks and steel helmets away and, when we felt confident that we had everything under control, we blew the whistle, indicating we were ready to move off. It was an ear-splitting sound, several keys higher than a Western whistle, and the signalman responded by pulling off the signal to show a green light to proceed.

Pulling away on the tight curve at Foxhall was always a struggle, particularly on a wet night with a head wind, but with sand run on the rails to assist adhesion, and the hand brake taken off the rear van by the guard, we were usually able to ease away off the curve and on to the main line. The amount of sand left alongside the rails here proved that other drivers had faced the same problems.

That night, as we left, wheel spin was more of a problem than usual, a shudder, a tremble, then wheels spinning with orange sparks showing up in the darkness. The sand was not running freely, so with the fireman's shovel I climbed down while the engine was in motion and ran to the front of the loco to shovel any earth or gravel from the edge of the ballast onto the rails. This was all right until we reached the crossover where I had to give up for fear of fouling the moving parts of the points. However, by this time, with gentle persuasion, *Trevithick* was on the move, so I climbed back onto the footplate. Reg was relieved that I knew what to do in these conditions. As a gentle movement developed, the steam pressure proved difficult to maintain, but we plodded on to Swindon with Reg 'nursing' *Trevithick* like a true engineman.

When we arrived at Swindon, we handed over to a fresh crew and reported to the Relief Supervisor. While we were waiting for our orders, a Swindon crew invited us to join them in a game of Solo. We were experienced players so the game went well until the unexpected happened and all four suits had been dealt. I just burst with excitement, saying to Reg "I told you so". For the second time in as many days I had seen this unlikely coincidence — a thousand to one chance. Poor Reg could hardly believe it. "Bundance declared" shouted the first player next to the dealer when he made his own trumps and laid them on the table — an unlikely but true experience which Reg was to relate many times.

The return trip from Swindon was soon organised by the controller; we had to work a train of petrol from Avonmouth Docks which was needed urgently for London Airport, twenty-two petrol tanks loaded with aviation fuel, with a '63XX' loco on the front.

By this time the early morning sky was flooded by moonlight. This was often the case after an air raid, giving the Germans a chance to see their way home. 'Attack in the dark but fly home by moonlight' was their strategy! Anyway, we were both feeling in high spirits as we were back on the footplate of a decent locomotive. We had twenty-two loose-coupled tanks, with an empty goods wagon attached to the locomotive, and another on the guard's van, to act as a barrier for any sparks that might come off the brake blocks of our loco or the guard's van.

We had been telegraphed ahead as 'URE', which meant that we must not be stopped, and had priority over other trains. Armed with this

Foxhall Junction, looking west towards Swindon in the early 1930s, with the transfer sheds in the Ordnance Depot in the right background.
C. L. Mowat

Foxhall Junction signal box as first built. It was later modified with a brick base.
National Railway Museum

knowledge, we soon got under way. Forty miles an hour gave us both a pleasant ride, and with a gentle downhill gradient, only a whisper of steam was necessary, once we had gained momentum.

Reg was singing in his lilting Welsh tenor, and I joined in. The light from the firebox door was reflected onto the side sheets, which acted as 'black-outs'. Reg, perched on the reversing rack, was still in a splendid mood and I was peering through the spectacle glass when the Automatic Train Control buzzer alarm sounded!

We had just passed Challow on the main line, but what was most unusual, we had received a caution signal from Circourt signal box. We braked hard, but found the weight of the train still pushing us on and our speed was not declining fast enough. I knew we would never stop at Circourt home signal and as Reg reversed the lever and opened the regulator, I hung onto the handbrake with grim determination. Half twisting my body, I looked over the side of the cab and saw the 'red' light of the home signal pass by. My senses became numb and my knees weak — we had committed a serious crime in passing a signal at 'Danger'. Our train eventually came to a stand about a quarter of a mile further on, and I raced back to the signal box, nervously anticipating a tirade of abuse from the Bobby. When I got there I found him calm and smiling. His mate at Wantage Road had not received the important 'URE' message so allowed another train to proceed off the relief line in front of us! He was therefore expecting us to overshoot and there was no question of our being reported for such a serious breach of the rules, and we were given permission to proceed.

I was still panting and breathless from running to the box, but with such wonderful news from the Bobby I found extra wind in my lungs, and bounced down the steps two at a time and ran towards my mate, Reg, who was naturally in a very worried state. This time I was panting with joy, and keen to tell him that we could now proceed. We could have been in collision with 20,000 gallons of highly inflammable fuel!

After that drama, our progress to Southall was mercifully uneventful, only stopping at Reading station to pick up a pilotman as Reg only signed the road that far. The 'URE' message ('important that ...... train should be worked punctually') had obviously got through, and we ran main line all the way to West Drayton where we were switched to the goods loop. At Hayes we berthed the train on the up relief loop (known as Barlow's Sidings, because of the old rail in the loop), next to more waiting petrol tankers.

Obviously, the signalman at Wantage who had let the freight in front of us had alerted the London controller that there was a 'cock-up' with the 'URE' message, and had sent another successful one.

When Reg wasn't available I was put with other drivers. One week, during the Blitz on London, I was teamed with Curly Barker. While I was walking to work, the early morning sky on the eastern horizon over the London area was glowing with stars of exploding anti-aircraft fire and criss-crossed with searchlight beams, while London itself was burning with incendiary bombs. It was an unforgettable sight, especially when viewed from the peaceful countryside around Didcot.

Our duty was to relieve a freight for Acton which was held in Didcot up running goods loop behind two others heading for the same area. No trains were being accepted ahead which meant that all sections between Didcot and London already held a train.

Taking over the footplate, we settled down for a long wait, some of which was spent playing cards. We even made our own draughts board out of a driver's daily record sheet, on which we drew squares and shaded the black ones with a pencil. We used small pieces of coal for black draughts and pieces of white cardboard from a cigarette packet for the white ones. These simple pleasures passed the time away while we drank tea made by boiling water in the tea can held on the shovel. Curly even taught me the moves for chess, though I never progressed beyond the novice stage.

When the silence was eventually broken by the ping-ping sound of the couplings being tightened up, we knew the train in front was starting to move to take up first place at the loop signal. As the brake van in front slowly moved off with a squeal from the brakes, we realised that it was our turn to move up in the queue, though only a train's length. The most frustrating part of these situations was never knowing when we would be required to move. With hindsight, there was always enough time to wander off and enjoy other more interesting activities but there was no

RAPID PROMOTIONS

Air raids were often the cause of delays as far back along the line as Swindon. This picture, taken on 23rd March 1944, shows bomb damage repairs under way at Paddington.
National Railway Museum

A typical wartime scene, with female ticket collectors and service personnel at Paddington on 28th May 1942. *National Railway Museum*

way of knowing that at the time. After several hours we eventually found ourselves at the head of the queue, but the traffic regulator at Didcot East Junction informed us we would not be moving for a considerable time as the block had again been put on. The night was chilly so we took out the deflector plate from inside the firehole and reversed it, tipping it upside down and placing one end of it back into the firehole and supporting the other on a large knob of coal. This gave us a trough, onto which we pulled back some of the red glowing embers from inside the firebox to provide us with a crude brazier to keep us warm. We just cracked the blower open gently to provide a mild draught to draw away the fumes and it was soon like an oven inside the cab. Glowing, flickering shadows danced on the inside of the blackout sheets which hung all round us to prevent any light escaping. As I sat on the upturned bucket with a lump of cotton waste for a cushion, thoughts flowed around inside my head of peaceful days to come, my eyes became leaden and I soon fell into a slumber.

When I woke up later, the morning sunshine was piercing through the cab window and the fire was almost out. The firebox was just a mass of clinker and unburnt coal. It was panic stations, the water in the boiler had fallen dangerously low and so had the steam pressure. We both worked like demons to rekindle the fire, which had previously provided us with so much comfort. We raked back the dying embers from the front of the firebox under the brick arch and searched the back of the tender for lumps of hard northern coal which would ignite more quickly. With the hot firebox and sparing use of the blower to draw up the fire, we managed to get the fire burning again — we were lucky! As the firebox became a mass of fire, the steam pressure began to rise again and we were able to turn on an injector to get some more water into the boiler and get things ship-shape again. By then it was mid-afternoon and at 4.30 we would be relieved, having been on duty for twelve hours. When they arrived, we wandered down to book off duty, having moved just 220 yards. We were ordered to take 12 hours rest and report for duty at 4.30 a.m. the next day.

Tired, ragged, dirty and hungry, I slowly trudged home with my satchel across my shoulder. Soon I was in the bath, and after being fed and watered, I listened to the 6 o'clock BBC news and the reports of the London Blitz. Lord Haw-Haw's (William Joyce) propaganda from 'Germany calling, Germany calling' telling of how London had suffered was soul-destroying but our spirits were never broken. In fact it gave us more determination than ever. I never heard a complaint whispered by any locomotive crews during this difficult period. That evening when I turned into bed, I was fretful of our future but tried to relax.

It seemed that my head had hardly hit the pillow when the alarm clock went off at 3.30 a.m. in time to get to work again at 4.30 a.m. Feeling refreshed, more relaxed and in better spirits after my 12-hour rest, I walked at a brisk pace to the station to report for 4.30 a.m., only to find we had to relieve the same train and engine still waiting where we'd left it at Didcot East Up Goods Loop! When we rang the train regulator, we were told to expect to proceed shortly, but it was 7.30 when we eventually had permission to proceed, and then only to the next signal box section at Aston Tirrold. There was then a movement every hour until we eventually arrived at South Stoke signal box (between Cholsey and Goring) at 9.30 a.m., only to be told that the block had been imposed again. By 10.30 we were in the pub at the bottom of the railway embankment; at least this was a civilised place to spend the next few hours. Little did we know that we were to spend the next day anchored down. The beer and food we had at the pub was so welcome that we were sorry when it was closing time at 2.00 p.m. We still had no idea when a movement was to be made with our train, and I vividly recall my mate wagering with me that we would be in the pub at 6.00 p.m. opening time. In fact, we did exactly that, and we were still there at closing time, 10.00 p.m. We had been on duty seventeen hours, and, just when we turned out of the pub, there was a movement as far as Goring & Streatley, where we changed over with a Reading crew who were taking a light engine to Didcot Loco.

Later that week, we were instructed to relieve on a train of fly ash for Newbury Racecourse via Reading West Junction. We were to take over at Didcot East Junction up goods loop some time after midnight, and the sound I heard as the train arrived I instantly recognised as the sharp tinny exhaust of a 'Yankee' engine. I was keen to have a go at a 'Yank', and George Cox and Reg Warr had just brought one from Honeybourne. Reg showed me over the principal controls, i.e. injector steam valve, water injector valve, blower, and the strange-shaped boiler gauge glass.

While working this train up Honeybourne bank through deep snow, on the run up to Campden tunnel, with pine trees on the bank sides laden with platelets of snow, Reg had felt it was like passing through the Rocky Mountains. The clear crisp blast from the chimney echoing from the snow-covered cutting sides sounding increasingly vibrant, on the steep rising gradient, broke the silence of the winter's night and they even had a Yankee whistle just like in a Western film!

The challenge had arrived, now I was to take over the 'Yankee' and experience yet another type of locomotive. The principle of all steam locomotives was the same, but there were different ideas of how to operate them. The cab was luxurious compared to the spartan footplates of Great Western engines; there were padded seats, arm rests, and even sliding side windows, which shut out the cruel winter nights. The boiler back inside the cab sloped slightly forward and gave more room on the footplate. There were low doors closing the gap between the engine and tender, and on the tender front there were vertical tool boxes either side of, and horizontally over the top

'Yankee' 2–8–0 No. 2148 with an up 'H' class goods on the approach to Oxford North. This could even be a train of fly ash.
R. H. G. Simpson

One night we were told that four USA locomotives had been stabled in the sidings at Didcot North signal box, the result of lease/lend between Great Britain and the USA when we stood alone in 1942. Although it was dark, several of us decided to walk up there and take a look at them, but, of course, we were very limited in what we could see, so it was something of an anticlimax. I could just make out the front of the smokebox which, smeared with oil, reflected what little light there was. The footplate was high and we all climbed up to look in the cab. It was designed for comfort, with sliding windows at the sides and padded seats, and was enclosed by the high tender. Surprisingly, the engine came complete with tools, which included a long-handled broom with bristles shaped like a sheaf of corn. This intrigued me, a mental picture crossing my mind of an American fireman in blue striped bib-and-brace overalls with red neckerchief and large peaked cap, sweeping the footplate like a Mississippi Mammy. This picture shows No. 1898 at Reading West Junction on 13th September 1943.
Maurice Earley

of, the coal shovelling area, which gave extra protection to our rear.

The steam regulator for these right-hand drive locomotives was completely different, it was horizontal and operated on a push and pull system at a horizontal angle. All the controls could be operated easily by sitting down on the padded seat!

The firebox was square and rather shallow, but had a rocking fire grate for disposal, operated by a thick iron bar which controlled the mechanical rodding just below the outside of the firebox hole. This enabled the fireman to clean the fire of clinker and ash residue, which fell into the hopper ashpan, which in turn was emptied onto the track. As there were no dampers, it was difficult to achieve fire control and steam pressure. Below the firegrate there was simply an open slit some 3-4in wide along each side to admit air under the grate. This may have been to allow for conversion to oil burning, which could be switched off when not required, but, of course, with coal this was not possible. These locomotives were destined for Persia later in the war and presumably converted there.

On the GWR we didn't use the Westinghouse brake which was available on these engines, so we relied on the straight steam brake on the locomotive only. The braking of freight trains had to be done with extra care as these locos were not very heavy and allowance had to be made for this when judging speed and inclines.

The water injectors were completely different to operate, a handle grip on a rod to open the steam valve to the injector below the footplate, and there was a wheel control for opening the water valve. All this could be done sitting down in the fireman's seat, what a luxury!

Another innovation was a boiler blow-down valve, which allowed the crew to blow out of the boiler all the sludge when necessary. 'Afloc' was added to the water in the tender beforehand but of course this was only carried out when being serviced on the loco depot.

They were free-running locos, but loose in the axleboxes which caused a side-to-side movement. One very unusual feature was the position of the sand boxes which were situated on top of the boiler to keep the sand warm and dry to help it to gravitate freely through the delivery pipes to the rails in front of the wheels. Of course the disadvantage was that the poor fireman had to carry buckets of sand from the furnace to the top of the locomotive. Imagine doing this in a howling gale, pouring rain, or frosty night.

The gauge frame was fitted with a corrugated type of glass which I am sure was never liked by our locomen. The water level was difficult to see at night time when we relied on an oil lamp. The safety valves were situated on the side of the boiler in front of the fireman's window. That morning at 2.30 a.m., while passing over Reading West Junction towards Reading West station, the safety valve started to warble, and I felt a tremor in the cab. I could see what was going to happen, but without any dampers to control the fire there was nothing I could do about it other than pray it would not blow fully. At this point, as we were rolling along an embankment, I looked out over the rooftops. The streets below were empty and dark, everyone was asleep — then, with a sudden and almighty explosion, the silence was shattered. Cascades of pure white steam soared out of the safety valves and into the night sky. I felt we must have woken half of Reading. I have often wondered how many people below awoke with a start that night or how many dreams accommodated the sound.

On arrival at Newbury Racecourse we reversed our train into the yard, signalled by an American soldier waving an electric torch, whereas we only had oil lamps. This was typical of the progress into the modern world by the Americans. The fly ash we were delivering was for the preparation of a new marshalling yard on Newbury Racecourse in connection with a prisoner-of-war camp.

While we were waiting to return with an empty train, I noticed a German prisoner-of-war making his way towards the high-security perimeter fence alongside the main line. He left a bundle wrapped in brown paper underneath the fence and shortly afterwards along came an Italian POW who had been working outside on the track. He examined the contents and concealed the package at the foot of the grassy bank. I was concerned at what I'd seen and telephoned the security centre. A USA sergeant, answering in a low drawl, realised what had happened and made three German POWs follow him at gunpoint to the spot I had described. He picked up the parcel and threw it in front of the POWs, demanding that they opened it. The Yanks were cross at discovering a gang of

Two passenger trains crossing at Upton & Blewbury station in 1937. This is where Reg and his mate picked up the wrong staff.
J. H. Venn

thieves and when the parcel was opened they found it contained a pair of USA army boots — a luxury in those days.

The sergeant sent an Italian POW to our locomotive to ask if I would like the boots. I accepted them with some remorse as I had got the POW into trouble. But I made good use of them; the large rubber soles were just the job for use on the footplate. They were a godsend during the war and lasted 12-18 months.

That week I was on duty for 104 hours and I drew £7-plus. But we didn't dare feel hard done by — we had it easy while others involved in the war effort went through hell. Our worst scenario was stopping near a pub, only to find it had no beer.

I thoroughly enjoyed my time with Reg Johns but, being together in the special No. 4 Relief Link, it was inevitable we'd have to part. Promotion was quick and along with several others he was soon moved up to No. 3 Link which required an increased road knowledge. He learned the route to Newbury and Winchester with me when I was doing a spare turn on the branch. I was able to pass on some useful tips, like showing him landmarks such as bridges, farm barns, cuttings, etc. and where to shut off steam. I felt I could not do enough to help him.

On the following pay day he said that he'd asked for me to be booked with him for the whole of his first week. He'd used his personality to pull off a concession with the shed foreman — a fiddle actually, because the duty was not in my link, but Reg told me had had asked, because I was as good as a 'passenger fireman' and knew the road blindfolded.

It was around this time that I also moved up to No. 3 Link and I was put with Roy Frewin, another new driver who'd spent all his time as fireman on the Wallingford branch. Despite his limited experience, he was an excellent engineman. We soon developed a good relationship and enjoyed many happy trips together. I was lucky again to have another good mate. However, I was soon to learn Reg Johns had been let down badly while working on the 6.45 a.m. passenger train from Newbury. At that time the branch was still a single line worked by the electric train staff system to prevent more than one train at a time entering the section. When Reg arrived at Upton & Blewbury station he had to surrender the train staff which had been his authority to occupy the line from Compton to Upton. The fireman usually did this by leaning out of the cab and hanging it on a lineside catcher post. The staff for the next section would then be collected off an adjacent post where it was held ready in a special clip. However, on this occasion the signalman had taken the Upton to Didcot staff out of the ETS machine and leant it against the platform fence, exactly where the loco usually stopped.

When Reg arrived, his mate jumped off the loco and for some reason also put the Compton to Upton staff against the fence alongside the other one. He then rushed into the signal box to make a phone call for relief at Didcot. On his return there was only one staff left by the fence, so he picked it up, jumped on board, and they left for Didcot without reading the name marked on it or noticing the colour. Panic and trauma ensued in the cab when, arriving at Didcot East Junction, they realised they had the wrong staff! It transpired that the signalman at Upton & Blewbury had picked up the same one that he'd put against the fence (Upton & Blewbury to Didcot) a few minutes earlier, whilst Reg's fireman had unwittingly also picked up the one he'd put there before.

When they realized what had happened, Reg's mate ran back two miles up the bank to Upton station, to exchange tokens. He borrowed the signalman's bicycle to return along the side of the track, on the down gradient. He corrected the offence very gallantly, but the traffic regulator at East Junction signal box would not let this pass unknown and HQ Control soon knew. Reg and his mate had committed a very serious offence and now they were to be disciplined.

He was a shattered man who vowed it would never have happened had I been with him. I'm sure he was right. Knowing him as I did, three days back in the valleys did him good. Nothing a pint of beer in the Celtic Club in Pontypridd could not cure. He came back the wiser, and once again his bubbly self.

A few months later Reg was transferred back to Abercynon in South Wales. Having spotted his name on the duty sheets and not knowing if he was aware, I called into his lodgings to break the news. His landlady, Mrs. H. Dibden, answered the door. She was a short, tubby woman, with large eyebrows, neat teeth and a broad smile. "You

Reg Johns. *Cty. Mervyn Johns*

want Reg, don't you?" she asked. I nodded, but when I saw him, he looked as if he knew what I had called for. He had already heard of his transfer, but presumably did not want to tell me face to face. We both felt choked at our parting.

I had been introduced to Welsh rugby, male voice choirs, how to play Solo, and the comradeship experienced in visits to the Rhondda Valley. My life was all the richer for these valuable introductions, but above all for having known a true Welshman.

No. 3 Link provided a more varied range of work and gave me wider route knowledge, but only months afterwards a number of the firemen including myself were temporarily moved up to No. 2 Link for ten months to take the place of a group of passenger firemen needed for driving duties during the doubling of the Didcot Newbury & Southampton line. 'The branch', as we called it, was selected to carry supplies from the northern industrial areas to the Channel docks

Didcot station in the mid-1930s. The boarded crossing, leading from the subway across the carriage sidings to the shed path, features on the right of this view. The water crane in the foreground, alongside the up main, was one of many we had to keep from freezing during the harsh spells of winter. It fell to the cleaners to keep all the braziers or 'fire devils' burning, flames often licking out of the tall stovepipes when they were stoked up. After the war, the corn exchange (the old wangle') seen in the left background on the edge of the station forecourt, became a garage. I bought my first car from there.
National Railway Museum

for shipment to the French coast. In preparation for 'D-Day', the route was uprated, bridges made stronger, and the northern part of the line was doubled.

Didcot Locomotive Depot supplied motive power for the civil engineers who had the task of bringing this route up to a higher standard. Eventually, the track carried troop and ambulance trains, as well as the components of the famous Mulberry Harbour project, and PLUTO (Pipe Line Under The Ocean). Vital food supplies for the invasion forces, petrol and military tanks, in fact everything necessary to conduct a military campaign was transported by rail.

Passenger services were suspended between Didcot, Newbury and Winchester in August 1942 to enable the necessary work to be carried out, and an alternative bus service was provided.

The Newbury branch bay and engine release loop. The straw on the cattle and horse loading bank was being burnt to prevent disease spreading between animals. *National Railway Museum*

A Newbury branch train in the bay in the 1930s. The horse-box was correctly marshalled so it could be left at its destination without shunting the whole train into the siding. *Collection P. Karau*

During alterations the branch came under the control of a railway inspector who arranged the locomotive requirements. Because of the need for extra men and locos, it was agreed that a special link (we called it 'the branch link') would be established quickly using passenger firemen who had passed for driving duties, and it was during this time that, on a spare duty I had a firing turn with my father who was one of the passed firemen acting as driver. I can't recall discussing our impending duties when we joined each other at the table for our midday meal — everything was the same as usual. After carrying out various domestic chores, we eventually set off together, Father on Mother's bicycle, with me following behind on mine.

While booking on duty, we had to suffer the inevitable humorous remarks. Predictably, I was called "Daddy's boy", while my father was accused of a 'wangle' and asked "How much did it cost?". However, it was all a friendly leg-pull.

We prepared 3376 *River Plym* to work an early evening freight for Winchester which would take us over a newly completed section of track. Because of this we had the Permanent Way Inspector with us on the footplate to 'roll the road'. This meant he would feel how the engine would ride over the new track, noting any defects, i.e. dips, looseness, etc. He stood behind the driver to view the approaching track. Of course he was unaware of our relationship, so Father suggested I drove, and I eagerly swapped places before the inspector came on board. He greeted me with "Can I ride with you, driver?". "Of course" came my reply.

During our trip my father carried on doing the fireman's work. I'm sure it was because he really wanted to show me that he was a good fireman. Not once did we interfere with each other's duties, each of us blending to make a good team. Eventually, the conversation between the three of us came to families. This was deliberately manipulated by my father who was clever at setting up a topic to wind someone up. He had laid the bait! Between shovelling, the inspector asked him if had any family. "Yes", Father said, "We are father and son". I could see the inspector was amazed to find such a situation on the footplate. Then came the vital question, which was father and which was son. Father looked very young for

P.W. Inspector Bill Nash, the permanent way inspector who travelled with Father and me over the Newbury branch. He really was a very pleasant personality.

his age and all the time I had my back to him, looking ahead through the spectacle glass. I enjoyed listening to my father setting up our passenger and my stomach was aching where I had held myself from laughing at the good, solid banter between him and the inspector. Railway work was far from our thoughts, but all the while our instincts and reflexes were alert to our job - it was second nature.

While we stopped at Newbury to fill our tank, Father carried on the fireman's work and when we eventually pulled away from Newbury, the inspector passed a complimentary remark on how well I handled the train. Father just stretched his neck, nodded his head and carried on firing. It was of no consequence to him. He had given me no help. I had to learn the hard way. When I was a young boy he'd thrown me in the River Thames and watched me struggle to reach the bank. He made me swim twenty strokes before helping me out. I knew he was behind me all the time. He'd had a hard schooling in the Royal Navy and expected me to be my own man.

The practice of relatives manning locomotives was stopped when the consequences of any serious accident were realised, so I was never rostered with Father again, and I can truthfully record that I learned very little from him.

Doubling the Newbury branch at Didcot East Junction in 1943.

National Railway Museum

I am sure his early interest in the railway was as a secure financially paying job, but, like most, he soon came to value the companionship enjoyed amongst railwaymen.

Early shift men working on the southern part of the line booked on at Didcot shed as normal and worked their engines down to Newbury where they'd receive orders. Those on relief turns would travel south of Newbury by road, gathering on the forecourt of Didcot station to await the arrival of the bus at 11.30 a.m. It went to Whitchurch first and then proceeded to any other point required, eventually collecting all those who had been relieved and taking them back to Didcot or sometimes to Newbury station, leaving the men to make their way back to Didcot by train via Reading.

I have vivid memories of another occasion when I was fireman on an engine sent to Woodhay with a brake van to rescue a 'crocodile'. This was a long low-loader goods vehicle with four-wheeled bogies at either end of a low 'well' type body. They were used for transporting military tanks or high loading goods and were consequently at a premium during the wartime years. Our guard was a Royal Engineer.

The whole Newbury–Winchester branch line was controlled by the Signal Inspector who had issued the necessary orders. The 'crocodile', which had been taken out of service with faulty brakes, was in a siding trailing from the down direction and, because of engineering work, there were no loops available at Woodhay or Highclere. We therefore had to proceed on to Burghclere with the 'crocodile' and brake van in tow in order to run round them and work back to Newbury.

After conferring with the signalman at Burghclere, it was decided that we would leave the brake van in the down platform, take the 'croc' out clear of the points at the southern end of the loop, uncouple it and let it roll down the gradient into the up platform where the guard would meet it and apply the brake. This was all straightforward enough if the brakes on the 'crocodile' had been working, but no-one had warned us that they weren't! While the guard ran alongside trying to wind the brake wheel on hard, he realised something was wrong and in desperation tried to chock the wheels with some of the fishplates lying around from the engineering work, but the wagon was already moving too fast. Determined to stay with his quarry, the soldier jumped on it and we started to chase after the runaway with the engine. The signalman watched the goings on and, in the knowledge that the engineer's crane was working at the bottom of the incline, had the choice of either allowing the 'croc' to become derailed at the catchpoints at the end of the crossing loop, or turning it out, with the guard still on board, towards the engineering works. He chose to let both the loco and the 'croc' run into the section.

By this time our tender was touching the buffers of the 'croc', and the brave soldier guard was lying across the floor, over the buffer beam, with the 'croc's' coupling in his hands. Each time we buffered up, the springs bounced the 'croc' away before the guard could couple up.

After several more failed attempts, I decided to make my way along the side of our tender and, slowly edging forward, I arrived at the rear. By this time, we were well on the way back to Highclere station. Holding on to the top lamp bracket with my right hand, I managed to get hold of the coupling he was holding out and

Burghclere station.
T. B. Sands

eventually drop it over the coupling hook of the engine just as the buffers came into contact. The musical sound of the coupling dropping on to the hook was relief beyond description. After shouting to my driver, we came to a gentle halt, greatly relieved that we were in one piece.

The rising gradient towards Highclere had helped us to rescue the runaway 'croc' whilst, further on and quite unaware of their narrow escape, the engineering gang worked on in blissful ignorance.

At the end of this eventful turn we were due at Whitchurch to meet our relief and travel back by the bus. However, we were delayed and when we eventually arrived we found the relief crew already there and learned that the bus had gone. We were stranded with no means of getting home, so we decided to head for the main road, the A34, and hitch a lift to Newbury.

After waiting by the roadside for a while, two military jeeps with only their drivers pulled up, amazed to see a locomotive crew thumbing a lift. With Roy in the leading car and me in the second, I was pleased to be heading towards Newbury and enjoying a convivial chat with the soldier driver. We were going along nicely until the hill approaching Burghclere when we started to slow down with mechanical trouble. The leading jeep got further and further into the distance until it disappeared over the hill,

A picture of me on a 'Castle' stabled on No. 3 road, opposite the stationary boiler at the back of Didcot shed during the 1940s. Didcot crews didn't get much chance to handle these engines. *Author's collection*

unaware of our problem. I was stranded on the roadside again, tired and lonely and decided to foot it once more. Bidding farewell to my brief companion, I slung my satchel over my shoulder and set off at a brisk pace, looking back occasionally at the driver whose back was bent as he peered under the bonnet. What a lousy end to the day!

After reaching the top of the hill, looking down towards Burghclere, I spotted the other jeep in the distance coming back in search. I swung my satchel around my head in a circle, waving like a windmill in full sail. The driver flashed his headlights, he had seen me — what a sense of relief. I could feel the tension drain from me as I sat on the roadside, now in a state of mind to appreciate the beautiful countryside while a solitary skylark was heralding Roy's arrival.

We all returned to the other jeep a couple of miles back and after a quick examination of the engine, the NCO driver decided to return to Newbury with the broken down jeep in tow behind.

In the spring of 1943, when the engineering work on the branch was completed, the passed firemen returned to their regular duties and I went back to No. 3 Link. I had spent most of my time in No. 2 Link with Percy Steel but I now found myself back with Roy Frewin. To the best of my memory, the work in No. 3 Link at the time included the following:

No. 3 LINK 1942-44 (12 turns)
THE 3.45 a.m. HINKSEY
Book on 1.40 a.m. Off shed 2.25 a.m.
This had been a No. 2 Link duty, referred to as 'the Cheltenham job', which had previously involved working from Didcot to Hinksey, then on to Honeybourne; here, we reversed onto the Stratford line and continued to Cheltenham where we took the engine on shed and returned home passenger. While I was in No. 3 link we only worked out to Hinksey, usually with a 22XX, 63XX or a tank engine, which we prepared. Coming off shed at 2.25 and running over to West Curve Yard, we formed the train for departure at 3.45 a.m. On arrival at Hinksey, we

A southbound 'H' class freight passing Hinksey South signal box. The yard here was built during the war with the help of Italian prisoners; the concrete supports of the drain running under the line at Hinksey North still bear some of their names. On the 3.45 a.m. Hinksey, we ran into the down reception line (on the left of the sidings) where we left our train for the Hinksey North pilot. The north sidings were used to sort all down traffic for the various destinations. Normally we ran light engine from here to Oxford shed for turning, but sometimes if we were in a hurry we didn't bother and worked back to Didcot tender first, after collecting traffic from the up sidings at the south end of the yard. This picture shows the safety valves blowing on No. 9008, but this was not often the case with these engines in their later years! The line on the left was a continuation of the down goods line from Radley.
R. H. G. Simpson

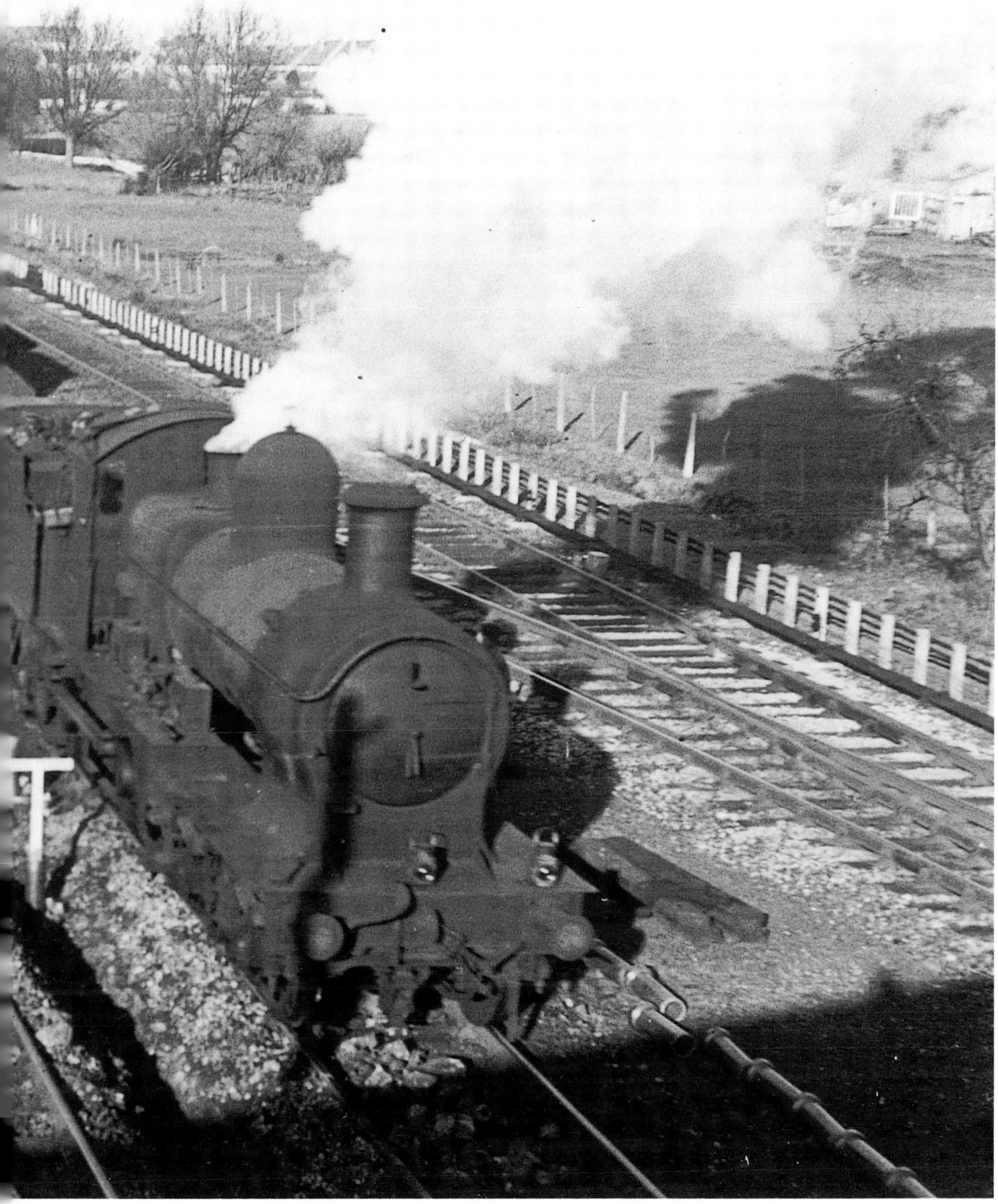

No. 6312 approaching Radley with the 10.40 a.m. Oxford to Didcot stopping train on 15th May 1948. The down goods line on the left and the up goods loop on the right were added during the war to ease congestion on the running lines. A Ministry of Food cold stores, built at Sandford during the war years, was served by sidings off the down goods loop, and on the Hinksey job we often called there to put off wagons. Unless they were occupied, goods trains were nearly always switched into the loops to keep the running lines free. However, if, for example, we were put into the up goods loop from Hinksey to Radley, in order to let a higher priority up train by, a good driver would keep his train rolling at such a speed that we would arrive at the signal at the end of the loop (the ringed arm on the right of this picture) just as it was pulled off in the wake of the faster train. That sort of timing avoided bringing the train to a stand and having to start up again.

M. F. Yarwood

did any shunting required before continuing on to Oxford to turn the engine. We then ran back up to Hinksey where we shunted the Up Yard to collect any wagons for Radley (which included traffic for Abingdon), Culham and Didcot, departing at 5.45 a.m. At that time, we shunted the yards on the way out, but in later years these arrangements changed and Oxford men served Culham on another job. When we returned, the train was put in at the north end of the West Curve Yard on the up goods line, known as the running road. We were usually required to do some shunting there before going back on shed.

In the early 1950s, the 3.45 a.m. Hinksey was superseded by the 9.0 Culham, an accommodation turn arranged to suit a driver who, for medical reasons, was no

A 'J' class freight pulling out of the up goods loop (just through the bridge) on its way south through Radley station. We didn't often call at Radley with traffic on our way back to Didcot, but if we did, leaving the train on the up running line while we dropped wagons in the yard, could delay other trains. If we called on the down journey, we usually backed the whole train onto the Abingdon line before shunting,

R. H. G. Simpson

Looking north through Radley station on 7th March 1949. *National Railway Museum*

We served Culham on the northbound trip, taking any southbound wagons with us to Hinksey, and back to Didcot with us on the return journey. This saved calling at Culham twice. The siding on the right of the top picture served the Fleet Air Arm. The lower picture shows the goods shed.

Roye England

RAPID PROMOTIONS

Looking north and south through Culham station. The Jolly Porter on the right of the left-hand view was used by crews on the fly.

Appleford Halt, looking towards Didcot.

John Boot

104   DIDCOT ENGINEMAN

longer able to fulfil the demands of normal duties. It became known as 'the Jack Wilkins' after the driver who worked it every day for years. He even had a regular engine, No. 1502 (built 1949), which had been transferred from Old Oak. With a short six-coupled wheelbase and outside cylinders with Walschaerts valve gear, No. 1502 used to waddle from side to side and bounce when running well. In the afternoon, the engine also worked the 3.20 p.m. to Hinksey yard and back.

4.30 a.m. WINCHESTER FREIGHT
Book on 3.30 a.m. Off shed 4.15 a.m.
This turn changed in detail through the years and I have described it in more detail in Chapter 6 with one engine. However, for many years it was worked by two 22XXs,

Reading 'Old Bank' connecting with the Southern Railway. This view, taken from Reading East Main box, also shows the Southern engine shed. On the Moreton job we usually pulled up at the signal further on down the bank, uncoupled and left the train there for Southern men to collect. We returned light engine via the running line alongside. However, sometimes we worked further on and set it back into the SR sidings.
Photographer unknown

This view from the cess alongside the down main, also shows the 'Old Bank' descending to the Southern and the stop signal with the fixed distant below. *National Railway Museum*

and on Mondays we carried the Newbury men's allocation of oil (in 5 gallon drums) and cotton waste, new service books and anything else required.

5.40 a.m. MORETON TO READING SR
Book on 4.30 a.m. Off shed 5.15 a.m.
For this job we were given a standard goods or a tank engine (sometimes one of the LMS '2F' 0–6–0s on loan during the war — Didcot had Nos. 3108, 3119, 3121, 3485 and 3564). We prepared the engine and ran light to Reading. On arrival there, we stopped in the station on the main through line while the guard pinned down brakes ready for the descent on the old bank to the Southern. We either left the train on the bank or carried on further and set it back into the sidings according to instructions. We returned light engine to Didcot, calling at Pangbourne, Goring and Cholsey shunting those yards as required before continuing light engine to Didcot shed. Before booking off we turned the engine and handed it over to another crew for the 11.40 Reading 'Fly' (later known as 'the Cecil Evetts'), which served all the stations to Reading and collected the wagons we had already shunted out earlier.

Looking back to Didcot East Junction box from the new up goods loop to Moreton Cutting. *National Railway Museum*

The new embankment widening the trackbed to support the up goods line to Moreton in 1943. The view on the left shows the accompanying extension to Marsh bridge over the main road from Wallingford. *National Railway Museum*

Fullscott bridge, extended to span the new up goods line. I used to play there as a child and when I was in the telegraph office I picked a huge number of mushrooms from the field seen on the right through the bridge. I took some home and sold the rest! The points through the bridge led to the two Moreton Yard reception lines. In practice, most trains were received in No. 1 road as the No. 2 reception line was usually occupied with traffic for Southall. As the water tank seen in the distance was either not provided or at least not connected when the yard first opened, we were given LMS 0–6–0 tender engines, instead of the usual pannier tank, so that we had more water with us. When the tender got low, we had to run up to Cholsey to cross over onto the down relief in order to return to Didcot to fill the tank. *National Railway Museum*

The sidings at Moreton Cutting were used to sort up goods traffic for onward conveyance. This picture, looking west, shows the 'back yard' shortly after completion in 1941. The sidings, numbered away from the goods loop were as follows: Nos. 1 & 2 reception roads, No. 3 for Hayes, No. 4 for Maidenhead and Slough, No. 5 Basingstoke, No. 6 exchange road for the two yards (front and back), No. 7 Sonning (power station), No. 8 for the Southern at Reading (old and new banks), No. 9 Tonbridge, No. 10 Feltham, No. 11 Redhill, No. 12 Taplow, No. 13 Reading West Junction, No. 14 Reading High Level, No. 15 Reading Low Level, No. 16 Cripple Sidings. There were two pilot engines here to sort all the traffic, one for the 'front yard' (roads 1-5) and one for the 'back yard' (roads 7-16).

National Railway Museum

This picture, taken in 1940, shows earthworks well in hand for the new yard. I was in the relief link while all this was happening, so working between Reading and Swindon gave me plenty of chance to watch progress.

National Railway Museum

Looking west over Moreton Yard in 1943. Moreton Cutting signal box which had previously controlled double junctions connecting the main and relief lines, was enlarged 1940/1 to accommodate a larger frame (104 levers) to handle the extra connections to the yard. It was manned in three shifts to give 24-hour coverage.
National Railway Museum

Looking east towards Cholsey, showing the new connections to the yard in 1940.
National Railway Museum

Both the down main and down relief refuge sidings were occupied by abandoned trains when this undated picture of Cholsey & Moulsford was taken. This is typical of what the whole system was like during the difficult war years, with long delays and shortages of crews.

Collection A. E. Smith

THE ROGERSTONE
Book on 4.45 a.m.

We relieved the 11.00 p.m. Rogerstone steam coal (the 'Roggy' or 'Long Tom') at about 6.00 a.m. We booked on 15 minutes beforehand, 10 minutes to read the notices and 5 minutes to walk to West End Box, where we took over the train on the up relief line. If it was on time, the Swindon crew we were about to relieve might be filling the tender with water prior to handing over. The loco was usually a 28XX (but occasionally a 72XX) which, after working all the way up from Severn Tunnel Junction, often had a pretty rough fire and a depleted tender or bunker. However, it used to be said that the 77 miles to London was 'all downhill' and that the top of the platform at Swindon was level with the top of St. Paul's.

The 'Roggy' conveyed loco coal for all the sheds along the main line and in the past is said to have conveyed 100 wagons, but in my time it usually had about 70. On arrival at Didcot, several wagons (usually ten or so) were cut off the front of the train, drawn forward and propelled back into the Baltic siding where they were left for one of the pilots to collect later. After taking water, we worked the train on towards Old Oak, dropping off wagons at Reading West Junction Yard for Reading shed, Slough yard for the shed there, West Drayton, where a pilot collected wagons for Southall shed from the rear of the train, and finally (with something like thirty wagons left) Old Oak Common. However, it was only on Sundays that we actually reached Old Oak because on weekdays we usually only got as far as Southall before being relieved at the end of our hours.

THE 'ABERDARE'
Book on 6.10 a.m. to relieve at 6.40 a.m.

The 'Aberdare' (5.35 p.m. Aberdare) was a train of about sixty wagons of 'traders' or domestic coal bound for West

This 1930s view was taken at Steventon before my time on the footplate, but it was nevertheless typical of the mixed trains I relieved with Reg Johns. These ROD engines would almost run without steam showing on the clock!   *T. J. Harvey*

Drayton. We took it over at Foxhall Junction and were allowed 25 minutes to walk over there. These official walking times were safe routes using roads and footpaths which kept the need to cross over lines, point rodding and signal wires to a minimum. However, we used to take the shortest route across all the running lines and sidings but keeping a sharp lookout. The official timings for walking gave us plenty of time. At the shed the clerk would tell us if the train we were due to relieve was on time or not, and there was a relief cabin at Foxhall Junction for us to wait in. When they arrived, many of these trains were subject to inspection by the C & W examiner, who took about 15 minutes to check all the vehicles. He felt the heat of wheel bosses, tapped all the wheels with his hammer and lifted the lids up on all the axleboxes. The lids were left open on any that needed the attention of the greaser who followed him round carrying a double-lid box of grease which was scooped out and put into the axleboxes with a metal-bladed spatula. Any vehicles with 'hot boxes' had to be shunted out of the train before it continued and this happened quite frequently. While all this was going on, I would spend the time pulling coal forward ready for the journey.

When we got going, progress along the main line with one of these long-distance trains was unpredictable. Because of our relatively slow speed, 35-40 mph, we 'looped the loop' all the way to Old Oak, signalmen frequently switching us into one of the numerous goods loops where we would be held out of the way so that we didn't delay any passenger or other higher priority trains. With only 3,500 gallon tenders behind the 28XXs, and even less capacity in the 72XX tanks (2,500), we needed to take water at various places. Many drivers would do their best to make whatever progress they could, but some would not mind being held everywhere and enjoyed clocking up the overtime as they managed to get just enough behind to miss a vital path in the timetable and had to be held out of the way. On top of all this, some of the extra signalmen taken on during the war lacked experience and, rather than let a long freight run whenever possible, instead played safe and switched them into loops to avoid the risk of hindering passenger trains. Old hand signalmen had become familiar with the attitude of many of the drivers and, in trusting the good ones to perform well, achieved a much more efficient flow of traffic. They also knew the bad drivers.

With all the factors involved, there was hardly a typical run, but a likely example might involve leaving Didcot with a full tender and topping up water on Goring troughs (there were no intermediate water columns between Didcot and Reading). We were very often held at Scours Lane, in fact if you got past there you were doing well, but were just as likely to be held at Reading West Goods box (opposite Reading shed) or around the back of Reading station, where we'd take water again in case of a decent long run ahead.

We would be lucky to get past Ruscombe sidings without being held there, but if we had a really good run and didn't get held at Waltham or Maidenhead either, then we'd probably have to stop in Slough yard for water. If we wanted to go into any of the loops to take water, we

No. 2816 with a down goods near Waltham c.1939. Unless changed footplates in an attempt to get home, we only worked the opposite direction towards London and travelled back on cushions.
C. R. L. Co

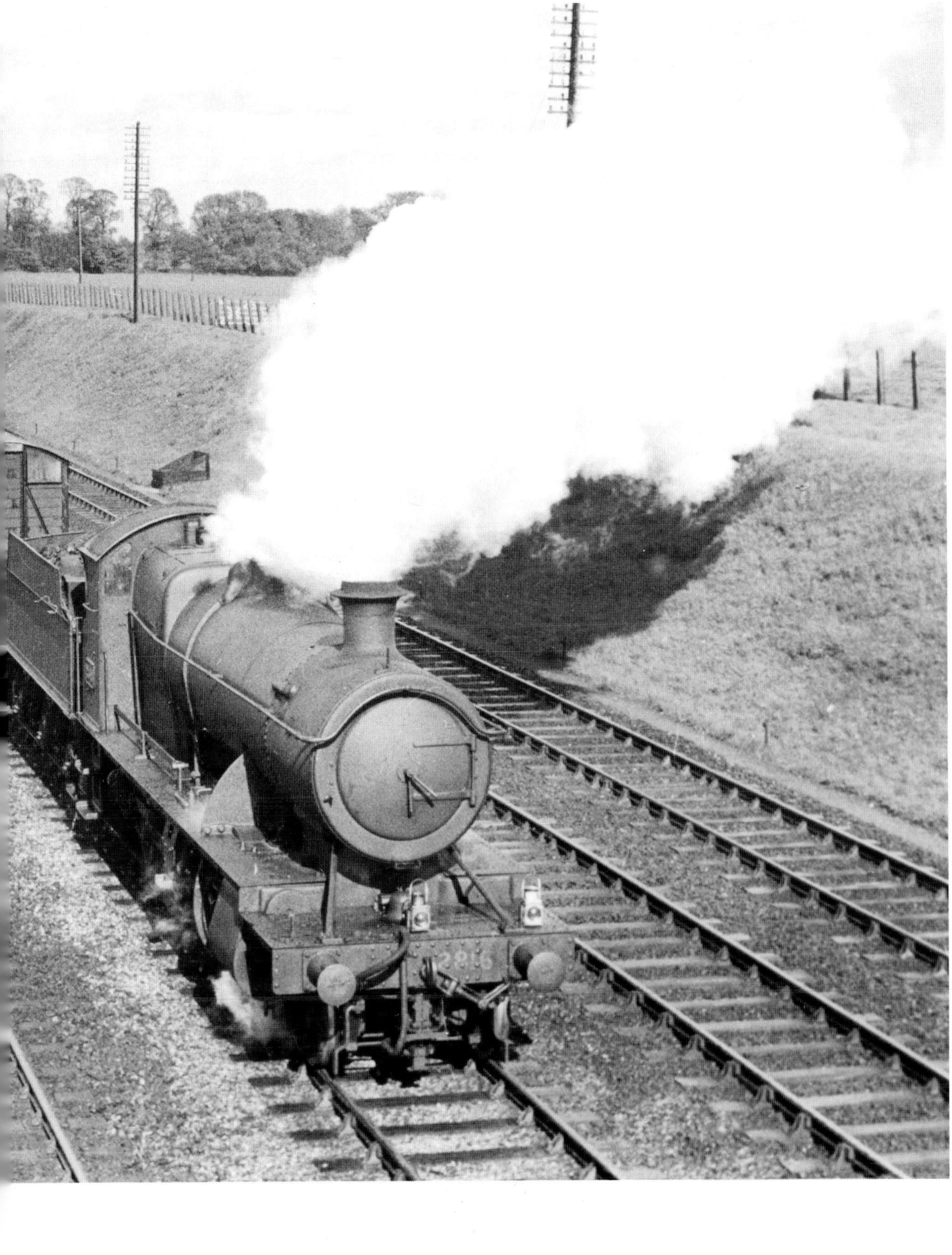

The 6.25 a.m. Swansea to Paddington train approaching West Drayton. Up coal trains were usually switched to the up goods line from Iver to West Drayton which was frequently the end of our journey. If this was the case, we stopped alongside the sidings shown above the roofs of the coaches in this picture, uncoupled and ran light engine to Southall shed (or wherever Control directed), leaving the local pilot to collect the wagons and put them in the yard for sorting. We were often asked to take the loco to Old Oak or back to Reading, either way travelling back to Didcot by passenger train.

C. R. L. Coles

gave a 'Cock-a-doodle-do' ('Crow' whistle) as we passed the preceding signal box and mime a drinking action of cup to lips so that the message could be sent ahead. The loop at Dolphin Junction was another favourite place to be held. On arrival at West Drayton, we were put on the 'up goods' line and either left the train there for the pilot to take over or backed it into the yard before going on to Southall shed.

If we were working a train through to Acton, we might get held out of the way in the loop at West Drayton, Hayes or Hanwell Bridge.

Of course the more delays we suffered, the less ground we'd cover during our hours of duty, so we'd have to arrange for a relief crew to take over and enable us to return to Didcot, most likely on the cushions.

If we suffered a really rough journey, it was sometimes possible to complain to Control and persuade them to arrange for a decent pathway to make up for it, otherwise it was a case of talking to the signalman to make other arrangements. If, for instance, we were held in the loop at Ruscombe, it was possible to ask Control to get the signalman to bring a down goods or light engine to a stand in order to ask the crew if they would exchange footplates so that we could each work back to our home depots.

Crews could refuse to co-operate and some did, but this was a usually good way of solving a common problem. If a relief crew could not be found, we told Control we would leave the train in the loop and run light engine to the nearest shed where we could leave the loco and make our way home. These trains, abandoned in loops because of the long hours and shortage of crews, were known as 'dead trains'. Some crews even threw the fire out and left the engine and train in the loop and, although rare, it was not unknown for relief crews to be ferried in taxis.

There were 'as required' or Control relief turns in each link for which Control would ring through instructions for a variety of work. Occasionally we had to take over on the 'Radyr' and 'East Usk' long goods or even the 'Long Tom' instead of regular men if they were running out of course. At one time the 'Long Tom' was worked by Southall men. The most wagons I ever worked on any of these trains was 80. There were usually something between 60 and 80 wagons. I can remember relieving the 2.00 a.m. Severn Tunnel—

A 30XX ROD working out of West Drayton yard, after putting off coal wagons, on its way to Old Oak Common in 1937. *C. R. L. Coles*

A 61XX heading through Compton with a northbound freight. When we were on the Hungerford 'Fly', most of the work at Compton was done on the southbound journey, anything for the north being left ready and collected on the way back. *T. B. Sands*

West Drayton domestic coal train, booking on at 4.40 a.m. with ten minutes to read notices and ten minutes to walk to West End box where the train was scheduled to be waiting on the up relief.

8.25 a.m. HUNGERFORD FLY
Book on 7.25 a.m. Off shed 8.10 a.m.
The 8.25 a.m. Hungerford Fly was marshalled in the up yard at Didcot. We prepared our engine and came off shed at 8.10, by which time the train had been pulled up out of the yard by the pilot, and the guard was taking his tally of the train. The early turn shunters took a break soon after 8.00, and assembling this train and drawing it forward was usually the last thing they did before having breakfast. We usually had a 57XX tank engine or a 22XX for this turn, but tender engines were not popular as we had to run tender first back from Hungerford. Only at Newbury was it possible to turn.

We had about 24 wagons and served most of the stations over the branch, stopping as required, often with 6-12 wagons of coal for Upton for 'the Atomic'. Water was usually tight on this turn and the tanks were as good as empty by the time we reached the water columns alongside the branch at Newbury East Junction. At Newbury Yard we picked up more wagons for Kintbury and Hungerford, leaving there with about 35. Although this was general traffic, much of it was domestic coal. At Hungerford we shunted the yard and had our meal break while being held out of the way for the down 'Cornish Riviera Express' which tore through Hungerford around 11.40 a.m.

We returned from Hungerford around midday, largely with empties which we left in Newbury yard, and picked up another local goods (the 12.30 p.m.), calling at all the stations up the branch again. On our way back to Didcot we were usually held out of the way at one of the stations to let an up passenger train (the 11.26 a.m. Southampton, 1.55 p.m. from Newbury) pass us. At Didcot we pulled up to North Junction and set back into the up yard where we uncoupled, ran round the train and went back on shed.

1.45 a.m. THATCHAM & COLTHROP
Book on 12.30 a.m. Off shed 1.30 a.m.
The 2.00 a.m. Thatcham conveyed supplies for the large American depot there and pulp for the paper mill at Colthrop. This job was in No. 2 Link during the war. We usually had a 61XX (often No. 6106), which we prepared, came off shed at 1.30 a.m. and backed straight onto the train which was left on the running road of the up yard before the shunters retired into their cabin for a meal. The train, usually around the maximum of 35 wagons, was made up with a brake van at each end to allow for a reversal of direction at Newbury. This was the first train over the branch and when we ran into Newbury, 'under the wall', we ran round to the other end of the train while the guard changed ends and made himself at home in the other van. Then, bunker-first, we set off up

the line to Thatcham where we were turned into the yard at Thatcham West Box. There was always a lot of shunting to do in the large yard serving the camp (a WD Ordnance Depot) before we continued to Colthrop Mill where we left our train on the up running line to drop off pulp and coal and pick up sheeted wagons containing large rolls of paper. On arrival at Reading West Junction Box, with about 20-25 wagons, we either backed the train into the old down yard or, alternatively, if it was for Reading West Up Yard, ran into the down goods loop and waited for a pilot to pull the train off from us and propel it into Reading West Junction Yard, or, if directed, backed it into the down yard. Either way, we worked light engine back to Didcot.

10.48 a.m. EASTLEIGH
Book on 9.48 a.m. Off shed 10.33 a.m.
The 10.48 a.m. for Eastleigh was a passenger link turn, but for a while it was in No. 3 Link. It was kept for men to retain their familiarity of the road over the branch to Winchester and Southampton. We used to book on at 9.48 a.m., prepare the engine, usually a 22XX, to come off shed at about 10.33. We left from No. 1 bay platform coupled to the coaches which had arrived as the 6.45 a.m.

A 22XX setting out from Upton & Blewbury on its journey across the Berkshire Downs to Newbury. During the construction of the DN&S, a navvy camp is said to have been based on the far side of the line in the right-hand area of the picture. *T. B. Sands*

Collecting the single-line tablet for Winchester from the signalman at Shawford Junction on the way back to Didcot. I think the fireman was Dick Hooper. *T. B. Sands*

Newbury service. After a 50-minute wait at Newbury, we left from the down bay at 12.30 p.m. and worked through to Eastleigh where we left our coaches in the platform and went on shed, turning the loco on the table or triangle. While we were there, we took water and enjoyed a meal break. We got to know some of the Southern men and often scrounged a couple of the towels or 'wipes' they issued to their men instead of cotton waste.

A large clock on some adjacent office buildings kept us aware of the time and when we were due off shed, we contacted the signalman by means of a route selector with an archaic dial.

When we got back to the station, our coaches were waiting in the up platform. We left at 2.22 p.m., again with a lengthy wait (40 minutes) at Newbury, taking water in the main platform, prior to backing into the up bay where we waited for departure time. We usually handed the engine over on arrival in the branch bay at Didcot. If there was no relief, we might have to take the engine on shed ourselves. For a short period the loco from this job was used as West End passenger pilot, working in the carriage sidings, particularly on the run up to Christmas.

THE SWINDON FLY
Book on 1.23 p.m. Travel passenger to Swindon.

After booking on, we walked back to the station to catch the 1.35 passenger train to Swindon. On arrival, we made our way to the shed to pick up whatever engine they had for us to work up through the Vale with the 2.40 p.m. 'Fly'. We could be given anything; my friend Sam Essex, for instance, remembers having No. 5040 *Stokesay Castle* which nearly wrecked the goods shed platform at Challow, its overhanging front end exceeding the limited clearance on a crossover there. The train was collected from Highworth Yard and called at Shrivenham, Uffington and Challow on the way to Wantage Road where we shunted the yard and left the train, running forward light engine to Didcot shed to book off around 7.00 p.m.

On arrival at Shrivenham with the Swindon 'Fly', we reversed the whole train back into the up refuge, and worked from there, putting off any traffic and picking up empty wagons. However, there wasn't much to do as we only left Swindon with a train of about 20 wagons and I think Swindon men had already called at all these stations before us with a down 'Fly' in the morning. This picture was taken looking west towards Swindon.
C. L. Mowat

Looking in the opposite direction towards Didcot, showing the sidings trailing from the down relief. The solitary wagon was probably a 'hot box' put off a down goods.
National Railway Museum

RAPID PROMOTIONS

A 1950s view of Uffington, looking towards Didcot with the Faringdon branch platform to the left of the station building. The pub in the station approach was another watering hole of ours!
P. J. Garland

We arrived at Uffington in the up loop and left our train there while we dropped off the usual two or three wagons in the siding (seen through the bridge) and collected any empties. When we finished, we usually pulled out of the loop directly onto the up running line, but if we needed water, the signalman sent us round the back of the platform to use the column at the opposite end of the station buildings, without blocking the main line. This picture also shows the single line to Faringdon curving away to the right.
J. H. Moss

Challow station, looking west towards Swindon. When we arrived with the Swindon 'Fly', we ran into the up platform, then backed into the up refuge where we left the train while we dropped off the usual two or three wagons. We didn't mind being held here with the 'Fly' when Freddie Monks was our guard. He had a key to the nearby pub so we could slip over for a drink even when it was closed.
J. H. Moss

We were often held at the signal beside the down relief in the distance of this view looking towards Didcot, but when we rang the signalman from there to find out how long we had to wait, more often than not he'd put the kettle on for us.
National Railway Museum

A stopping train held in the down relief for an express to clear. *A. Attewell*

RAPID PROMOTIONS

Up and down relief lines extended all the way from Wantage Road to Challow, so we were rarely held in the platforms. During the war, I spent many hours waiting on the relief lines, never knowing when we'd have to move. Again, if we were within a reasonable distance of the station, the signalman would usually put the kettle on for us. The relief lines can be seen stretching towards Challow in the distance of this view looking west at Wantage Road in the 1930s.
C. L. Mowat

No. 5348 with an 'F' class freight in the up platform at Wantage Road in 1937. It was probably on its way from the up goods line where it would have been held out of the way of higher priority trains.
H. E. Simmons

On the Swindon 'Fly' we stopped outside Wantage Road station, on our way from Challow, and left most of our train on the up relief (to the west of the platforms). There were usually about half a dozen or so wagons for Wantage, which might include supplies for the RAF at Grove and traffic for the Wantage Tramway. Marshalled at the front of the train, these were uncoupled and taken through the platform, out onto the up main and backed over the long crossover into the yard where another engine from Didcot was waiting to take over. We simply left the wagons there and returned light engine to Didcot, leaving the other engine to sort the yard and take any outwards traffic and empties to Didcot together with the rest of the train we'd left on the up relief. At this time, during the 1940s, the other engine came off shed at 2.55 a.m. to work what was known as 'the Challow'. The engine for this turn varied; it could be a Standard Goods, a 22XX or, as was often the case during the war years, one of the LMS 0–6–0s which ran light engine down to Wantage Road, calling to sort the yard at Steventon on the way. On the return journey it called at the Army Food and Supply Depot at Lockinge, and at Steventon to pick up the wagons left ready earlier. *C. L. Mowat*

In the 1940s the yard at Steventon was shunted by the light engine from Didcot to Wantage. As mentioned, it called to do the work on the way out, leaving any traffic ready for collection on the return journey to Didcot. In later years all this changed and we served the stations between Didcot and Swindon on a down Swindon 'Fly' in the mornings. This picture was taken looking towards Swindon in the 1930s.
C. L. Mowat

A closer view of Steventon goods shed.
P. J. Garland

After working the 5.52 Winchester, we walked through the town to the Southern station and travelled home on the cushions via Basingstoke and Reading.

The Southern Railway station at Winchester, looking down the line towards Eastleigh.

H. J. Stretton-Ward

5.52 p.m. WINCHESTER
Book on 4.52 p.m. Off shed 5.37 p.m.

This was a 22XX turn. After preparing the engine, we came off shed and over to the branch bay to couple onto the three coaches (sometimes six) which had previously formed the 1.55 p.m. Southampton to Didcot. We stopped at all stations to Winchester and took the loco on shed. We used to carry out our own disposal here, but later the Winchester shedman did it for us. We travelled home passenger on the Southern via Basingstoke and after walking through the town, usually had time for a pint in the SR staff club near the station.

11.40 p.m. POOLS
Book on 10.00 p.m. Off shed 11.00 p.m.

The engine for the 11.40 p.m. Pools to Yarnton, usually a 28XX, was sometimes already prepared for the crew who would then take the engine straight off shed to the up yard to assemble a train of empty coal wagons from various 'Flies' put off from various places as directed by Traffic Control.

We usually had sixty or so wagons which we took to Yarnton for transfer to the LMS or onward conveyance to Worcester or Banbury. This was often a short duty but

The bridge below Hinksey South yard. The line in the foreground was a goods loop from Radley provided during the war.
R. H. G. Simpson

This freight heading north through Oxford station was typical of the trains we worked from Didcot.
Barry Warr

Hinksey yard from the south, looking towards Oxford. These sidings, also provided during the war, were used for traffic from the car works at Cowley.

we never knew what work would be required of us at Yarnton where we might spend some time shunting or work a freight back to Hinksey Yard before taking the engine on to Oxford shed and returning home on the cushions.

Wartime arrangements in particular were subject to change but for a short time around this period a light engine was sent to Lockinge Ordnance Depot to shunt in preparation for the Swindon 'Fly', and after it had called, place any wagons left by it.

I think it was worked by a relief crew, but I had it as a spare turn with an LMS 0–6–0. The tenders of these engines were fitted with coal rails which required extra attention while trimming the coal. They were often damaged by heavy lumps of coal while they were being filled. These engines were on loan to the GWR and when they first arrived around the beginning of 1940 they had no seats or coal-watering pipes.

We arrived at the Lockinge depot at 12.30 p.m. and worked under the instruction of Shunter Higgs, a real country character with a reddish bronzed complexion, moustache, and a cap cocked onto the back of his head. I knew him from my time in the Telegraph Office at Didcot when he was a shunter in the passenger yard. Many of the older railwaymen showed great kindness towards us younger firemen and in a rich Berkshire accent he asked if I would like a rice pudding as his wife worked in the canteen. He knew rations were short. Proud of his ability to please, he left the shunting pole tucked into the handrail supports at the side of our cab and strutted off with swinging arms and disappeared into the canteen door. He soon reappeared with a broad grin, carrying an enamel bowl of rice pudding — my favourite dish. "Here you are, my lad, get that across your chest." He even provided a spoon. Blended with grated nutmeg, creamy milk and topped with brown skin, it was wonderful. "If you're on the job tomorrow, I'll arrange the same", was all he said when I gratefully handed back the empty dish.

CHAPTER SEVEN
OVER THE BRANCH

"FIREMAN Barlow, Fireman Barlow", shouted the call-boy beneath my bedroom window. Today I was on the 3.5 a.m. Winchester goods, so the call came at 1 o'clock in the morning. I hastily turned on the light in response so that the family and neighbours were not further disturbed, then settled down in bed again, hands behind my head, for a few moments of comfort and peace.

Going to bed in the early hours of the evening never really suited me. I would lay there, tossing and turning, anxious that if I fell into a deep sleep I might miss the call-boy's shout, and be late for work.

The night before I had laid out everything I needed. My overalls were in the outside lavatory, and my dungarees, short jacket and an old pair of trousers hung over the kitchen chair. Waiting to be packed into my box were the ingredients of my breakfast, bacon, bread and eggs, with a small piece of lard, for a 'fry-up' on the shovel, and a piece of cake, tea, and a small bottle of milk. I also took a hand towel and some soap. The food varied, sometimes my parents would pack me off with home-baked pasties, meat sandwiches, a raw onion that I could bake on the boiler gauge frame, and fresh fruit. I even took my Sunday roast on an enamel plate, covered by another plate held together with a cloth tied on top by its corners. This could be re-heated in the cab by leaving it on the steam fountain on top of the firebox.

The fresh night air would always revive me and, wide awake, I would begin to enjoy my surroundings as I cycled to the station through the silhouettes of familiar landmarks on a dark September morning in 1943. Approaching Didcot station, the silence was punctuated by the sounds of shunting in the up yard. That morning I felt certain I could recognise the sound of No. 5735, pulling out a freight train. Even though she was working over a quarter of a mile away, I could hear a pause in the rhythm of beats as she laboured under a heavy load. I knew she was trying to pull the train up from the up yard.

The driver persuaded her to give just a bit more power, but a damp dew-covered rail caused her to shudder and slip. In the distance, sparks, smoke and steam came from her chimney, shooting into the canopy of darkness above the floodlit yard. Like a small volcano, she continued for a few seconds and then stopped suddenly. I could imagine the sand lever being pulled in the cab, and, as the sand poured onto the rails in front of the leading wheels, she found the grip she needed.

Sparks momentarily floated in the wind like fireflies, their brilliance lasting some distance from where the 'volcano' had erupted. Gently, confident once more, the exhaust beats resumed with an ever-increasing rhythm. Light from the open firebox door stabbed the darkness with a beam of yellow brilliance. I knew she had won!

Access to the shed was via the subway connecting the platforms, up the steps at the far end and over the up carriage sidings by means of a boarded crossing, the surface of which was a good indicator of frost conditions. When I reached the top of the steps, the train on which I was to be fireman had been positioned on No. 1 running road, and there, as I had thought, was No. 5735 being filled at the water column.

From the other side of the crossing, the route was down the south side of the coal stage. Cycling was now allowed on the footpath, but with human nature being what it is, most men would ride the rest of the way. After putting my bike in the cycle shed, I walked over the boarded crossing, checking the time shown by the huge clock on the wall above the foreman's window before entering the shed. It was nearly 2.10 a.m. so I was almost on time. The interior of the shed was already filled with choking yellow smoke, a real 'pea-soup' atmosphere, which lingered when the various engines had been lit up. This indicated that Welsh steam coal was being used — slow to burn from a cold start, but once the fire had got going it was excellent.

The first port of call was the lobby where we booked on duty with the clerk through a kind of ticket window into the office, then a look at the duty board in the lobby. The board was glass, with notices, etc. fixed on the glass from a passage behind it. This was done by the roster clerk who shared his office with the shed foreman. The late notice board (always painted red) was the next to study before signing for any notices handed to us. We were allowed ten minutes for reading them. Examining the duty board, I saw that I was on No. 2221, the assisting engine, as far as Newbury, on the 3.5 a.m. Didcot to Winchester freight. This pleased me as I knew she was a good engine. The train engine was 2289, with driver Albert Haycroft and fireman Sam Essex, who would work the train through to Winchester. After careful study of the noticeboard, I couldn't find any speed restrictions or signal alterations.

The clerk in the office always had a cheerful word for us. It was his responsibility to make sure that the train crews appeared physically fit to take charge of the locos. It was all done in such a discreet manner that the majority of men never even realised it was being done!

Then I went into the cabin to collect a few things from my locker; I kept some old overalls there for preparing, an oil feeder and some spare cotton waste in case it was not available.

The next call was the stores to collect the keys for whichever engine was allocated to us. At this time the tools were still padlocked on the engines. I collected the oil 'bottles' (cans), a large 'bottle' of mineral oil for all the bearings, a medium 'bottle' of thick vegetable oil for the lubricator, and a small bottle of paraffin. We used to ask for 'six, two and one, and ¼lb waste', sign for it, and then it was off to prepare the engine. On leaving the stores, I was confronted by engineman Haycroft who began the usual jocular banter between footplate crews: "I suppose we shall have to push you all the way", as we were to assist him over the 'Linger and Die', and "Make sure you keep out of our way!". It was all so early in the morning, but with these words ringing in my ears, I didn't rise to the bait, but simply replied, "You will have to take second place today, Albert, we will be leading." A cheerful "Come on, let's get on with it", was agreed between us and we walked on through the shed to find our locomotives.

As my arrival was later than Sam's, he was already on 2289 which was berthed on No. 1 road outside the shed. For some reason, I was always a late arrival so early in the morning! My engine was on No. 4 road in front of the building. No. 2221 looked a sorry and silent locomotive, with sulphur-coloured smoke rolling out of her chimney and black flakes of soot dancing along her boiler. She was completely lifeless — not a whisper of steam anywhere.

At eye-level, as I climbed onto the footplate, I could see the cab was full of choking smoke. A tongue of yellow and black flame licked out of the small hole in the closed firebox doors, everywhere was covered in a film of black soot, even the glass on the steam pressure gauge was covered in a velvet blackness. This quiet air of neglect was deceptive, her power was just waiting to be aroused!

I wiped the grime from the left-hand side of the cab, and hung my clothes on one of the hooks just below the cab roof. The other one was left for the driver's clothes. Next I opened the blower valve to create a draught through the firebox. Fortunately, there was just enough steam pressure to draw the flames and fumes back into the firebox, a much happier state of affairs. The oil 'bottles', one for cylinders and valves and one for the various bearings, were placed on the dish above the fire-hole to warm so the oil would flow freely when the driver arrived.

I cleaned the boiler gauge glass and its protector, and lit and fitted the gauge lamp onto its bracket. I could now see the water level; the boiler was half full and inside the glass tube, the water was 'breathing', a sure sign that she was on the boil, and feeling the temperature of one of the boiler washout plugs confirmed this was the case.

With the blower on, an active hissing could be heard from inside the boiler, and, after wiping the film of soot from the pressure gauge, I could see the needle registering a few pounds per square inch.

The firebox was the next area to examine. There were no unusual sounds to be heard, such as leaking tubes or fusible plugs, but, because the fire was still 'green', it was necessary to light a ball of cotton waste soaked in paraffin, and throw it on the brick arch to provide enough light to examine the tube plate and fusible plugs and the arch itself.

Before disturbing the fire, which would create a dense smoke, I had to examine the smokebox. I lit the flare lamp and, holding it in one hand, climbed around the outside of the cab and made my way along the footplate to the front of the engine. The smokebox door was secured by two handles in the centre, one to lock the door and the other to screw it up tight. Inside I examined the blast pipe and jumper ring and baffle plate, making sure everything was in position. I could also see through the tubes to the light inside the firebox – a sure sign that all was well.

The smokebox door had to be closed securely to maintain the vital draught on the fire. Then, while I was still at the front, I lit the engine headlamp and placed it on the bracket on top of the smokebox in front of the chimney.

After stowing the coupling sideways on the hook on the front buffer beam, I climbed in the pit underneath the loco. The pit was messy and often filled with water, ashes and clinker, but I had to examine the ash pan with the front damper open. It was essential that the area was free to allow the passage of air through the fire grate. The fire bars were also noted as in position correctly. These areas of examination took time and patience, but it was necessary that everything was right if the loco was to steam efficiently. By now Roy Frewin, my driver, had arrived.

After climbing out of the pit, I got back up in the cab and pulled the sand lever a couple of times, then got back down again and tapped the sandbox pipes in front of the leading wheels to check the free running of sand. Often these were choked with wet sand which wouldn't discharge, and the only remedy was to scoop it all out with an old tin can and clear the delivery pipe by tapping it with a spanner until it was all empty. One of the fitters would often help out with this sort of problem, then we had to fill it up again with dry sand.

The other headlamp was then put in place over the left buffer of the tender with the shade in position to show a red light. With the outside examination completed, it was now time to prepare the fire and raise the steam pressure, the gauge by this time reading 45 PSI and the blower having become even more powerful.

The long metal pricker or poker was eased off the rack on the tender. Some 10ft in length and 1 inch thick, this was pushed deep into the fire through slightly open firebox doors. The glowing lumps of coal were then distributed around the grate by using the 'L' piece attached to the end of the pricker.

The fire bars at the back of the firebox were then rubbed with the pricker to knock any residue of ash or old clinker through into the ash pan below, leaving the grate nice and clear. Spreading the fire had a dramatic effect on the steam pressure and the needle began to rise more quickly. Under close observation, it could actually be seen to move.

The water in the gauge frame was now breathing, panting, rising and falling, as the steam pressure rose, and, opening the firebox doors, I could see the white-hot fire hungry for more coal. At this stage I still chose hand-selected lumps the size of coconuts, which were placed around the firebox in a saucer shape, with more in the back corners behind the doors, and less under the brick arch.

The idea was to keep an open hot mass of fire in the middle, and allow the corners and sides to fill the centre by the oscillation of the moving loco. After building up the fire, it was left with the back damper open and blower on gently, to allow the fire to burn through evenly until the boiler pressure reached 200 PSI and the safety valves lifted.

The boiler injectors were tested earlier but now I tried them again in turn to ensure they were working properly, and left one running to fill the boiler. The coal watering pipe worked off one of the injectors, so, while it was on, I hosed down the inside of the cab, the boiler back and floor, blasting away the coating of soot and small coal. At last the entire footplate smelt and felt a cleaner place!

In the meantime, Roy had prepared all the lubricating oil wells, big end shaft, gear linkage, etc., examining the loco with an experienced eye as he did so. Now the loco was ready, it was time to move to the water column. Often, as a fireman, I was allowed to do this while the driver positioned himself by the column and shouted "Whoa!" when the tender filler was in line with the water hose.

Before moving, the steam brake was put on to hold the loco while the handbrake was taken off the tender. I also closed the cylinder cocks to avoid showering the driver who was standing just in front, by the water column. With the steam brake handle returned to its upright position, the brakes came off and the regulator was eased up gently until the power could be felt as the pistons urged to turn the wheels. As that moment arrived, the regulator was soon closed; sufficient steam had been released into the cylinders for the engine to roll forward the short distance to the water column.

When the leather hose had been put into the manhole on the tender, the water was turned on and the leather bag swelled like a balloon, with water cascading everywhere except in the tank! Standing below, drivers sometimes got soaked and bad-tempered, whereas I stood back on the tender while they turned the water on.

All was well now. She was blowing off at the safety valves and the firebox doors were open to dry off the footplate and provide some light. In preparation for the trip, I oiled the firebox door guides to make them open and close more easily. Using the pick, I trimmed the coal in the tender and examined the emergency equipment, the cannister of detonators and two red flags, before stowing them safely back in the toolbox.

I went to the cabin to make a can of tea and on my way back I climbed up onto the footplate of 2289 to have a word with Sam and Albert and let them know we were ready to leave. With his cloth cap at a slight angle, and a cigarette in his mouth, Albert was relaxed on his seat, the reflection of the firelight on his features portraying contentment. A chuckle and a nod said it all. Everything was ship-shape and they were ready. When I got back to 2221, Roy, my mate, had lit his pipe and the scent of his favourite tobacco was drifting around the cab, another scene of contentment so typical of the relaxed manner of these men. I told Roy that Albert was ready and that he would follow us up to the shed signal where he would couple on to us.

With the can of hot tea keeping warm on the dish, we moved slowly off to the sound of a sharp blast on the whistle, to warn that we were leaving the shed, and idly crept up to the departure signal.

As we cleared No. 1 road, on our way to the shed signal, No. 2289 was slowly following, with alternating blasts of steam issuing from the cylinder cocks, hissing loudly and rising to shroud the engine. The scene was made all the more dramatic by the safety valves blowing in the damp morning air, the clouds of pure white steam contrasting with the dark surroundings. When we arrived at the shed signal, Roy held the engine on the steam brake and I went down to the back of the tender to wait for 2289 to arrive. It was the practice for the fireman of the standing locomotive to couple up, but, just prior to buffering up, Sam jumped off and came to shine some light from his gauge lamp. It was always good practice for both crews to satisfy themselves that the two engines were coupled together. The coupling of the leading engine was used, the front coupling of the second one being safely secured on the stowing hook with the screw lever knob placed inside to link! The vacuum pipes were then coupled together and, having satisfied ourselves that the coupling was secure, we removed our head and tail lamps and took them back to our cabs.

Before getting back on the engine, I pressed the button on the shed signal telephone. One long and two short presses aroused the East End ground foreman, who lowered the signal, and we were off.

We ran clear of the shed points and backed the engines towards the up yard where the shunter called us onto our train with a white light. He stood alongside the buffers of the leading wagon and swung his hand lamp steadily from side to side. It was my job to keep a constant watch on his signal. I kept the driver informed and when the light changed to green, he slowed the loco down to a creep as the shunter was telling us we were almost on the train.

A red light was shown just prior to buffering up and, during the split second taken to relay this to the driver, the buffers clanged gently as the loco came to a stand against the train. When the shunter had coupled up, he took the brakes off the leading wagon, which took up the slack of the couplings. While Sam took the lamp from the tender, I put a lamp on the bracket in the middle of the front buffer beam, below the smokebox. One high, one low in line, was the 'F' headcode carried by the 3.5 a.m. Winchester freight.

We could see the station clock on platforms 6 and 7 showing exactly 3.5 a.m. This clock is now one of my most prized possessions, bought when it became redundant. It still has 'GWR' on its face.

It was time to depart and our guard was alongside the engines, giving the loading to the drivers. There were forty wagons, twenty No. 1's, fifteen No. 2's and five No. 3's. These numbers indicated the class of traffic: 1 — coal, coke or patent fuel, 2 — other minerals, 3 — general merchandise, and were used in the calculation of loading. The weight of our train was 330 tons, not including the tare weight.

On the footplate, a couple of mugs of tea made all the difference — I always regarded the tea-can as one of the most important pieces of equipment carried on the loco!

While we drank our tea, the loco sat quietly, the firebox doors were open, and the blower was just cracked open. We were now only waiting for the all-clear. Once the yard inspector had obtained 'line clear' from the east signal box, he gave us permission to pass the stop board by the shunters cabin in the centre yard, and pull up to the signals controlling the departure from the goods yard. We couldn't see the guard when we left as the back of the train was hidden round the corner between the rows of vans and wagons on the adjacent curved roads. He would tell us he was going back to his van and we would pull away slowly when he'd had time to reach it. We might only pull up to the signal, but it was usually off, displaying a small green light, and the lowered signal arms could also be seen in the floodlighting.

When we moved off, the reversing lever was in full forward gear, the cylinder cocks were closed and oil was floating up the glasses of the sight feed lubricator on its way to feed the valves and cylinders. There was a full boiler of water and 200 lbs of steam on the clock. With both hands clasped around the smooth handle of the regulator, Roy gently opened and closed it while the loco responded to the steam entering the valves and pistons. No. 2221 moved away with a quiet gasp of exhaust from the chimney.

The full weight of the train could be felt as we worked steadily sideways over the various point crossings, from Didcot East Junction box across the main line to the Newbury branch.

On the approach to East Junction box, I looked back on my side to catch a glimpse of the guard's van coming round the corner by the East End ground frame by the end of Platforms 6 and 7. I waved my hand lamp towards the back of the train from the driver's side as we negotiated the right-hand curve towards the Newbury branch, waving it up and down to raise the guard's attention. Strictly speaking, he should have responded by showing a green light, but he usually gave a white light from the verandah of his brake van – the train was complete. Roy acknowledged with a cheerful response on the engine whistle and nicked back the reverser to 35 per cent cut-off and eased the regulator open very gradually.

The gentle curve of the branch as it left the main line caused the wheels to squeal for a moment, and the silence of the morning was now being broken by the sharp crisp beats of exhaust from the chimney.

The safety valves were now simmering with a whisper of steam escaping. No. 2221 was beginning to fly along the rails, as though she knew her business. Behind us, the wagons rumbled, and from the right-hand side of the loco came the steady 'tick-tick, tick-tick' of the vacuum pump which grew faster as the speed increased to 35 miles an hour.

By now the train engine 2289 had started to give us some assistance – we could hear its exhaust and see the chimney over the back of our tender. Albert was gently getting into unison with us and as the gradient became steeper, so the beats became louder. When I looked back, I could see flashes of light as Sam was opening and shutting the firebox doors, and, as he added each shovelful of coal, varying emissions of black and grey smoke were carried with the steam continually blasting out of the chimney.

With the draught through the firebox, I could now see that the white-hot mass of fire was eager for a fresh supply of coal. It was time to get down to it myself, so I gripped the shovel with my right hand and opened the firebox doors with my left. With feet slightly apart, to keep my balance, I soon slipped a shovelful of Welsh steam coal into the hungry firebox, bouncing the heel of the shovel onto the back of the firehole ring. A twist of the wrist directed the coal to wherever it was needed as I kept a mental picture of where each charge was placed. The smoke from the chimney was greyish-black as it passed overhead. This was good combustion.

The smell of smoke excited my senses and a feeling of exhilaration came over me, particularly as the pressure gauge responded to my efforts with a white feather of steam from the safety valves.

Each physical movement of coal shovelling took only a few seconds and a rhythm was soon developed – a bit like a dance. My partner was the shovel and the music was provided by the chimney beating time like a base drum, supported by the sounds of the vacuum pump, the rumbling of the wheels, and steam whispering from the safety valves. I had always wanted to be an engineman and here I was – young fireman Barlow – full of confidence, rattling south towards the Downs on the high embankment which strode across the Hagbourne fields, on a hard-working locomotive responding to my every touch. Sheer joy! Peering ahead, the distant for Upton and Blewbury showed a bright green – we had a clear road. Surveying the dark surroundings below, I watched the spent steam and smoke drift across the tops of the trees we were leaving behind.

As we rattled through Upton and Blewbury station, the 'bobby' watched from his signal box, with one hand on the lever frame, the other above his head, indicating all was well. As we passed, he put one of the levers back, returning the signal behind us to 'Danger'.

Our next signal was about a quarter of a mile away, but Roy and I kept peering out of the right-hand side of the cab to make certain it was green. As we expected, it was.

The gradient before us was long and steep, 1 in 104, so I shovelled more coal into the firebox using some of the better lumps I could conveniently lay hands on, and the driver eased the regulator further open on to second valve. It was all teamwork. The firebox doors were closed and the injector turned on to top up the boiler. The sound of the injector singing away could be heard as the water level in the gauge glass began to rise higher.

As we reached the cutting, I turned off the injector, then, as the cutting sides deepened, the sound of each beat of exhaust rose higher and higher on the approach to the first of three overbridges which Didcot crews dubbed 'Faith', 'Hope' and 'Charity'.

I opened the firebox doors again and fired all round the box. Opening and closing the doors along this stretch provided a never-to-be forgotten spectacle, with the white chalk sides of the cutting suddenly illuminated with splashes of firelight. It was like passing between two icebergs in a thunderstorm, with flashes of light trapped by the cutting sides and the overhead cloud of greyish-white steam billowing from the chimney. The train engine contributed to this dramatic spectacle with plenty of power and its own sharp blast contained between the deep cutting sides. Amid the fierce echoes, I looked back to watch the sparks being thrown out of their chimney with the harsh exhaust, the hiss of steam from the safety valves showing that Sam was in control. When the safety valves calmed briefly, I knew he was using the injector to top up the boiler, but with all the heat in his firebox they were soon merrily simmering away again. The two of us were acting in unison, teamwork to be proud of.

Nearing 'Hope' bridge, the tension of the train's weight became more apparent as the gradient increased and, with the reverser at 30 per cent cut-off, the cab developed a gentle sideways rock, as the engine began to slow. Passing under the high three-pillared 'Hope' bridge reminded me of the inside of a cathedral as we made for the deepest part of the cutting.

A set of catch points along here protected the bank we'd just climbed from any runaways, and then there was 'Charity' bridge and the gradient began to level out. As we finally came towards the end of the enormous cutting, the reverser was eased back to 25% cut-off, with the regulator back on first valve. With the safety valve blowing, I opened the firebox doors and put the injector on; everything was in our favour.

As we reached the level on top of the Downs, Albert gently eased 2289, finally shutting off and drifting, leaving us to work the train. This was normal when two engines were coupled together, the driver of the front engine being responsible for the braking. It was only possible for one driver to handle a train.

Streaks of silver grey on the eastern horizon greeted us as we headed across the open downland towards Churn Halt, and the dawn chorus was just beginning.

To experience this is always stimulating, but even more so from the footplate of a steam loco, out in the fresh air with just a cool breeze blowing into the cab, birds on the wing, and the sun appearing over the horizon.

A misty haze floated low over the meadows, and curled away from the pressure wave in front of the loco, finishing up in turbulence to our rear.

Rabbits hastened to the shelter of the many warrens in the embankments, startled sheep bounced away from the railway fence, and once I even saw a fox carrying a chicken as it slunk across the meadow, satisfied after its night of hunting.

Reading signals during the half-light of dawn or dusk was never easy and spotting a green signal light or semaphore arm was only possible if we knew exactly where to look. Special care was needed in these conditions. On this occasion the distant signal for Compton was displaying a green aspect, so we continued coasting along until well past the post where the gradient rose slightly. Over the hump where the gradient fell, the couplings tightened as the guard applied the brake on the van. The regulator opened slightly to gain speed through Compton station, where the 'bobby' cheerfully waved a duster from inside his signal box, which we acknowledged by a short, sharp blast from our whistle.

On the other side of the station there was a short cutting, then, on the falling gradient on the approach to Compton crossing, our speed was increasing and steam was shut off. An overbridge and another distant signal showing green marked the approach to Hampstead Norris. We faced a steep gradient beyond the station so I filled the firebox with fresh coal while the regulator was shut. It was always best to fill the firebox when no blast from the chimney drew in cold air. I had also filled the boiler during the slack period. As we drew nearer to the station, Roy gradually opened the regulator until it was fully across the guide, and the reverser was dropped to 40% cut-off. We had approached the dip at 20 miles an hour with tight couplings and gained speed until we passed under the bridge, where the gradient suddenly altered to a distinct dip.

Our speed was now 45 miles an hour, and we were racing to keep away from the wagons and keep the couplings tight until the whole of the train was on the rising gradient, then a pluck could be felt as the drawbar took the strain. If you misjudged the speed of approach to the dip, and opened the regulator at the wrong time, a terrific snatch would take place, with the serious risk of snapping a coupling. Such timing was an art developed by experience. Many drivers I fired to never mastered it, whilst others were real experts. With Roy it was a gentle tug, and looking back along the train I noticed the guard's van was safely in tow as it came under the overbridge with its side lights winking. Some guards would lean out of the van and raise an arm to indicate that all was well.

When the train was travelling on a left-hand curve, the fireman was expected to look out on his side to check that the train was following in a proper manner. During the hours of darkness, you could see sparks from any brakes that were seized on, or broken brake gear scraping along the track. In the daylight we kept a look-out for smoke from hot axle boxes, or displacement of a load on a wagon which might look lopsided. These were all potential hazards. If the guard in the rear van noted any problem, he would try to attract the driver's attention by snatching his hand brake on and off at intervals to cause warning jerks which might be felt on the engine. He would also show a red flag from the van.

The dip at Hampstead Norris was always difficult with one engine, so it needed all the experience of the two drivers to make sure each knew exactly what was expected of the other. Therefore Albert on 2289 did not open his regulator until the whole of the train was on the rising gradient. He had left the speed to us — perfect handling by two Western drivers. These experiences held me in good stead in later years.

As we tackled the steep gradient, I gave the firebox a stir with the pricker, and she responded with a flurry of steam from the safety valve. Roy, smiling happily, was now satisfied that he had maximum power to call on. The gentle rocking on the footplate was like being in a cradle, and the warmth and rhythm was making it easy to feel drowsy! There was many a time that I took a deep breath and put my head outside the cab to shake off the feeling.

Passing Hampstead Woods, my nostrils filled with the musty scents of pine mingling with poplar and elm, each tree having its own distinctive odour. The pressure gauge was steady on 200 psi, and the right-hand injector was gaining on the boiler. It was wonderful to be alive on a morning like this.

Knowing that the end of heavy gradients was near, we could drift down off the escarpment towards Newbury, and passing Pinewood Halt the regulator was closed, leaving only the jockey valve open to provide steam to the lubricator, and for a moment I watched the droplets of oil still rising up the sight glasses of the lubricator, to feed the valves and pistons.

The distant signal for Hermitage was at 'caution', indicating that the stop signals would be against us some quarter of a mile ahead. I screwed the handbrake down on the tender and held the weight of the train as we gradually decreased speed. The home signal was at 'danger', but, as we approached, it was lowered, as was the inner home signal, but a red flag was being exhibited from Hermitage signal box. Roy acknowledged by a short blast on the whistle, and stopping at the signal box the 'bobby' told us that the section ahead was clear, but the junction was blocked. This meant that Newbury East Junction would carry out a shunting movement, ahead of our approach to Newbury. When he was satisfied

When we arrived at Newbury with the 3.5 Winchester Goods, we stopped on the down main, where the assisting engine was uncoupled. As soon as the left-hand signal was pulled off, we ran forward into the down platform, leaving the train engine to pull the train through the station on the down main to Newbury West box where it stopped for water before continuing on to Winchester. In the meantime, after the backing signal at the end of the down platform had been lowered, we reversed out of the platform and stopped 'under the wall' below the cottages, to wait for the London newspaper train. We had to keep quiet if we were to avoid Newbury Annie's chamber pot!

C. L. Mowat

that these instructions were clearly understood, the signalman lowered the starting signal for us to proceed to Newbury.

Although there was a falling gradient on the approach to Newbury, the train was tightened up until the canal rise, which was just like a camel's back, just past the distant signal for Newbury East Junction. This was a fixed distant, always at 'caution'. The hump was approached slowly and as more wagons came over the top, so the tender handbrake was screwed on progressively tighter. The handbrake was always used in these conditions, the engine brake being held in reserve in case it was needed. In our case there was no problem as we drifted over the hump and started the descent in complete control towards the home signal in front of the road bridge. As expected, it was at 'danger', but a blast on the whistle, a few seconds pause, and the arm was lowered. Easing the handbrake, we proceeded towards the sharp curve where the squealing of wheels on the check rail always heralded our approach into Newbury. Roy acknowledged a green flag from the signal box with a short whistle, and we proceeded under caution to Newbury Middle Box.

During the approach to Newbury, I let the fire burn down, and the boiler water level drop to leave room to control the steam. The firebox was hot so she would generate steam easily if required, but if the boiler level was too high and the safety valves started blowing off noisily, I wouldn't have been able to keep it quiet and we might annoy those asleep in Railway Cottages, above the embankment. One particular lady here, who we called 'Annie', would lean out of her bedroom window in a rage, waving a towel at us, and shouting for some peace and quiet if we left the safety valves blowing hard. Her bedroom was just above us, and we were always a bit wary as other drivers had told us of chamber pots being emptied over the fence, and down onto locos! It was certainly difficult to keep such a free-steaming loco as 2221 quiet — but we didn't fancy the alternative!

We left the train here, so Sam climbed down and uncoupled us, at the same time putting up headlamps on his engine ready for the next stage of their journey. We were booked to go into Newbury yard and prepare the pick-up goods for Winchester which we took as far as Woodhay, but our first task was to 'tail' the Westbury paper train. We therefore moved off the train and ran forward into the down platform. When we were out of the way, Albert drew the train through the station on the down main and stopped by Newbury West box to take water before continuing on to Winchester. In the meantime we backed out of the platform, took water, and waited 'under the wall' until the paper train arrived. While it was in the platform, we coupled onto the last vehicle which was detached before the train continued to Westbury. When it had been unloaded, we took it over to the goods yard where we prepared our train. However, before we started shunting, we took a break.

For most enginemen the highlight of these early morning trips was breakfast, and I was certainly feeling hungry now, so while we were sitting still in the yard, I used the opportunity to cook some bacon and eggs on the shovel, which I washed down with scalding steam and water from the coal watering pipe. The blade, worn by continual use, was already shiny — the wash only removed the coal dust. After being rubbed by a wad of cotton waste, it was clean as a new pin, better than some frying pans I have seen. I put a lump of lard in and allowed it to melt by placing the heel of the shovel joint into the firebox, where the fire was now just quietly glowing red. I put two rashers of bacon on the blade first, and as soon as they began to crackle, I broke two eggs on the lip of the shovel and dropped them into the sizzling fat. Quickly removing the shovel from the firebox to allow it to cool, the bacon and eggs continued to cook.

My mouth was truly watering as the smell of cooking wafted around the cab. I turned the bucket upside-down for a seat and placed it in a corner of the cab, and gently eased the shovel with its contents into position onto the fireman's seat which served as a table. With my back to the firebox and the shovel serving as a plate, I sat down to enjoy my favourite meal. I cannot begin to describe the pleasure from this feast!

In the meantime, Roy had made a can of tea and was enjoying having a yarn with the shunters in their cabin. The sugarless tea washed down the eggs and bacon and the inner man was well satisfied. Furthermore, there was no washing-up to do!

Warm and comfortable in the cab, and with a satisfied stomach, I relaxed into a doze for a while, but I had a startled awakening by Roy who struck the metal fall plate with the coal pick. Time to start work again!

The shunters were ready for us to assemble our train for the stations to Winchester. When this was done, I shovelled some more coal forward ready for use, while Roy checked round the outside of 2221 and oiled the bars and pistons.

In the firebox the red embers now had a dull appearance, and there was no sign of flames. The solid black coal lumps that I'd placed while we had breakfast had burned away. I opened the blower valve and rubbed the pricker or poker along the firebox grate to prevent any clinker from forming on the bars. As the fire livened up, several shovels of coal were sprinkled around the sides and it soon developed a bright appearance.

I had a general tidy up on the footplate and washed the floor down with the pep pipe (on cold winter days the smokeplate was taken out of the fire hole to dry up the wet footboards) and we were ready for the next leg of the trip over the Winchester branch.

We had twenty-six wagons, an average load, mainly consisting of agricultural requirements and house coal. With the blast from the chimney, the fire came alive as we pulled the train up to the ground disc or dummy, at the end of the sidings. We had excellent quality coal, with 95% carbon and hardly any residue. The energy produced was terrific. The white ash was so fine it was like talcum powder and was soon cleared by the blast through the fire.

We had a quick check of essentials around the cab, the boiler gauge frame was showing two-thirds of a glass, steam pressure was 180 psi, the back damper was half open, the front one closed and the firebox doors were left open. The gauge on the tender showed three thousand gallons of water. The sight glasses of the lubricator again showed droplets of oil rising steadily. All these things registered with just a glance to a trained mind.

When the dummy came off at 7.50 a.m., we realised that the first passenger train to Winchester, leaving Newbury from the down bay at 7.45, had cleared the section and we would follow it along the main line to Enborne Junction.

As the home signal was lowered, I exchanged hand signals with the guard, and we were under way. The regulator was opened gently to take up the slack couplings, and after the guard had given us the tip that his van had a tight coupling, the regulator was opened further and the sound of exhaust bounced between the surrounding buildings as we pulled away from Newbury.

A rising gradient with catch points lay some 400 yards beyond the starting signal on the approach to Enborne Junction. The smell of burning coal drifted into the cab, and the rising boiler pressure hastened when the regulator was eased as we approached the junction at 20 miles an hour. I put on the right-hand injector to fill the boiler and prevent the safety valves from blowing as any escaping steam might obscure our view of the signals.

A gentle nudge was felt on the front of the loco as we negotiated the points taking us onto the branch line. Having no pony wheels to lead into a curve, there was always a sideways rocking movement with 22XX locos.

Once again we were able to enjoy beautiful countryside as we ran across the farmland on our way to Woodhay. On the curved approach to the station we both kept a sharp lookout for the outer home signal. It was at 'danger', and I knew a northbound passenger train had already arrived at the station.

When we gave a blast on the whistle to let the signalman know we had seen the signal at 'danger', the arm was lowered and we rolled into the station where the 7.5 from Winchester was waiting in the opposite platform.

We had a couple of wagons of traders coal for Woodhay, so shortly after the passenger train had left, we ran forward with them and backed into the yard, leaving the rest of our train in the platform. Quite a bit of locally cut timber was loaded at Woodhay for use as pit props, so besides a couple of empties there was also a wagon load of timber to take with us.

With the coal wagons 'on the engine' (coupled behind the tender), we collected the outgoing vehicles and put them on to the train in the platform, running back over to the yard to place the coal wagons. The guard worked quickly, pinning down brakes and swinging the couplings with his shunters pole and we were soon back on our train in the platform, ready to continue our journey.

Although the line had just been improved as part of the war effort, the doubling only extended as far as Woodhay, so from here onwards we were back to single-line working. As we pulled out of the station, the signalman leaned out of the window of the box to hand me the single-line token to Highclere, which I showed to Roy before hanging it on the clothes hook in the corner of the cab. Much of the steady climb to Highclere was on an embankment overlooking fir trees and rhododendrons which looked beautiful in the spring.

The approach to Highclere was marked by a deep cutting where the gradient changed to fall through the station. There was never much traffic here, so with no need to call that morning, we simply exchanged tokens on the way through to Burghclere. The guard used the handbrake in his van to keep the couplings of the train taut on the way down into the gentle dip midway between Highclere and Burghclere, Roy using just enough steam to maintain our speed up the bank the other side to take us into Burghclere station, where we came to a gentle stand in the platform and handed the single-line token to the signalman.

This was as far south as we would go. We had to leave the footplate we'd become so familiar with to work back to Didcot with the next northbound passenger due into Burghclere in a few minutes time. We had left Woodhay around the booked time of 8.20 a.m., and, without calling at Highclere, we had saved the 11 minutes allowed in the timetable for any work there, so now we had plenty of time for the changeover.

Before leaving the engine, Roy destroyed the brake, put the reverser into mid gear and opened the drain cocks while I screwed the handbrake on hard and put the chain on the handle. Then we climbed down and walked across to the north end of the opposite platform to wait for the 7.32 from Southampton (8.14 Winchester) which we would work through to Didcot, leaving the Winchester men to work our train south on the

No. 3448 *Kingfisher* at Woodhay in the 1940s. This locomotive was always a pleasure to work on. She ran like a well-oiled sewing machine. I found these locos far superior to any of the BR Standards.
G. L. Hoare

turn I'd cut my teeth on a couple of years previously.

As soon as their train had come to a stand, we exchanged a few words with the Winchester men as we boarded the footplate of No. 3448 *Kingfisher*, a loco of the 'Bulldog' class. My first impression was the lower level of the footplate, and compared with 2221 everything felt strange at first. However, the previous crew had left everything spick and span, so we had nothing to grumble about, and they had already exchanged tokens with the signalman on their way into the station and left the one for the section ahead, to Highclere, hanging in the corner of the cab. We had three passenger coaches weighing 96 tons, a free-steaming loco with a healthy fire, and a full head of steam in the boiler. We were all set to leave and there was little to do as the gradient was falling most of the way to Newbury.

I left the firebox doors open, the back damper half open, and the front one closed, which just kept her from blowing off at the safety valves. We were gliding along effortlessly, with just a whisper of steam coming from the chimney. She rode freely, with ease and comfort. The bogie wheels and the low-level profile of this type of loco made all the difference.

It was my experience over the years that of all the locos I worked, including the modern BR Standards, the earlier locos such as 3448 always gave a more comfortable ride. It seemed to me that the more modern the engineering, the poorer they rode!

On the way back, we called at Highclere and Woodhay and, on arrival at Enborne Junction, the outer home signal was lowered as we approached it. Roy blew the whistle in acknowledgement and found the signalman was exhibiting a green flag from the signal box, a warning for us to proceed to Newbury as the section was clear, but the junction or platform approach beyond was blocked.

The signals came off just ahead of us as we approached Newbury, shepherding us in, and on the signal post outside the station a small signal with 'CO' came off, calling us in behind another passenger train already occupying the platform. The reason for proceeding under the warning now became apparent, the 7.15 Frome was running late that morning and we were being let in behind it. We rolled in gently and stopped six feet away from the end of the train in front, near to the station clock which was underneath the verandah. It was 9.22 and the passengers for London on our train normally got off and waited here for the 6.25 a.m. Weymouth which left Newbury at 10 a.m. However, the 7.15 Frome (which should have left at 8.53) was too good an opportunity to miss, so as soon as we came to rest, passengers from our train rushed past to catch the one in front. Leaning over the side of the cab, I watched the guard standing ready with his watch in his hand, the station master, looking very important in his gold-braided uniform, cheerfully hurrying the last passengers to their seats.

The guard gave two sharp blasts on his whistle, followed by two more, an impatient sound to hasten any stragglers. Then the station master gave the 'All Clear' by raising his arm above his head, the guard lifted the green flag, and, with a quick flick of his wrist, the square unfurled and was waved in a semaphore arc — 'Right Away'. As the train pulled away, the guard jumped on to the running board of his van, and then moved inside, closing the door behind him and putting his head out of the window to watch the train safely out of the station.

The platform line was now clear and, as I watched the tail lamp on the last coach take a sudden lurch to the right over the points to the up main line, we could hear the loco being nicked up, as the sound of the exhaust faded away into the distance, leaving behind a cloud of steam and smoke, only gradually lifting in the morning breeze.

We would normally have come to a stand alongside the water column on the platform, so now we had to move up to take water. I therefore went back to tell the guard who closed all the doors and waved us forward with a hand signal. When arriving with a passenger train, considerable skill was required to stop a train in exactly the right position for the leather bag on the jib to be placed into the tank. If we didn't get it exactly right, we could only move again with the cooperation of the guard after the passengers had alighted. Time wasted through misjudgement could cause delays, so many drivers worked to a mark on their side, like a lump of coal or a fishplate (or even a chalk line) placed on a Monday in the hope that it would remain there for the rest of the week on that duty.

Our departure time was 9.35, so with the extra time taken to move up to the column when the London train had gone, we had to work quickly to take water and shovel some coal forward ready for the journey. I had built the fire in the shape of a haycock, with the hump underneath the doors, using hand-picked lumps at the back, and with the dampers open, I partially closed the firebox doors, and opened the blower valve slightly to ease the draught through the fire. Grey smoke was coming from the chimney, assisted by the hiss of the blower.

The banner disc signal on the gantry indicated that the signal at the end of the platform obscured by the bridge was off, and the minute hand on the large clock under the verandah was already pointing to our departure time, so our guard blew his whistle and raised his green flag. Our departure with a local train was quite a contrast to the prestige and fuss over the London train. There was no station master and, with rather less passengers, we slipped away quite anonymously.

No. 3448 pulled away with ease, and the feel of movement under our feet again was pleasant. Rocking gently from side to side, she rode over the points leading on to the up main line, then the junction points of the branch, nudging her way around the curve, eager to get away. Roy had to ease her back; the check-railed curve had a restriction of fifteen miles per hour, but once clear, the regulator was opened, the reverser reined back to 20% cut-off and she was given her head!

The speed increased to something like the 45 miles an hour restriction for this particular route. The limit was not always adhered to, the temptation to increase speed being very great.

It had turned out to be a clear day and with everything in our favour we could enjoy the surrounding countryside.

The firebox was now a white-hot mass, a perfect fire which was reflected in the steam pressure rising with ease. After I had placed about six shovels of coal around the sides and corners, I opened the firebox doors slightly. The extra

Newbury station, looking west. We took water at the column on the right, on our way back to Didcot with the Southampton train. *Lens of Sutton*

draught through the firebox was deflected by the smokeplate over the bed of fire, burning the carbon which would have issued from the chimney in the form of thick black smoke had the doors been shut.

However, 3448 was proudly showing signs of good combustion and each beat of the exhaust was followed by mushroom clouds of grey smoke which drifted upwards over the landscape.

As the safety valves began to simmer, showing maximum steam pressure, I put the injector on. The sounds of the injector purring away were always pleasant to hear, but a sudden change alerted my sound reflexes — a splutter or sudden burst of exhaust steam from the overflow required prompt attention. Generally, the injectors worked perfectly, but there was the odd occasion when problems did develop. Of course, during the hustle and bustle of footplate work or just admiring the scenery, there was always the chance of forgetting to turn the injector off again. This would cause the boiler to overfill and prime or just lower the steam pressure.

I soon learned to keep seated as much as possible when running at speed. It was very hard on the legs, and keeping balanced on the footplate was an art — like learning to skate! On rough-riding locos that needed extra attention in order to keep up the steam pressure, I would often finish a trip with aching limbs and knees weak with muscle tension. Sometimes I would even wake up at night with an attack of cramp.

Knowing the route was everything and I soon got to know where steam was needed and where drivers would close the regulator, which was usually done at landmarks such as a particular milepost, a bridge or a farm. Coming into stations, the blower was turned on and the firebox doors opened to clear the chimney of smut and thick black smoke. A gentle stop was also essential.

Our trip to Didcot over the 'linger and die' was pleasant and effortless. No. 3448 was a dream of

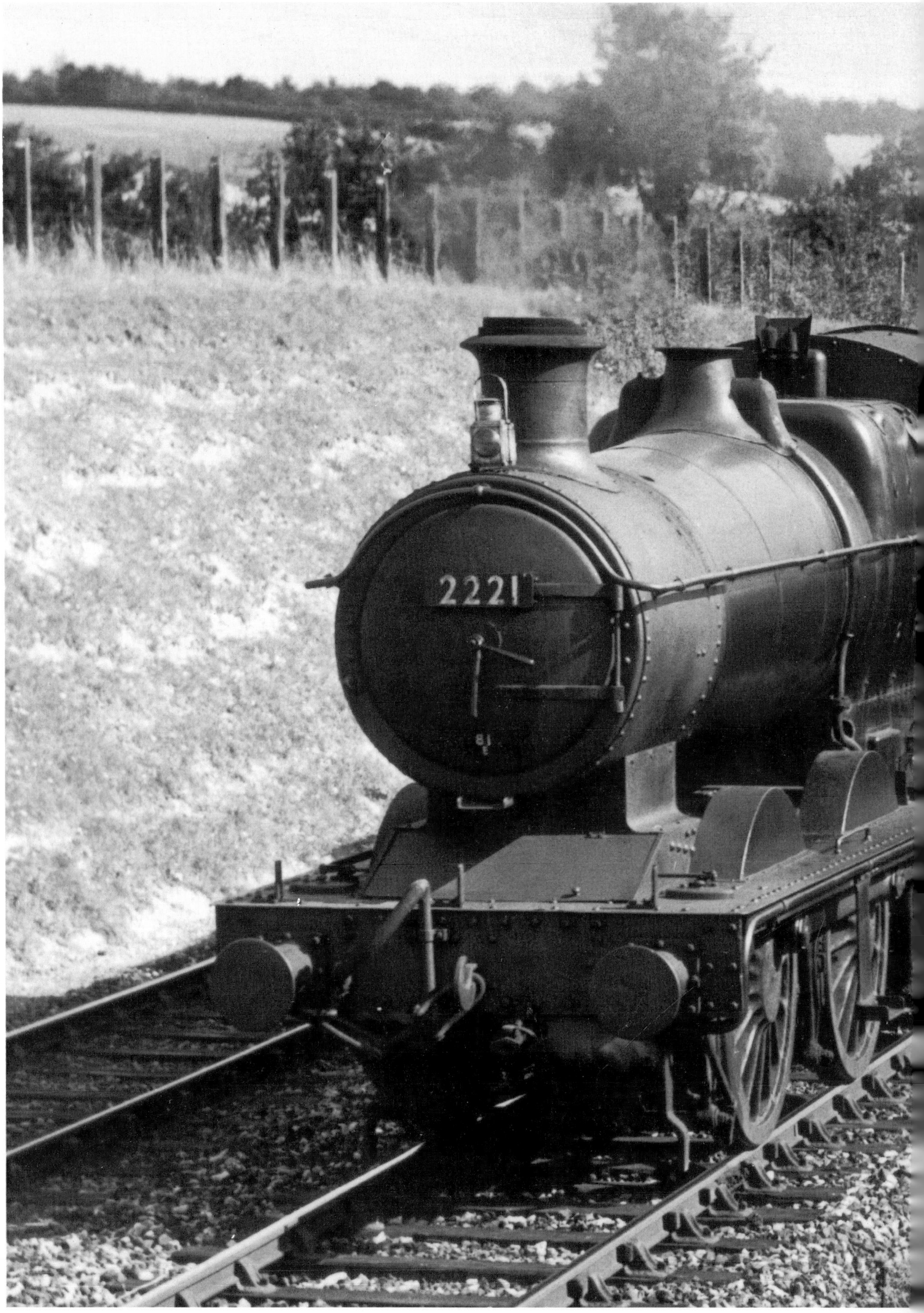
2221

No. 2221 heading north between Hampstead Norris and Compton Crossing on its way back from Southampton to Didcot. The Hampstead Norris up advanced starter can just be seen in the background. No. 2221 was a very free-steaming loco. *J. F. Russell-Smith*

No. 2289 going on shed after working the 6.9 p.m. from Reading on 16th August 1947. The large ROD tender was an instantly recognisable feature although I don't think it was paired with it for that long.
H. C. Casserley

a loco to work on and we only had three coaches to pull. When steam was shut off, with just the jockey valve left open at the top of the Downs, I knew we had finished, and a drift or free-wheel to Didcot East Junction was all that was left. What a contrast to the outward trip with 2221! The sounds of the track as we sped through the cutting varied from a dull thud to a high rumble as we passed over the strata of chalk-rock underneath the track.

As we came into Upton and Blewbury, a panoramic view of the Thames Valley greeted us, stretching across to Oxford in the north, and Bledlow Ridge in Buckinghamshire, high in the Chiltern Hills, to the east, one of the finest views anywhere on a clear morning, with the sunlight behind you. This was a real bonus for all our hard efforts, and cheered me as we drifted down the incline to Didcot and the end of our duty.

No. 3448 was like a well-oiled sewing machine as she responded to every control. I had let the fire run down to a thin layer over the fire-bars, so that she would arrive on the shed ash-pit with as little as possible. I rested the shovel handle on to the side of the tender coal hole, the blade of the shovel on the other side, filling the hollow of the shovel, hand-basin fashion, with hot water from the pep pipe to wash our hands. While doing this on one occasion, my gold signet ring slipped off my finger because of the soapy foam I had on my hands. It was a treasured possession, given to me by my parents as a 21st birthday present. I watched as it bounced up and down on the footplate before disappearing into the hole at the back of one of the damper handles, to fall underneath the loco and disappear for ever. We were moving at 45 miles an hour, so I never thought I'd see it again.

On arrival back at Didcot shed, we berthed 3448 on the ash-pit road. Knowing how I was feeling about my loss, Roy suggested that it might be worth looking underneath the loco just in case. As I crawled underneath between red-hot ashes, to my utter amazement, directly in front of me there was my signet ring stuck in a lump of grease on the brake gear below the ashpan. I still wear this ring today, and it has never been off my finger since.

My attachment to 3448 gained a new dimension that day!

CHAPTER EIGHT
POST-WAR SERVICE

I don't remember so much about my time in No. 2 Link, partly because by this time serving as a fireman had become such a routine part of my life, but in truth mainly because in 1947 I met Winifred, a rather special girlfriend who I was later to marry.

Our serious courtship began when Winnie appeared one evening outside Didcot station waiting for me to return from Worcester at about 11.30 p.m.

Working a train with a '28XX' and forty 20-ton coal wagons laden with sugar beet for Kidderminster was always a slow, steady trip. Percy Steele and I took over at Didcot North in the late afternoon and made our way to Worcester (Wyldes Lane) via Oxford and Honeybourne. Working through the peak of the evening passenger train service meant hopping from goods loop to goods loop. At Radley we were put in the down goods loop and, after slowly running through Hinksey marshalling yard, we were held at Hinksey North signal box where we waited for a margin between evening rush-hour traffic. With a heavy load of over 800 tons behind, progress was slow up the heavy incline to Blockley station. Having passed through Campden station, we pulled up at the stop board where we pinned down the brakes of enough leading wagons to satisfy Percy that the progress of the train would be sufficiently checked for a safe descent of the bank. This was vital when the driver had only the brakes on the locomotive and tender to control the train. When he was happy, Percy sounded the whistle which indicated to the guard, who had been pinning down the brake handles, that he could make his way back to his brake van. The train was then pulled away against the brakes, which helped restrain it on the falling gradient, especially through the approaching Campden tunnel.

The tunnel always had a musty smell. Dampness was the locoman's worst enemy. A heavy load such as ours could soon start a wheel slide, and if the wheels locked up we were out of control. The tunnel was therefore negotiated with extreme caution. If the speed increased even slightly, the hand brake was screwed down on the tender; the vacuum brake on the locomotive was used only occasionally to help the fireman to screw the tender hand brake on even harder.

After drifting down to the Honeybourne stop board, the fireman always released the brakes on the wagons. I often did this job, easing the brake levers free with the handle of the coal pick, to

BERNARD BARLOW c.1949

save the guard walking up to the front. Still on a falling gradient, we soon passed Evesham and Norton Junction. On arrival at Wyldes Lane, it was always a welcome sight to see our relief waiting to take over and work the train on to Kidderminster. We were instructed to work back a train of empty mineral wagons to Yarnton which was waiting in the up loop, but it was rather an anticlimax to find an 'Austerity' class locomotive waiting for our attention. Forty-five empty wagons and a head wind blowing from the east did not make for an easy return trip.

The coal was dry and dusty, and choking clouds hung in the cab as I picked and cracked the large lumps into manageable sizes. The sprinkler system was damaged and not operating, and the coal watering pipe was missing. The only means we had of damping the coal was the bucket occasionally filled by opening the water level rod on the side of the tender. I sloshed the bucket of water over the coal but it was completely inadequate and ran off like water off a duck's back. The whole cab was a mess, and with not even a handbrush we were paddling in coal dust and mud with only a shovel to scrape up the mess. We had been left a sorry state of affairs and everything we touched was coated with fine dust which stuck to our skin. My mate went to the signal box and demanded thirty minutes or more to try and get ourselves sorted out. This we duly did, filling the tank, making up the firebox with lumps of coal and topping up the boiler, making sure both injectors were working properly. After a while, we came to accept our lot, and did our best to keep the dust under control. A can of tea always made these situations less painful, then I was ready to face whatever lay ahead.

Despite the dusty coal, the loco steamed very well, the safety valves hissed away as we climbed up Honeybourne bank, with the bank engine behind helping out. On the curve approaching the cutting before the tunnel, we could see the banking engine working reasonably well, the intermittent flashes of firelight showing in the

A banker at work on Campden Bank. It always gave us a good feeling to look back over our tender and see the banker working hard; the Honeybourne men were always helpful. The constant gradient meant there was no need for them to couple up. When they left us at Blockley Crossing, they whistled 'toot toot' in farewell, leaving us with the full weight of the train.
Philip Hopkins

dark as the fireman opened and closed the firebox doors between each shovel of coal. Sparks were spewing out of our chimney, as the steam drifted away behind. A cylinder pressure valve blowing all added to the scene. The 22XX gave us valued assistance, leaving us at Blockley signal box when its work had been done.

By now the coal dust was even more of a nuisance and my eyes had begun to smart, and my nostrils were feeling caked, so I decided to use my hand towel as a mask over my face. This helped but my eyes still had no protection from the clouds of coal dust which were swirling around the cab.

Throughout the journey I gradually came to terms with my lot but I was so relieved when we passed Combe Halt and felt the rising gradient towards Yarnton. When we arrived, we ran past the signal box clear of the ground disc and were directed back into the yard. Here we had relief as our train was to pass onto the LMS line to Bletchley.

The wait for a lift to Oxford station seemed endless but eventually we cadged a lift on a light engine returning to the shed. After another wait on the station, we caught the last passenger train, the 9.50 p.m. to Didcot, to find my girlfriend waiting outside. Winnie was literally a sight for sore eyes.

Having just come off this rough trip, I was in no fit state to meet a girlfriend! I had a black face, oily hands, overalls full of coal dust, and my lips were caked with a mixture of sweat and coal dust. We must have made a pretty picture as she linked her arm into mine, and we walked home to East Hagbourne together. It was fortunate that the enveloping darkness hid us from prying eyes! When we arrived at her parents' house, I asked her if they had minded her being out so late, but she didn't reply. It was only many years later that I learned the truth. Winifred had gone to bed at 9 o'clock and at 10 p.m. she had crept quietly downstairs again while her parents were fast asleep, and had walked through the darkness to meet me. Her devotion was a secure anchorage during my railway career. No man could ask for more.

She did not come from a railway family and had no idea how my work would affect the routine of normal family life. Like myself, she was from the Berkshire Downs, country born and bred. Living close to nature, and keenly interested in the animals and plants around the farm cottage where she was raised, helped to forge her natural

The entrance to Didcot station, where I found Winnie waiting for me. The waiting room above (from down main platform) was the venue for the regular weekly St. John Ambulance classes.
National Railway Museum

Honeybourne Junction, looking east along the main lines towards Oxford.
C. L. Mowat

Still looking east, this time through the adjacent span along the relief lines to and from Stratford.
Photographer unknown

Looking in the opposite direction towards Worcester. When we reached Honeybourne with the Tyseley freight, we had to reverse direction, so we ran through the station and into the sidings on the right. There we uncoupled from the train and turned the engine on the triangle by running along the Stratford branch, reversing onto the Cheltenham line at East Loop Junction, then back under the bridge on the north loop and back through the station and onto our train. In the meantime the brake van had been put on the other end by the pilot. We left for Cheltenham via the west loop.
Photographer unknown

POSTWAR SERVICE

This view east towards Oxford was taken from the bridge shown on the opposite page. The pair of relief lines on the left can be seen curving away in the distance towards Stratford and the north, whilst the adjacent up and down main lines to Oxford continued straight on. We were put in the goods loops on the right, behind the south signal box, when we went to Worcester. *Photographer unknown*

instincts of common sense and a calm orderly manner. In spite of the strains, tensions and disorganised hours of duty which affected our family life, we have a successful marriage.

Our courtship lasted from 1947 to 1950, when we married (appropriately) on Lady Day, the 25th March. It was a wedding to be proud of, and as it turned out, I was marrying the East Hagbourne Carnival Queen, so I felt fortunate that I had placed a ring on her finger two years earlier, as many other young men were hovering around.

I shall never forget the day we bought the diamond ring, from a jeweller at Swindon. As we left the shop, Winifred could hardly wait for me to place it on her finger. As we stood there, the sound of an express train could be heard rattling through Swindon. The continuous shrill sound of the whistle seemed to me symbolic of our future lives together.

As far as I can remember, the time I spent in No. 2 Link more or less coincided with our courtship and I have attempted to record the turns in the link at that time:

No. 2 LINK – 1947-50. (12 Turns)

3.45 a.m. POOLS, SEVERN TUNNEL JCT
Book on 3.15 a.m. Off shed 3.30 a.m.
The engine, a 28XX, was prepared for us ready to take off shed and run to West Curve Yard to pick up or assemble the train of empties. We picked up more at Hinksey and set off for Gloucester. At Honeybourne we ran into the platform and set back onto the Stratford line and, running under the Oxford & Worcester line, we continued our journey via Winchcombe as far as Lansdown Junction where we usually got relief. We travelled home passenger.

THE 'TYSELEY' FREIGHT
Book on 3.20 a.m. Relieve the 1.5 a.m. Swindon to Bordesley at 3.45.
This was a 'double home' turn which normally involved lodging at Tyseley, but during the war 'double home' work was suspended and for some time afterwards we only worked this train as far as Honeybourne. The train, an 'F' freight, started out from Swindon. We relieved the Swindon men on the West Curve and worked the train as far as Honeybourne. (In postwar years we went 'double home' to Tyseley via Stratford-upon-Avon.) Our train home didn't stop at Honeybourne so we rode on to Evesham where we jumped off and waited for the first passenger train of the day from Worcester. Guard Hall regularly worked this train and locked off a compartment for us. He usually greeted us with "This way

Didcot — got yer bed". The train started filling up from Moreton so the reserve compartment, towards the rear near the guard's van, was very welcome.

4.00 a.m. LIGHT ENGINE TO NEWBURY
Book on 3.00 a.m.
We prepared our own engine, a 63XX, for this turn and ran light to Newbury where we carried out any shunting required in the yard, then ran out to the Racecourse to turn. Afterwards we waited in the sidings under the wall for the arrival of the 6-coach 6.22 a.m. train from Reading in the down platform. We backed onto stock and a shunter coupled us onto the last three coaches. The Reading men and their 43XX worked the front portion on to Winchester (one of the few times Reading men worked over the branch) and we took our stock over to the up platform ready to work the 8.10 a.m. which called at Thatcham and then ran fast to Reading where we ran into No. 3 bay. A pilot collected the empty stock, releasing us to run light to Reading shed and travel home passenger back to Didcot.

By 1951, this turn had changed, and the 8.10 from Newbury to Reading was worked by Reading men. We were given a 36XX pannier tank (often 3622) which saved turning when we got to Newbury. We ran to Newbury assisting the 4.30 Winchester freight, changed footplates with the Newbury men on the previous day's engine, and worked it back with the 6.45 a.m. passenger to Didcot, the coaches for which were already in the bay. However, I can alternatively remember working the 7.45 to Reading and even assisting a freight.

11.10 a.m. DEPOT TO HANWELL BRIDGE
Book on 9.55 a.m. Off shed 10.55 a.m.
This wartime job pre-dated Moreton Yard and was kept going through to the 1950s when Didcot Ordnance Depot was being cleared. It was a 49XX, 28XX or 'Austerity' duty. We prepared the engine and ran light to the Hump sidings via Foxhall Junction where we collected a train of Ordnance traffic, largely vans. We might call at Moreton Yard but were otherwise right away. When we got there, we took the engine to Southall Shed (or elsewhere if Control wanted it) and travelled back on the cushions.

4.45 p.m. MORETON–SOUTHALL
Book on 3.15 p.m. Off shed 4.15 p.m.
The engine for this duty was usually a 28XX or WD 2–8–0 which we prepared and worked light engine to Moreton Yard to pick up the 4.45 p.m. 'F' freight which we worked through to Southall (arrive about 8.25 p.m.) where we took the engine on shed and returned on the cushions unless required by Control.

5.25 p.m. MORETON TO HAYES
Book on 3.45 p.m. Off shed 4.45 p.m.
This was similar to the previous job, we even used to meet up with the crew of the 4.45 p.m. Moreton in the hostel canteen at Southall (on the down side of the road bridge) and return together. If we had a really good run, we could get to Paddington in time to catch the 9.25 p.m. or even the 9.50 but otherwise it was the 11.50 'Plymouth Sleeper'. If we missed that, we had to hang around at

Southall-based 3859 pulling out of the front yard at Moreto 11.45 a.m. with what is thought to be the 4.00 a.m. (Sund Severn Tunnel Junction to West Drayton 'H' class freight on September 1946. This picture shows the depleted tender afte long journey. The pump house on the left supplied the w columns.
M. F. Yaru

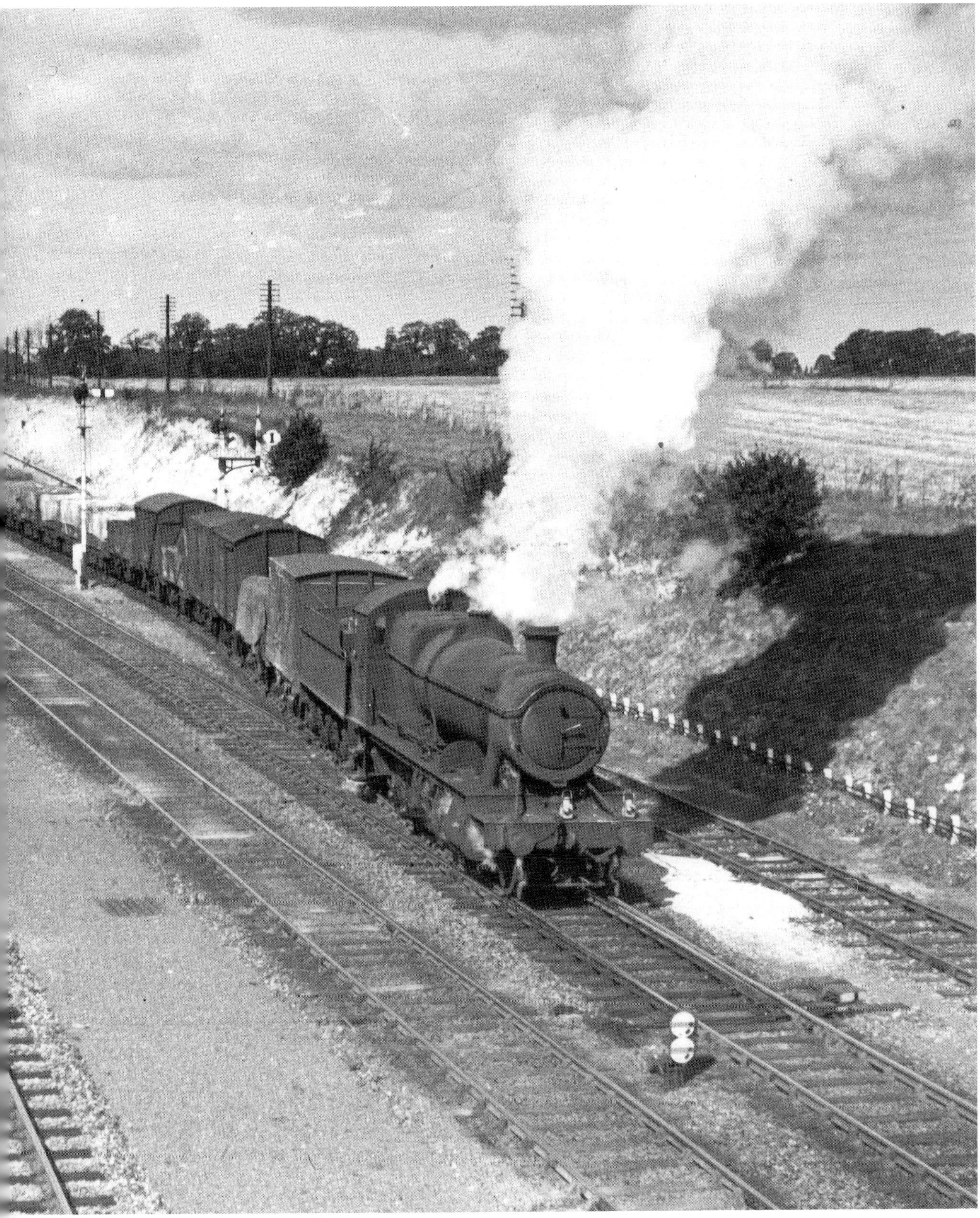

Paddington for the 3.30 a.m. papers which, although made up of parcels vans, included a passenger coach with three compartments. It was travelling home in the dark on one of these trains that the subject of route knowledge came up. I confidently claimed I could tell where I was in the dark anywhere between Paddington and Reading. We were sitting in the first coach behind the engine and my mates pulled the blinds down and peeped out to check where they were before asking me. I was sitting over one of the bogies which helped me to feel any pointwork, and by listening to the sound rebounding from cutting sides, punctuated by bridges and stations, I managed to give the correct answer at each location with great pride.

During the 1930s, 'Star' 4–6–0 No. 4038 *Queen Berengaria* was moved around the system, being variously shedded at Old Oak, Shrewsbury, Worcester, Swindon, Weymouth and Westbury. She is shown here awaiting departure from Platform No. 2 at Paddington during one evening in the mid-1930s.

Another 'Star', No. 4021 *British Monarch* (from Oxford shed), at the head of the 11.15 p.m. Paddington to Slough train on 31st December 1947, at which point the old company had less than an hour's existence ahead of it. *Collection Peter Winding*

Right: The 'Night Mail' alongside Platform 1 in 1936. In my time we often caught this train, which left at 9.50 for the West of England via Newbury. We changed at Reading and during the war years travelled in the front of the train. However, later on, following complaints from passengers who objected to sitting amongst loco crews with dirty overalls, special compartments were reserved for us. The later Mail passed Didcot at 11.20 and this was the one I could hear from my window in Wessex Road. *H. L. Boston*

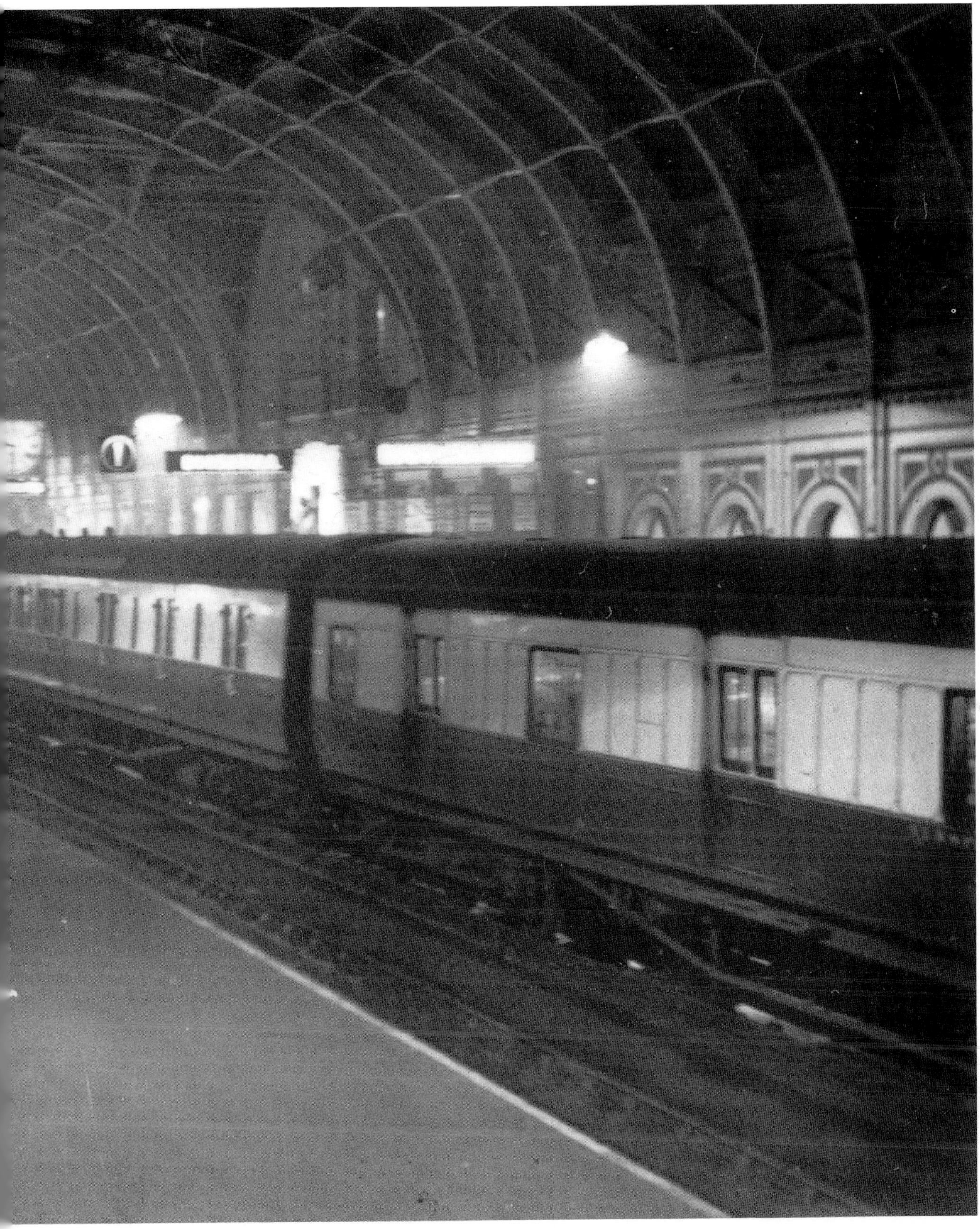

The pictures on these pages show the night-time chaos at Paddington with the huge quantities of mail, newspapers and parcels taking over the station. We were often stranded amongst all this if we missed the 11.50 Penzance after working a coal train to Southall.
National Railway Museum

POSTWAR SERVICE

Night activity at Paddington, with 'Star' No. 4062 *Malmesbury Abbey* waiting at No. 8 platform, c.1937. *C. R. L. Coles*

Another view of the night-time loading, again in 1937. *C. R. L. Coles*

The train in No. 1 platform was probably the 12.55 a.m. to Carmarthen newspaper & parcels train. After its departure, stock for the 2.30 a.m. (Bristol) and 3.25 (Oxford & Banbury) newspaper trains would be moved into No. 1 platform (at about 1.00 a.m.) for loading. Vans from Fleet Street were driven onto the platform, so the newspapers could be transferred directly into the stock, van drivers being assisted by porters and the newspaper staff who travelled on the train. Naturally, at this time of night, everything was closed, and all we could do during the hours we were stranded there was make ourselves a pot of tea in the porters room. There was no food to be had anywhere. We often slept in the waiting room or, in the summer months, on a seat on the platform, until the stock arrived and we could settled into a compartment. Being able to relax in this way helped us to overcome the tensions, but on one occasion, having worked long hours, I was so tired that I fell asleep in the train and didn't wake up until we arrived at Oxford. Then I had to wait all over again for another train home!

L. E. Copeland

POSTWAR SERVICE

Paddington, 9.10 p.m. on 10th September 1952. It was the normal arrangement that the 9.15 p.m. to Reading left from Platform No. 3 (left) and the 9.25 (Mail and Passenger) to Neyland from No. 2 (right). However, if the 9.25 was duplicated, one part would run from Platform No. 3, which may be the case here; the Reading train would then depart from an alternative platform. Watching strings of trolleys being weaved between all the obstacles on the platform always intrigued me. I really admired the skill of the drivers.

National Railway Museum

Another night-time view of 4062 at Paddington, this time in the late 1940s.

C. R. L. Coles

THE BASINGSTOKE TRIPS
Book on 4.00 p.m. Off shed 5.00 p.m.
I don't recall working this turn myself, but as far as I know it was a 61XX job which involved working light to Moreton sidings and making two trips to Basingstoke, returning light engine from each one. The first left Moreton at 6.35 p.m., the second at 9.10 a.m. the following morning.

6.5 p.m. WESTBURY
Book on 5.05. Off shed 5.20 p.m.
This was another turn subject to change. It was a No. 3 Link turn at one time and I remember that it had previously been worked by Newbury men with an engine prepared by a Banbury crew. Because of this situation, no-one at Didcot shed checked the engine, and one day, after the Banbury men had left, the engine sat there blowing off. I don't know how much water they'd left in the boiler but no-one looked and before the Newbury men arrived there was a sudden bang as the fusible plug went.

The engine was usually a 28XX which was prepared for us. We collected our train, a 'J' freight, from the Centre Yard (it had been marshalled in the Up Yard). It was the last train of the day over the branch to Newbury, although it had previously (and was again later) routed via

No. 7204 leaving Didcot shed, and signalled for the up relief line on 16th August 1947. This engine was sent initially to Slough in June 1946 though it was transferred to Didcot in March 1947 to join the other three.
H. C. Casserley

No. 7204 again, this time at Reading General with a train for the Southern, probably from Moreton Cutting c.1947. A loose engine coupling like this always bothered me. It should have been hung up to avoid damage.
Maurice Earley

The new junction with the Southern at Reading — the destination of the Moreton three-tripper. The signals on the gantry read from left to right: up relief and distant; up main and distant; new junction to SR up loop; new junction to SR up branch. Photographer unknown

Reading. At Newbury we sometimes picked up a few more wagons before continuing to Westbury where we put the engine on shed and came home on the cushions. We caught the 12.36 a.m. Westbury (Taunton to Wolverhampton) parcels to Swindon, then the Neyland sleeper to Didcot, arriving at 2.49 a.m. If we were late into Westbury, we would catch the early Salisbury & Bristol train to Bath, and the Penzance sleeper to Didcot, though this did not get us back until around 6 a.m.

9.15 p.m. SWINDON PASSENGER
Book on 8.55. Relieve 9.10 p.m.
After booking on and reading the notices, we walked over to the Swindon bay and took over the 9.15 p.m. to Swindon. This was usually a Swindon 49XX, which had spent its day running between Swindon, Didcot and Oxford. At Swindon we took the engine on shed and carried out the disposal, then went into the cabin by the west loop, at the back of the station where we often met up with a Cardiff crew and the Didcot men from the 'Kensington Cakes'. Control used us as required, which usually meant we worked back with the 10.10 p.m. Bristol to Banbury 'D' Freight (Swindon 12.8 a.m.) which picked up at Highworth Yard, waiting on the relief line while the extra vehicles were put on the back of the train by the pilot there. When we arrived at Didcot at around 1.47 a.m., there was usually some shunting to do before the relief crew took over.

Alternatively, we often worked out of Swindon at 11.36 p.m. with the 'Milford Haven Fish' which we relieved in the station and took to Paddington with a scheduled arrival of 1.20 a.m. This was hauled by a 'Castle' and ran under 'C' headlamps which meant we were permitted to run at 60 mph. This was one of the few chances which Didcot men had to work a 'Castle'. We usually arrived in Platform 11 where we were relieved and returned passenger.

THREE TRIPPER
Book on 9.15 p.m. Off shed 9.30 p.m.
The engine for this job was one of Didcot's 72XX tanks (Nos. 7214, 7228 and 7252 were all at Didcot in the late 1940s) prepared for us by the men who prepared the 12.55 Crewe. We ran light to Moreton to work the 10.00 p.m. to Reading, putting off wagons at Reading West Junction on the way to High Level where a pilot took them on down the bank to the Southern. We 'hooked off', took water and ran down the bank enough to clear the 'dummy', then as soon as we got the road, returned light engine to Moreton.

On the next run we left at 12.30 a.m. and took the train to the SR new junction, returning this time along the down main to Didcot. We picked up freight from 'the Alexandra Docks' for Moreton Yard, where we made up another train for the Southern and worked it to Reading New Junction, and finally ran light back to Didcot shed.

10.00 p.m. BANBURY TO HACKNEY FREIGHT
Book on 11.40 p.m. Relieve 11.55 p.m.
This was another 'F' freight, destined for Hackney (Newton Abbot). This turn, which we kept to retain road knowledge to Westbury, was worked for three consecutive

Moreton Yard on 4th July 1953. The train on the down main was a through working from the Southern, headed by No. 6866 *Morfa Grange* and signalled for Oxford. *R. C. Riley*

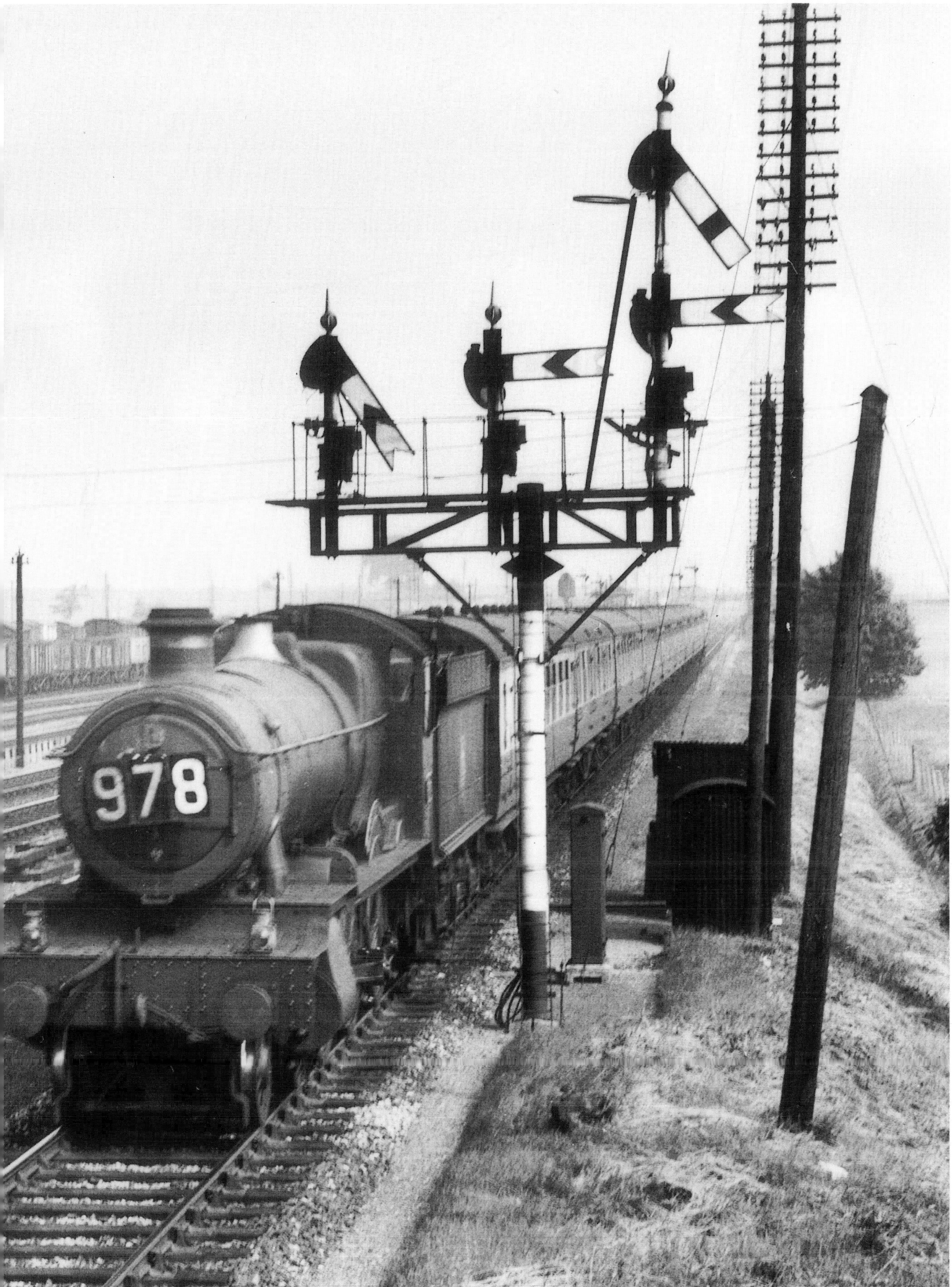
978

An up goods heading away from Aynho during the 1930s. During the Blitz on Birmingham we spent many hours in the down goods loop on the right of the picture.
Roye England

nights, perhaps Monday, Tuesday and Wednesday. We spent the remaining three nights of that week 'spare'. After reading notices, we were allowed ten minutes to walk to the up gully (the up goods loop on the avoiding line), where we relieved a Banbury crew on a 28XX. In later years we sometimes picked up wagons at Reading but at this time we worked straight through to Westbury (via Reading West Junction) and got relief at Heywood Road. From there Control might give us further orders but usually we travelled home passenger, catching a 3-coach train for Bath which left Westbury around 6.15. At Bath, the refreshment room was open so we waited in there for the 7.10 Bristol which stopped at Didcot.

After all the upheaval of the war, the railways took a long time to settle down, and the years that followed brought what seemed continuous changes. Nationalisation itself had no noticeable effect but the old practice of taking promotion on an all-line basis was changed. Under this system we had to take up a post wherever a vacancy arose, according to seniority, but the new system allowed men to apply for vacancies in order of preference. Enginemen who'd been away from home during the war years gradually returned to their home depots, particularly as retirements came up. For a while the retirement age of drivers had been lowered to 60 but now it was back up to 65.

During this period I had been in and out of No. 2 Link as required and consequently never had a regular driver. However, when I eventually left No. 3 Link my first mate was Percy Steele. He was a typical locoman who liked his pint, enjoyed company and was always helpful.

One trip with him on a freight to Banbury lingers in my mind. On an early afternoon during the winter of 1948 we arrived in the goods loop at Fritwell and Summerton, only to discover that we were behind seven other freight trains. The block was truly on. We had already been on duty several hours so I left the engine and settled down in the brake van of the train in front. As the evening approached, we had only moved up one place and when I rang the signalman at Aynho, who wasn't very helpful, I was told we'd be lucky to move before the morning. As the night dragged on, I occasionally returned to the engine to fill the boiler and keep the fire up. I also kept an eye on the water level in the tender tank. I kept dozing on the hard wooden bench inside the warm brake van, but I was not completely relaxed – I was fretful that if I fell into a long deep sleep the fire would go out on the engine or the boiler level get dangerously low. I was also hungry, having emptied my box of food many hours ago.

Half asleep in the early hours of the morning I suddenly became aware of the 'clink clink' sound as the couplings were tightening down the train.

A sudden jolt accompanied by the squeal of brakes and the van was on the move. I had to make a hurried exit from the van, so, still half-dazed, I stumbled into the open air, through the verandah doorway and down onto the footboard, and finally jumped onto the ballast without stumbling down the bank into the flowing stream below. I strolled gently back towards the engine where I found Percy Steele already sitting on his

The bridge at Aynho from which the pictures opposite and below were taken. The road also passed under the Bicester line about 200 yards to the left, serving Aynho Park platform.
H. J. Stretton-Ward

An empty stock train passing through Aynho on the up main.
H. J. Stretton-Ward

seat waiting for me. As I climbed up very slowly into the cab, he said he was hungry, thirsty and tired.

It was not until mid-morning that we arrived at the exit signal from the loop and I walked to Aynho signal box to ask where we might get hold of some food at such an isolated spot. I was surprised to be told to call at the pub in the station yard. Without even waiting to receive directions, I was off to the station and soon knocking at the door. Eventually, a pleasant elderly lady came to the door wearing a long dress down to her ankles. The white apron, which was tied round her small waist, could hardly have emphasised the contrast between us more. I was tired and dirty, with oily overalls and scruffy boots. I didn't have to say anything; before I could speak she asked me into the bar and then disappeared into her kitchen and came back with the top of a cottage loaf and a huge thick slice of home-cured bacon, enough to feed both of us. She even filled two bottles with draught beer for us. Only then did it dawn on me

The King Alfred Head (now the Great Western Arms), where the landlady Betty Walton gave us food and drink, features in the background of this picture.
A. Attewell

Aynho station and signal box.
J. H. Moss

Looking north towards Aynho Junction from Aynho signal box, showing the goods yard on the left, the up goods loop on the right, and the flyover in the distance, carrying the new line from Paddington.
National Railway Museum

that she'd fed the other crews who'd been stuck in the loop and so half expected me.

What an oasis — and what generosity was shown to me that day. I will never forget her kindness. Walking back to the engine, I was taunted by the smell of the bacon, and there's no need to say how much Percy and I enjoyed that feast.

Soon after we'd finished, we were told that a relief crew were coming up from Banbury on the local passenger train, so we left the engine and walked up to the station. As we still had thirty minutes before the train arrived, we called at the pub to express our appreciation. At least, that was Percy's idea, but I felt it was really to have another pint! When the train arrived, it was full, so we jumped into the guard's van where we found a lady guard. I remember the alcohol had begun to take effect on Percy who was a bit full of fun with her.

A few months later Percy was promoted to No. 1 Link and I was put with Jim Burridge who took his place in No. 2 Link. He was a Cornishman and a pipe smoker, his favourite tobacco being Condor Twist. He used to cut off a stick of twist, roll it in his hand, stuff the pipe full to the brim and light it off the gauge lamp. We might politely have been described as incompatible; the

ROD 2–8–0 No. 3033 on No. 5 road at Didcot shed in the early 1950s. These engines were not very popular with GWR enginemen. They had no real life about them (they certainly weren't exciting) and maintaining steam pressure was often difficult. The ride was also uncomfortable and very monotonous. If we saw one of these approaching when we were waiting to take over an up goods, our morale sank to a low ebb and we didn't set about the job with the same enthusiasm.
Photographer unknown

two of us just didn't get on together, and he often interfered with my work. Once we had been teamed, we had to make the best of our co-existence, but fortunately I was not with him long.

I recall an embarrassing situation on Bath station when Jim, the guard and myself were waiting for the up Penzance sleeper. Sunshine was streaming into the station early one summer's morning, straight through the thin dress of a young lady who was standing to the east of us on the platform. The outline of her figure was very apparent and prompted Jim to sound a wolf whistle, not once but repeatedly until she turned round. When she saw us, she hurried down the platform and tore me off a strip in front of the other passengers. Just because I was the youngest of the trio, I took the blame and felt I'd been set up.

By the time I reached No. 1 Link, or the Passenger Link, as it was known, I was acutely aware of the ability of the drivers I served with. Some had such a natural ability that they were truly at one with their machine. I could even recognise some long before their arrival by the sound of the exhaust or the speed they took over junctions. Unfortunately, some drivers couldn't handle a wheelbarrow, and didn't have a clue how to nurse a loco along to get the best results. Some were 'Tub Thumpers' who would open the regulator far too much, with the reverser well

A snapshot of me on a Standard Goods at Newbury when I was on the Sunday train to Lambourn c.1948. I felt the lined black livery applied after nationalisation was an attempt to cover the identity of the GWR — but it didn't kill the spirit.
Author's collection

Fitter Arthur Brinkley and fitter's mate Bert Paice on 4318 at Didcot shed in September 1949. Arthur was a really nice chap, very down to earth and an excellent fitter. Some were not at all responsive to problems reported by loco crews, but he was always helpful and had a warmth about his manner.
G. W. Sharpe

down the rack, creating excessive blast on the fire, using too much coal and water and leaving the poor fireman 'arse up, head down' shovelling in coal as fast as possible to keep up the steam pressure! Other enginemen would only use as much power as was necessary, letting the train run on down gradients, gathering speed to assist uphill work. It was all a matter of knowing the road and what your loco was capable of.

Letting the passenger train run with power off at high speed until the last moment, then applying the brakes at high speeds, was the most economical method of train running. One or two accurate brake applications by a confident engineman could save tons of coal. The opposite would be the engineman who kept applying the brakes many times prior to stopping. This could create an inefficient trip, and cause the fireman a lot of hard unnecessary work.

In the Passenger Link I was very fortunate in being teamed with a driver who had all the qualities I admired. His name was George Brown, better known as 'Paget'. He was a true engineman, with the belief that it was better to wear out the engine than the fireman! An engine could be replaced but not a good fireman. He was a short man with medium build, rugged features and a jovial personality. He commanded respect and the line of demarcation between driver and fireman was never broken. During my six years with him I was never allowed to drive, oil up or even turn on the water column. Even when he was feeling under the weather, he did it all himself. He was the captain and trusted no-one. In fact I used to refer to him as 'Captain'. The time I spent with him just flew by because of our understanding — even when he tried to give up smoking. They were brilliant years and I was very content.

Working with George for six years taught me all the finer points of enginecraft. He would 'nick-up' an engine very early, and let her settle in her own rhythm; the speed would increase just as quickly as if she had been thumped away. It was also much more economical. Often he would have the lever nicked up too high, and the pressure valves on the cylinder covers would blow, but only until the train gathered speed.

He would keep the blower turned off, and the ejectors closed to save energy and usually only made one brake application when stopping at a station. They would remain on almost until the stopping point and then be released. His stops were gentle enough not to spill a full glass of water — real skill when travelling at 60 or 70 mph, with a load of 350-400 tons!

Paget would always make sure that the engine coupling was correctly placed over the coach hook, and that only four threads were showing on the screw. This indicated that the coupling was tight. He never failed to check this and I adopted his habit which held me in good stead.

During my time in the Passenger Link the jobs were as follows:

No. 1 LINK — 1950-55
THE SALOP PARCELS
Book on 2.35 a.m. Relieve 3.00 a.m.
This train was the 10.15 p.m. from Shrewsbury with a 49XX, and from time to time vans were detached on arrival at Didcot. We took it over in Platform 5 and

Paget Brown, my driver in the passenger link for five years. This picture was taken in his garden off the Broadway in Didcot.

This Modified Hall approaching Reading with a down express for the West of England main line, presents a similar scene to our arrival with the Weymouth Boat Train which we worked as far as Reading. The relief crew were waiting to take over at the other end of the platform, leaving us to travel back to Didcot on the next available train. *Roye England*

worked it to Paddington on the up main, calling only at Reading. We took the engine back to Old Oak Shed where we had a cup of tea before preparing another engine for the 8.30 Weymouth Boat Train. We had a 69XX (often Old Oak's 6960) which we worked light engine to Paddington and backed onto the stock in Platform 1. On one occasion, we had 5026 which was such a free steamer that as I put on each shovelful of coal, the safety valves hissed, then fell again. Paget said "Mate, you're playing 'God Save The King' on the safety valves!" We ran fast to Reading where we were relieved by a Reading crew, then made our way over to the down relief platform to take over another 49XX on the 9.45 'stopper' to Didcot. This had been worked down from Paddington by Reading men.

When we arrived at Didcot, a relief crew took the engine on shed and another engine took the train on to Oxford.

7.4 a.m. BIRMINGHAM
Book on 5.00 a.m. Off shed 6.00 a.m.

We prepared the engine for this turn, usually a 59XX but sometimes a 63XX, and came off shed at 6.00 to steam-heat the stock in the platform. In the summer we sat in No. 1 running road until the coaches were put into the down relief platform. We worked through to Banbury, stopping at all stations and on arrival got relief, and worked the 8.38 a.m. Banbury back, running non-stop to Oxford. At Oxford another crew took over and we crossed over to the down side to relieve Didcot men on a

168   DIDCOT ENGINEMAN

36XX which had worked the 9.48 a.m. from Didcot. We took the train into Jericho sidings, ran the engine to the other end of the coaches and worked them back to Didcot as the 10.40 a.m., and took the engine on shed.

7.10 a.m. PADDINGTON
Book on 5.00 a.m. Off shed 6.00 a.m.
This was the top job at Didcot, a commuter train worked with a 59XX, calling at all stations to Reading, then Slough and Paddington. When we came off shed, the stock (up to 11 coaches) was already in Platform 7. Of course there were regular passengers, but one who sticks in my mind was a rather elegant business woman with dark hair who arrived off the 6.15 a.m. Swindon train and usually got in the first compartment behind the engine. We knew when we saw her we'd soon be off. We were crossed to the up main, and at Cholsey connected with the branch train from Wallingford. At Goring there always seemed to be a few stragglers running from their cars, but if we touched the whistle they ran faster! At Tilehurst we could see

At Cholsey, waiting passengers, including those from the Wallingford branch train (in the bay on the left), were told in advance if we were going to arrive at the up main platform (on the right of this picture, the other side of the nameboard), so they had time to cross over there by means of the subway which connected all the platforms.
R. C. Riley

The up and down relief platforms at Goring, looking towards Didcot. With the 7.10 or 8.5 Paddington, we always came to a stand with the tender at the top of the platform ramp. Goring was usually quite crowded with passengers and, as a fireman, I often looked back on my side to a latecomer running along the approach road. I always told Paget who'd say "Let him come" and if the guard had already given the 'Right away', he'd simply remark "You're not watching".
Lens of Sutton

We couldn't find a single picture of the 7.10 Paddington. but this view presents a very similar scene, with the morning shadows. It shows 4951 on the up main, on the approach to Tilehurst with the 8.20 a.m. Swansea–Paddington on 17th September 1955. From this point we could catch sight of the footbridge spanning the line from the Thames towpath to the Roebuck Inn.
R. C. Riley

Tilehurst, looking east towards Reading. When we were booked to run along the up relief, and there was a goods train ahead of us, we were often switched to the up main at Cholsey to avoid delays and crossed back to the relief at Scours Lane. *Roye England*

No. 5093 arriving at Reading station with an express for Paddington on 23rd April 1950. Arrangements varied over the years but I think we usually ran into the up relief platform. Then, if we were non-stop from Reading, I changed the lamps here to display the 'A' headcode. *W. Gilburt, cty. Kevin Robertson*

POSTWAR SERVICE

The black smoke from this express speeding through Twyford on the up main, indicates that the fireman had just put on more coal. Hard coal made more smoke and burned away quickly, but on a good trip with decent Welsh coal, if I made sure the firebox was full at Reading, the fire would often last all the way to Paddington.
N. D. Mundy

Twyford East signal box.

D. B. Hart

Looking west, back towards Didcot with an 'F' class freight approaching Maidenhead on the up relief in 1957. We didn't always call here — timetables changed, but if we were still on the up relief, we would cross to the up main at the other end of the platform. On goods work we might stop at Maidenhead for water which provided us with an opportunity to make a can of tea in the porters room (on the up relief platform) where there was always a kettle on the boil.
J. H. Venn

MAIDENHEAD
JUNCTION FOR
WYCOMBE LINE
MAIDENHEAD
JUNCTION FOR
WYCOMBE LINE

passengers running over the footbridge as we pulled into the station.

Timing was everything on this job, so we checked our progress by the clock on top of Reading station, then the Maidenhead tower clock which stood on the forecourt there, the Horlicks clock at Slough, Scotts Emulsion at Southall, where a clock was part of a mural of a fisherman in a sou'wester hat lugging a fish, the clock on the yard inspector's office at Acton, and the one on the offices at Old Oak carriage sidings. Running past at about 70 mph, we needed a minimum of four minutes from there to arrive at Paddington on schedule. It was important to arrive on time (not early) and there was nothing more satisfying than rolling to a stand at the buffer stops of

Continued on page 186

Maidenhead station, looking west with the Wycombe branch platform on the right. The clock tower was at the bottom of the station approach on the right, just out of the picture.
J. H. Venn

Taplow West signal box.
D. B. Hart

Some drivers I worked with never had a watch and it was a great feeling to break off for a moment and see one of the well-known clocks we relied upon displaying the expected time as we sped by. This view, looking west at Slough station, shows the Horlicks Factory tower on the right, behind the goods yard. The Horlicks clock was seldom faulty, even during the war years. Slough engine shed can be seen on the left, alongside the Windsor curve.
National Railway Museum

Another view of Slough on the same occasion, this time looking in the opposite direction through the platforms towards Paddington.
National Railway Museum

No. 1027 passing through Slough on the up main with the 8.40 a.m. Westbury to Paddington. We seldom had these engines although 1002 was stationed at Didcot during the final years of steam. On fast trains to Paddington I had started to run the fire down after leaving Reading and by the time we got to Slough I would level the remaining fire with the pricker. This was stowed in the rack on the tender and great care had to be taken in trying to keep within the loading gauge when handling it. I would only do this where there were no bridges or gantries. During my time, a fireman was killed handling a pricker while passing under Fulscott bridge.
J. F. Russell-Smith

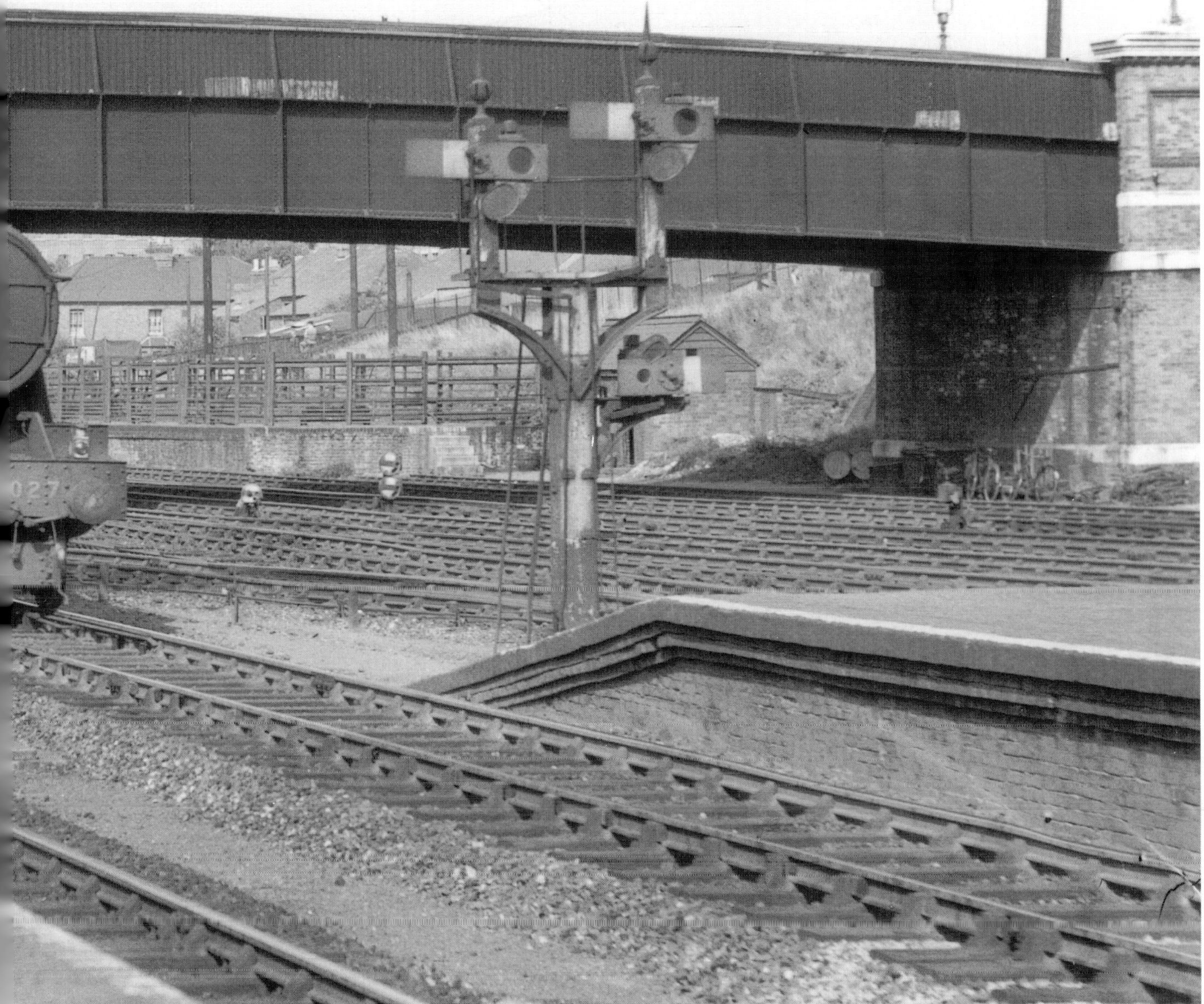

Iver station with, in the foreground, the up goods line which ran from here to West Drayton.
Lens of Sutton

No. 4080 running through Southall on the up main. The whole route is full of memories, the gasometer in the background, for instance, is where Reg Johns and I left the petrol train mentioned in Chapter 6, and the engine shed, where we used to take the 28XXs from the up coal trains, was on the left behind the photographer.
C. R. L. Coles

POSTWAR SERVICE

The east end of Southall station, looking over the main line and east yard from the engine shed. *National Railway Museum*

Longfield Avenue, just outside West Ealing, the beginning of the colour light signalling which took us all the way into Paddington. *National Railway Museum*

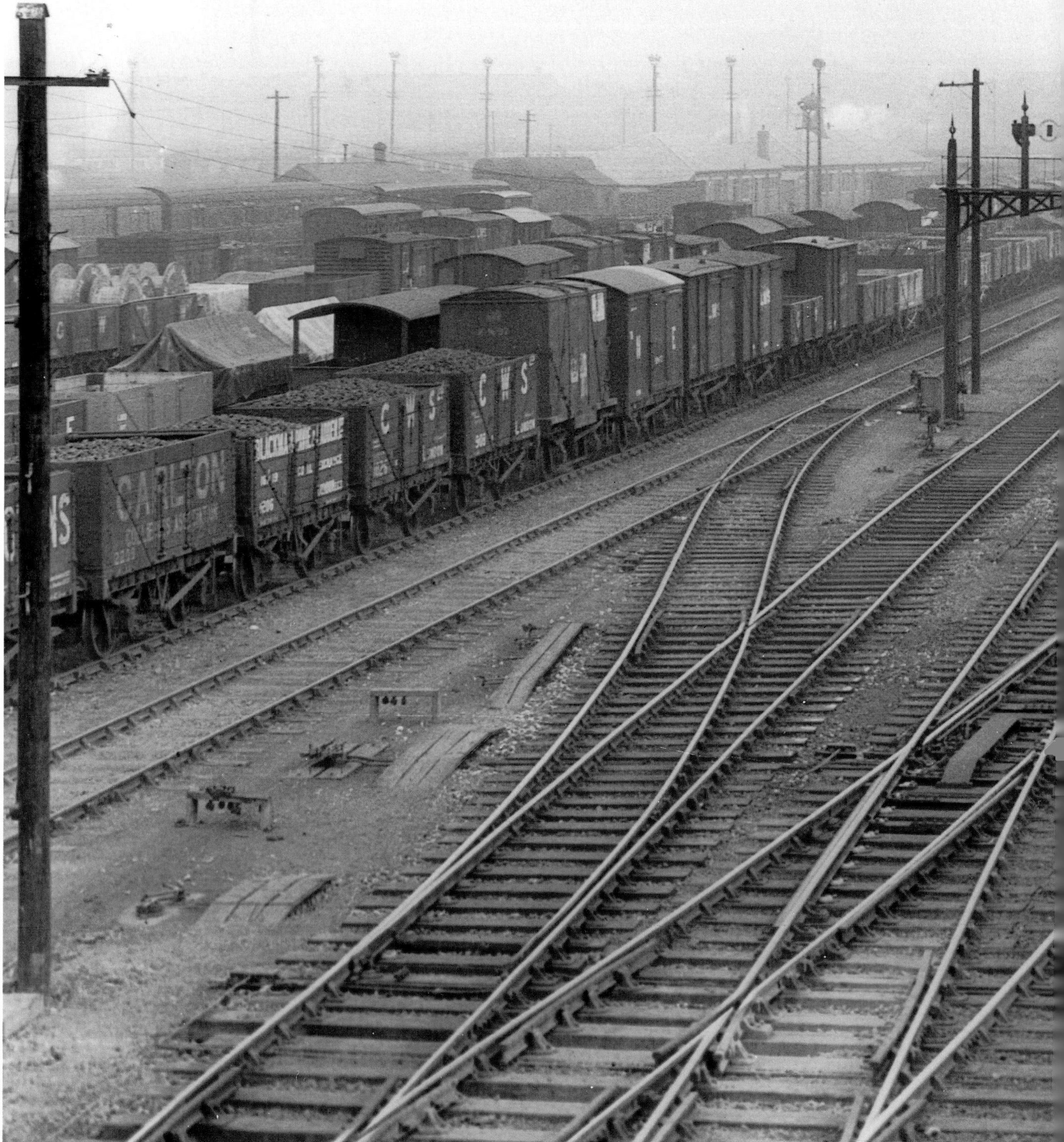
CARLTON
C W S
C W S

Old Oak Common, looking towards Paddington, with the engine shed and carriage sidings on the left. The clock on the yard offices and mess room on the left, opposite Old Oak Common West signal box, was another timepiece we relied upon. We needed four minutes in hand here to arrive right time at Paddington.
National Railway Museum

No. 4995 passing Westbourne Park with a stopping train on the up main in July 1948.
R. F. Roberts

The scene at Subway Junction, looking towards Paddington, with the up relief and up main on the right of the picture near the carriage sidings.
National Railway Museum

POSTWAR SERVICE

The illuminated 10 mph sign just before the station reminded us of the speed restriction as we ran into the tightly curving platforms.
National Railway Museum

The coaches in the foreground of this picture, looking over the final approach to Paddington, were standing on the No. 1 up engine and carriage road, the down main and the No. 2 up engine and carriage road.
P. J. Garland

This 1950s picture, looking west from Paddington station, gives the impression of a very orderly state of affairs, but I can assure readers that throughout the 1940s this was not the case. The unavoidable neglect throughout the war years took its toll and the bomb damage and general dilapidation through the backlog of repairs and maintenance still lingers in my mind. It took a long time to get straight again.

M. W. Earley

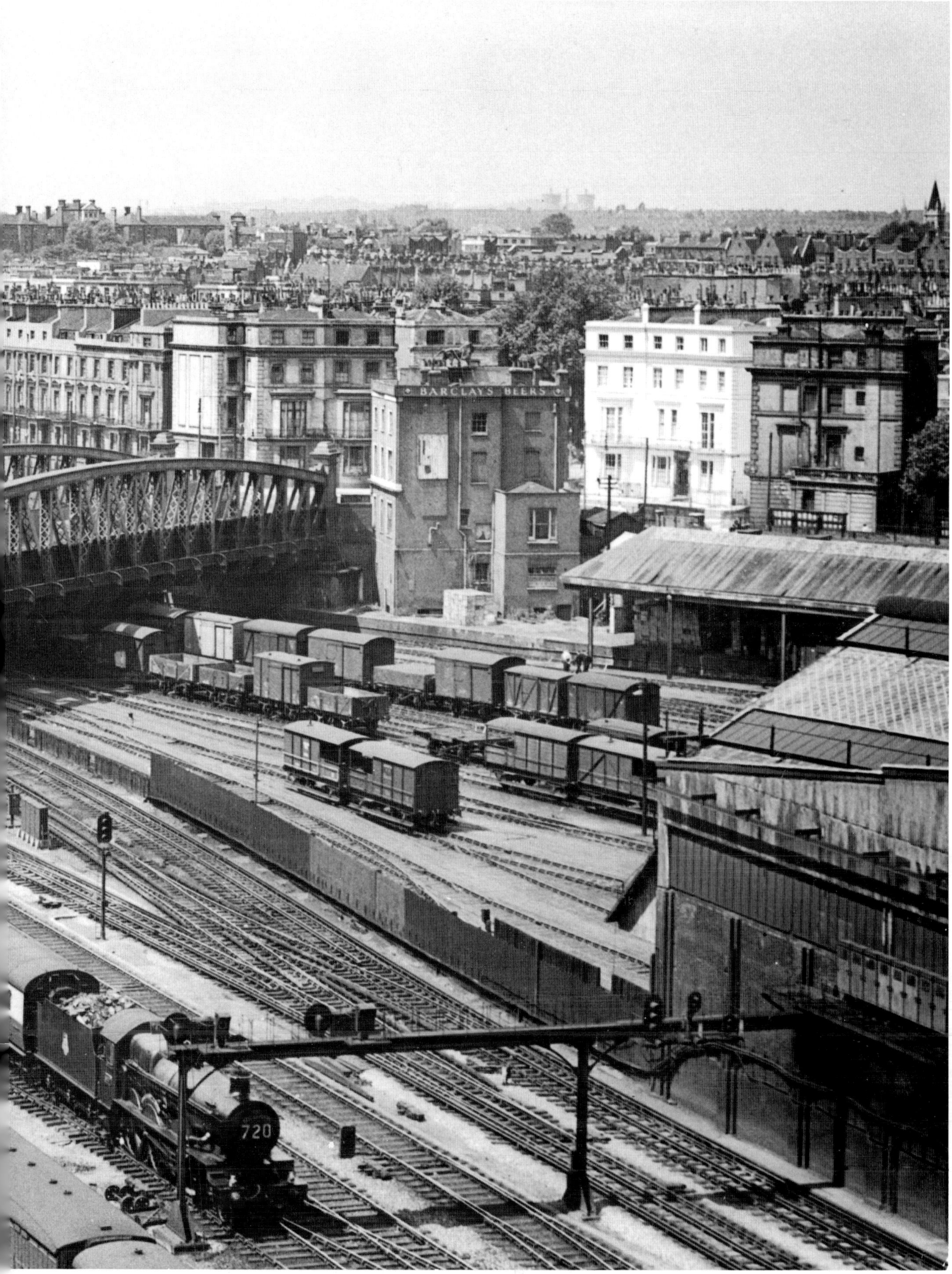
BARCLAYS BEERS
720

Platform 9 or 11 as the minute hand of the clock above the lawn jumped to 8.35. The passengers were generally pleased and many gave us newspapers as they passed by. It was a good feeling to lean out of the cab after a good trip and enjoy the thanks.

A relief crew took over the engine here, freeing us to walk down Platform 1 to the mess for a cup of tea.

Occasionally, on spare turns, while I was still in Link 3, I worked the 7.10 a.m. Paddington. On one occasion when we arrived with the platform on my side, I stood watching all the commuters pouring out of the coaches and hurrying past the engine on their way to the underground trains. Many raised their hands to us whilst others wished us a friendly 'good morning' and handed up a daily paper they'd finished with. It was a lovely feeling, that is until my driver demanded that I sat down and let them see *him*! I had just shovelled a couple of tons of coal and kept the engine on the mark in order to achieve this prompt arrival and now I was being told to hide myself. He sat on his seat like a proud bandmaster; the orchestra

The approaches to Paddington viewed from Platforms 9 & 10, with the parcels line on the left and Paddington Goods Depot on the right. Train-spotters were part of the scene and always keen to have a look in the cab. *L. E. Copeland*

In 1947, many (though by no means all) trains bound to or from Slough, Uxbridge, Windsor, Hayes, Reading and Aylesbury used the suburban platforms (Nos. 13-16). Before the war, through Great Western trains for Aldgate and Liverpool Street also passed this way. This picture shows No. 6152 waiting to depart from one of the suburban platforms on 24th June 1947. Without doubt these were my favourite tank engines. Free running, free steaming and comfortable, they rode exceptionally well and were so highly thought of by Slough men that when one of their engines came to Didcot shed, we found it had been fitted out with lino! *H. C. Casserley*

The clock over the lawn seemed friendly as the minute hand nudged to our time of arrival, but frowning when we were over five minutes late! This picture was taken in 1952. *National Railway Museum*

Passengers leaving Paddington on the arrivals side in 1946. *National Railway Museum*

The lawn at Paddington on 28th June 1955. After arrival, I was often sent off the engine to one of the bookstalls if the papers we collected didn't include a 'Mirror' or 'Express'.

National Railway Museum

QUEUE
B
FOR YOUR
HOLIDAYS
C
HALIFAX BUILDING SOCIETY
Savings and Home Loans
Boots
EXCURSIONS
JULY 1955
LEFT LUGGAGE LOCKERS
REFRESHMENTS

The Great Western Hotel along Praed Street enclosed the end of Paddington station, the road down the near side of the building leading to the departure entrances whilst the arrival side was at the other end.
National Railway Museum

had responded to his demands and at the end of a shining performance his audience were showing their pleasure and he was taking a bow.

It was all very different whenever we were late. Although it was often through no fault of ours, passengers would make rude remarks and pass by with irritable expressions, tut-tutting. On those occasions the bandmaster was inconspicuous!

The train we worked back to Didcot varied over the years. At one time we waited at the buffer stops until our stock was pulled off us, then we followed it out and turned the engine at Ranelagh Bridge where we also filled the tank and had a can of tea. We worked back as pilot engine on the front of the 9.45 a.m. Worcester, a 'Castle'-hauled train with an Old Oak crew which we double-headed as far as Oxford to get the engine back.

8.05 a.m. PADDINGTON (successor of the 8.42)
Book on 6.15 a.m. Off shed 7.15 a.m.
This was another 59XX turn similar to the 7.10 Paddington. We collected a 10-coach train from the carriage sidings and backed it into Platform 7 after the departure of the 7.10. Our train stopped all stations to Maidenhead, then Slough and Paddington. After the empty stock had

Two views of the departure side of Paddington station in 1946. *National Railway Museum*

Oxford was the point where the locos on the cross-country trains between Birkenhead and Bournemouth were changed. The picture below shows a Southern Railway engine signalled for the yard, where it would wait to take over when the Great Western engine came off.
Philip Hopkins and H. J. Stretton-Ward

been taken off us at Paddington, we turned the engine at Ranelagh Bridge and backed into the parcels sidings (or sometimes Platform 13) to couple onto the 11.40 parcels which had about 6-8 vehicles. This stopped at Southall, Hayes, West Drayton, Slough, Maidenhead, Twyford and Reading to pick up mails. At Didcot we were put into Platform 7 and went on shed, but sometimes we went into the carriage sidings where the passenger pilot took the train off us and put it into Platform 7 for unloading.

7.38 a.m. SOUTHAMPTON
Book on 6.30 a.m. Off shed 7.15 a.m.
This was a 22XX turn. After preparing the engine, we came off shed at 7.15 and backed onto a 3-coach train already in Platform 7. We called all stations to Southampton and back — 42 stops in all!

At Southampton we left our coaches in the platform and made our way to the turntable. When we'd turned the engine, we cleaned the fire, one side at a time. The coal we had then (imported from America) was all small stuff with poor carbon content and plenty of stone residue, and on one occasion I remember the fire was so poor that by the time we'd shovelled the rubbish out, the remaining fire had gone out. My driver, Paget Brown, was a bit worried about this and went off to the nearby allotments to see if he could find some kindling wood. He returned with a couple of orange boxes and, using a few odd lumps of hard coal I managed to find at the back of the tender, we soon had a fire of sorts on the go again. However, when we were back on the train, we only had 120lb on the clock, so with the guard's co-operation, we pulled the strings on the coaches to release the vacuum reservoir and left Southampton without any brakes. By the time we got to Eastleigh, the fire was healthy and we soon had enough pressure to restore the reservoir so that we had brakes again.

When we got back to Didcot we pulled into the down relief platform and handed the loco over to another Didcot crew who worked a freight train forward from Didcot West Curve to Yarnton.

8.45 a.m. OXFORD
Book on 7.59 a.m. Relieve 8.14 a.m.
We picked up this train in Platform 5, taking over from the Old Oak crew who had brought it down as the 6.20 a.m. from Paddington. We were all stations to Oxford where we put the stock into the down carriage sidings and took the engine on shed. We took an engine over at the coal stage and prepared it ready for the 9.30 a.m. Bournemouth to Birkenhead train which had an engine change at Oxford. We then made our way over to the up platform and relieved either Chester men or Oxford men on the 7.40 a.m. Birkenhead to Margate. We worked the train non-stop to Reading, passing Didcot on the avoiding line. At Reading a Southern engine was put on the train and we took ours on shed. Then we walked back up to the station and took over a 61XX in the platform to work the 3.45 p.m. to Didcot. The engine was at the end of its duty and

always low on coal. When we got back to Didcot we took it on shed.

Again details changed and later on we worked the 3.45 with an engine prepared on shed — a Southern engine or BR Standard. Once on this turn I remember running into a terrible thunderstorm when we reached the cutting by Aston Tirrold box. I was with Paget Brown and we were travelling on the down relief. I recall the brilliant mercury colour of the rails in front of us as the lightning danced on them. It was a frightening experience, but Paget merely opened the regulator and said "Come on mate, we'll catch the Devil up". We went faster but never seemed to close the distance between us and the dancing flashes, but all the time we were hurrying home.

Our surroundings were now like a boiling sea, with torrents of water cascading around us. In places the rails

Oxford loco shed, situated to the north of the platforms. The old building was very inadequate for the volume of work, locos mainly being prepared outside in all weathers. *R. H. G. Simpson*

An up train running into Oxford station. This might have been the Birkenhead to Bournemouth service which the Southern engine was waiting for. *H. J. Stretton-Ward*

were under water, which we were afraid would enter the ash pan under the loco. A tree had been struck by lightning, and was hanging precariously down the cutting, just clear of our track.

10.50 a.m. EASTLEIGH
Book on 9.35 a.m. Off shed 10.20 a.m.
This was another 22XX turn similar to the 7.38 a.m. Southampton already described, placed in a lower link to enable more men to retain route knowledge.

12.42 p.m. SOUTHAMPTON
Book on 12.20 p.m. Relieve 12.35 p.m.
Again this was a similar turn to the 7.38 a.m. Southampton except that we walked over to the bay where the engine was already on the train. It had been out in the morning as an extra passenger pilot (West End), so by the time we took over, the fire was already dirty.

1.15 p.m. SWINDON
Book on 12.00 noon. Off shed 1.00 p.m.
After preparing the engine, a 61XX, we ran over to the West End bay where the stock was ready for us. We stopped all stations to Swindon, put the stock into the carriage sidings and remained there as standby engine. If we had a 59XX or a 63XX we turned on the factory table at Rodbourne Lane, then ran up the up goods loop to West End sidings by the Gloucester curve opposite the signal box, and stood there. We worked the 5.50 p.m. stopper back to Didcot with the same engine and put the stock into the carriage sidings before going on shed.

One evening on this turn, Paget wanted to get off home early so, to save time, we tried to run straight on shed before anyone realised we'd left the stock in No. 6 platform. As soon as we came to a stand, I uncoupled the engine and we moved off smartly. However, it didn't work

Swindon Junction, looking west from the end of the platform. The up goods line where we stood after working the 1.15 p.m. to Swindon, was in front of the main offices in the middle of the picture to the left of the Gloucester curve. *C. L. Mowat*

No. 6108 at Didcot on 16th August 1947. *H. C. Casserley*

as the shunter in the East End ground frame realised we were due to put the stock away and began to get very cross, but Paget handled the situation very well and calmly said "It's OK, we're only drawing forward for water!"

3.45 p.m. PADDINGTON
Book on 3.15 p.m. Relieve 3.30 p.m.
This was one of my first turns with Fred Essex, but filling in for another fireman before I was in Link 1. It was a prewar turn but it still existed when I reached that seniority. We relieved Didcot men with the 2.42 p.m. passenger train from Swindon in No. 6 platform. It was a 59XX turn, stopping all stations to Slough, then Ealing Broadway and Paddington. From Paddington we travelled out to Old Oak on an empty stock train and picked up the engine for the 6.10 'Kensington Cakes'. We were given a 29XX on which the ATC shoe had already been clipped up on shed in preparation for working over the electrified lines to Kensington to pick up a train of about twenty vans (including parcels vans and long siphons) from the Lyons factory there. We worked this train to Didcot on the

No. 5082 with a down express on 16th August 1947, speeding through Didcot past the passenger pilot which can be seen in the middle sidings. Train No. 460 was carried by the 12 noon Bristol (Temple Meads) to Paddington in 1947. In this instance, the fireman of the return working hasn't removed the boards!

H. C. Casserley

down main after stopping at the signal under the overbridge at Old Oak while a fitter, who was waiting there for us, dropped the ATC shoe. At Didcot we were relieved by No. 2 Link men who took the train on to Swindon.

PASSENGER PILOT, 'EAST END' (3 shifts)
Book on 4.15 a.m. Off shed 4.30 a.m.
A 63XX was kept on duty at Didcot as passenger pilot throughout the day and night. The engine, which 'faced uphill' towards London, was prepared by another crew who booked on at 3.30 a.m. We came off shed at 4.30 a.m. in time to 'tail the papers'. The 3.25 from Paddington to Banbury was a newspaper train with sorters on board, stopping at Reading and Didcot. One of them, a local man Willie Gifford, used to get off the train when it arrived in the up relief platform. The van for Didcot, a long siphon, was uncoupled and left in the platform for unloading while the train continued to Oxford and Banbury, leaving Didcot at 4.40 (this was the train I caught to Oxford as a lad porter). We collected the empty vehicle and took it over to the carriage sidings. It was taken back to London

No. 6359 waiting to come off shed on 12th October 1949. During the summer months, if we could smell the sewage works in the background (behind the noticeboard), the wind was from the east and we knew we had good weather.
H. C. Casserley

A 43XX cab photographed at Didcot in 1959.   *J. H. Russell*

on the midday Oxford empty parcels vans which left for Old Oak around 12.45 p.m. We then sat in the carriage sidings on the front of the carriages for the 7.04 Banbury. Later on, we put these in the down relief platform, then put the three coaches for the 7.38 Southampton into Platform 7, and as soon as this had left, we put the stock for the 8.05 Paddington into the same platform. If we were steam-heating in the winter, we would often couple the stock for the 7.10 and 8.05 together so they were piped through for warming.

For much of the duty we were on standby in case we were needed in the event of a failure, so we kept a good bit of fire in. If the pilot was needed for a down train, it had to be taken on shed for turning but we were very rarely called upon. Old Oak men wouldn't bother Didcot shed because we only had a small engine which they didn't want to take themselves. If their engine was giving trouble and it was possible to reach either Swindon or Reading, there would be a 59XX or a 'Castle' on standby for exchange. We were more likely to be asked to go on the front of a train to assist.

The footplate was never a comfortable place for just sitting around on standby, especially on cold winter nights when there was not much shelter from the bitter winds, so we spent as much time as possible in the warmth of the shunters cabin which we had to ourselves. There was a telephone if we were needed and we stood the engine alongside.

We were occasionally called upon for marshalling trains but otherwise we put stock in and out of the carriage sidings and 'tailed' trains on the relief line, some parcels vans, but mostly taking horse-boxes off trains from Oxford, Swindon or Newbury and transferring them to others for forwarding. Empty horse-boxes were kept in the No. 1 carriage siding. There was the occasional defective vehicle to remove from a train, usually a 'hot box', and take to the cripple siding where many of the repairs were undertaken. The C & W Foreman at Didcot had a team of 6 wagon repairers, 5 examiners, 4 greasers and 8 carriage cleaners under him. The carriage cleaners prepared the stock early each morning while it was still in the sidings.

Book on 12.05 p.m. Relieve 12.20 p.m.
The relief crew took over the engine in the carriage sidings. This was a slack period for pilot work. There was an up stopper, the 10.25 a.m. from Swindon, which arrived at about 11.15 with a newly outshopped engine on a running-in turn. We collected the coaches from this train and put them into the down bay for the 1.15 p.m. Swindon. The engine went on shed, turned and stood 'over the table' for the afternoon. It worked back to Swindon with 'Paddy's Mail' which left Didcot at 6.05 p.m., calling at all stations to Bristol.

We might have tailed a passenger train with van before collecting coaches from the Winchester bay for watering and a C & W examination in the carriage sidings. We later returned them to the bay for the 5.55 Southampton. Without much to do, it was easy to get bored stuck on the engine waiting for the passenger shunter or the foreman passenger shunter to give us our next instructions. I would often sit on the upturned bucket, cushioned with cotton waste, reading newspapers collected off various trains.

In my time, Rich's sidings, curving away through the gate, served an oil depot, tank wagons being delivered there in the mornings by the centre yard pilot. The points here were unlocked using an Annetts key released from Didcot East Junction box.

Left: The east end of Didcot, showing the 'Middle sidings' where the passenger pilot sat between the pairs of relief and main lines. The Didcot, Newbury & Southampton line can be seen running along the right of this view before turning away to the south.
L & GRP

The signalman's view over the station from Didcot West End signal box. The signal on the left with the ringed arm was for leaving the West End yard, the catch point just beyond protecting the running lines if the signal was passed at 'danger'. In shunting the west yard, we frequently needed to run out past the signal onto the up relief or across the Oxford branch, whichever was available, but when we were shut in again, the signalman rang an electric bell on the outside of the signal box to draw our attention to his action. He left the bell ringing until acknowledged by the loco crew or the shunter. The building on the left of this view housed a guards room, shunters room, yard inspector's office and a lavatory. The relief cabin was to the left, just out of the picture.   *National Railway Museum*

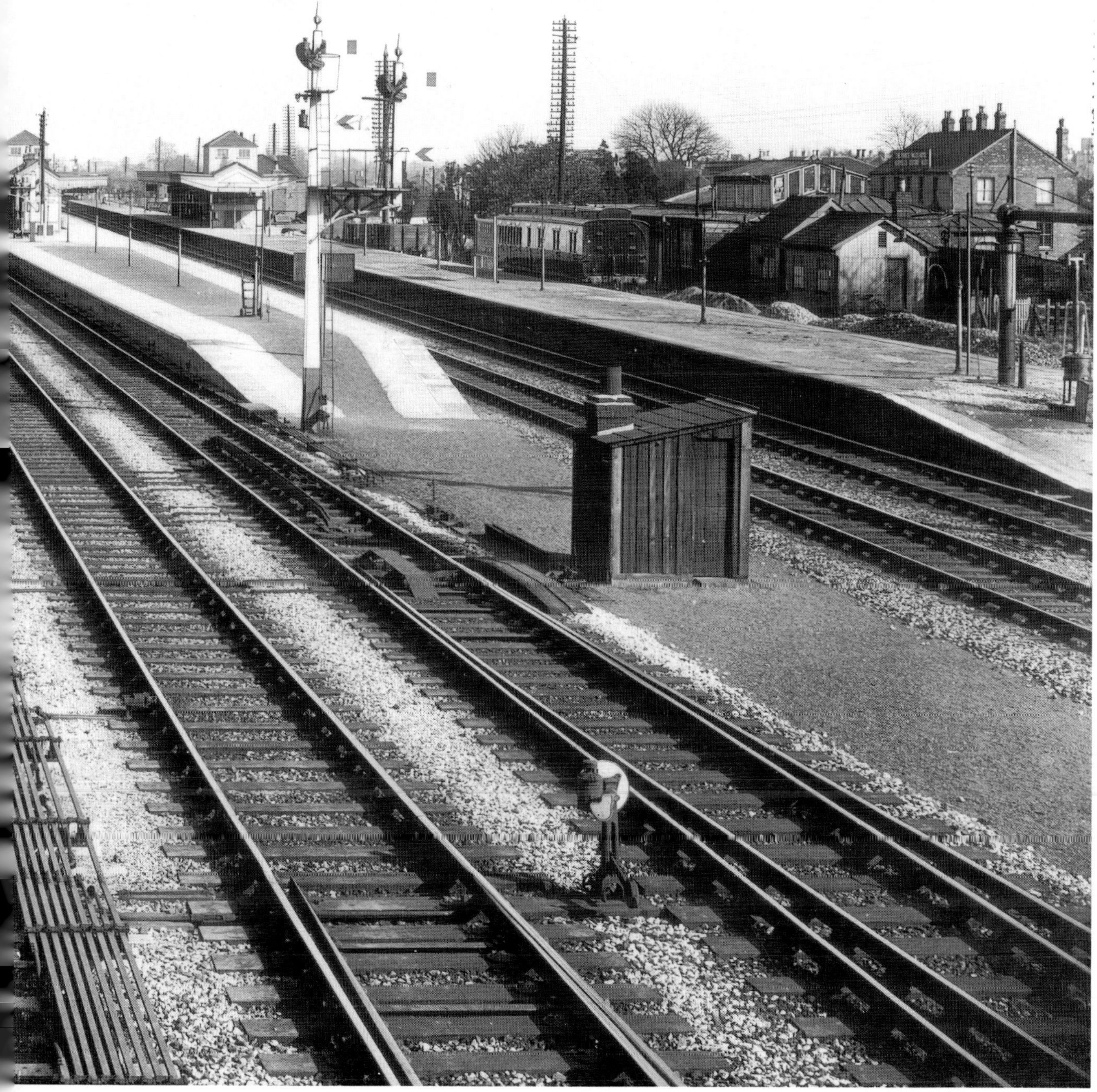

Looking west, along the up main platform, towards Swindon. The large nameboards were removed during the war years for fear of observation from enemy aircraft. Smaller ones with about 3-inch high letters were often placed under the verandah. *J. H. Moss*

The goods shed in the west yard. A hooter to summon workers to the provender was mounted on the tower in the background. A short blast was sounded at 7.50 followed by a longer one at 8.00 a.m. The lunch hour was marked by blasts at 12 o'clock and again at 1.00 p.m., and at the end of the working day it was sounded at 4.50 and again at 5.00 p.m. when workers streamed out of the provender and the Ordnance Depot (which also had a hooter). There were bicycles everywhere and pedestrians walking briskly down the footpath from Foxhall bridge to the station to catch the 5.20 Didcot to Reading train. As young lads, we never had watches, so when we heard the 5 o'clock hooter we knew it was time to go home. During the war an air raid warning siren was mounted on top of the tower and sounded short blasts when enemy aircraft were sighted. The floodlit yard and all the station were plunged into darkness, sometimes even before we heard the siren, and everyone took shelter. The subway served as protection at the station and shelters were also provided at the engine shed and behind the West End box. When it was over, the 'all clear' was a long wail on the siren. An ack-ack gun was also set up on top of the provender tower but I think this was only used once against a lone enemy aircraft. *A. F. Carpenter*

Looking south-east round the Oxford branch curve, with the Baltic siding in the foreground and West End signal box on the right. The bell mentioned on page 200 was mounted on the corner of the building. *Cty. Brian Lingham*

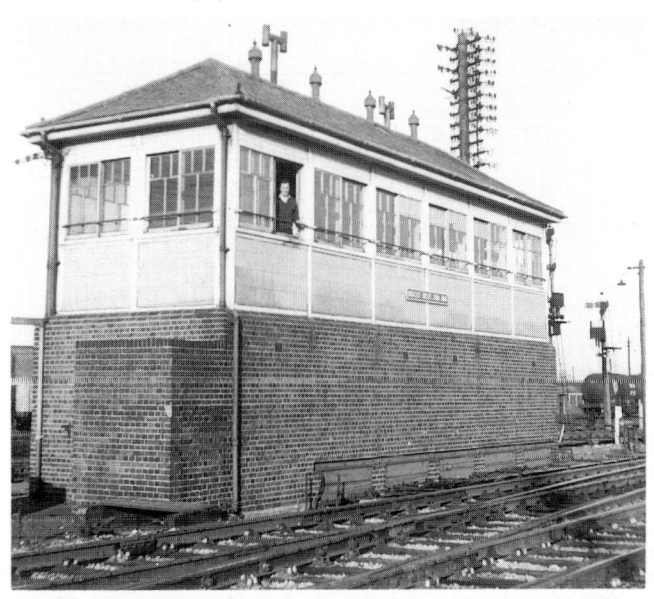

Joe Moore looking out of West End box. The new brick base was an air raid precaution.

Jim Gardner in West End box. He was an excellent signalman respected by all. It was quite common for successive generations of a family to work for the GWR and his was a typical example. His grandfather had been a signalman at Didcot, his father 'Jimmy' was in the telegraph department and his son Jack also became a signalman. *Collection Jim Gardner*

Looking towards Paddington in the mid-1950s, with the West End bay on the right. The corrugated iron shed at the end of the up relief platform was an oil hut where signal lamps were cleaned and filled, whilst the hut in the distance was the carriage and wagon examiner's shed. He walked all over the site to meet the various trains due for examination.

No. 7901 running into the up relief platform with what appears to have been the running-in turn from Swindon. This train often had a loco which was being run-in after a major overhaul. The most memorable one I saw on this turn was 3440 *City of Truro* which arrived at Didcot with loco inspector Curley on board.
Brian Wright

Looking along the up main platform towards Paddington, with the three coaches used on the Newbury line in the bay on the right.
Lens of Sutton

The old up main starting signal and bracket for the Newbury branch. The picture above shows the replacement. *P. J. Garland*

No. 9305 coming out of the centre yard towards the up relief on 16th August 1947. The white ash on the steps and footplate was left over from when fire was thrown out.

H. C. Casserley

Although it was quiet for most of the year, we certainly made up for it on the two weeks before Christmas with all the extra parcels traffic involved. The sidings were absolutely chock-a-block with extra stock drafted in from elsewhere.

In earlier years, the 12.20 men took the 'stale' pilot to work the 5.20 p.m. passenger to Reading, and a fresh engine and a crew from a lower link covered until the 8.55 relief. At that time, the pilot engine was changed daily at 5.0 p.m.

Book on 8.40 p.m. Relieve 8.55.
During the night, the stock for the 7.10 a.m. (11 coaches) and the 8.05 a.m. (9 or 10 coaches) arrived separately and we put them into the carriage sidings, with the shunter riding in the furthest coach, calling us in with a hand lamp.

We put a couple of parcels vans on the rear of the 11.40 p.m. Oxford in Platform 5, and at 2.25 a.m., the 1.5 a.m. West London Milk Empties arrived in the down relief platform and left a couple of vans for us to collect and put into the carriage sidings. We also 'tailed' the 10.15 p.m. Salop Parcels. In a bad winter we would be called on to steam-heat stock through the small hours and the train engines were often booked out one hour earlier.

We took the engine on shed at 4.30 a.m. when the morning crew came off with the fresh engine.

No. 6329 shunting the carriage sidings, probably on pilot duty, on 12th October 1949. *H. C. Casserley*

No. 2936 running into Didcot on the down relief, with the 5.8 p.m. Reading–Swindon on 16th August 1947. The passenger pilot seen in the background on the 'middle siding' was facing 'downhill' whereas they were usually 'head up', i.e. facing towards Paddington.

H. C. Casserley

The 'middle siding' features again in this picture looking west along the down relief towards the station in the early 1930s. The train staff catcher on the left was used by the firemen of trains off the Newbury branch, the signalman from Didcot East Junction box walking over the boarded crossing to retrieve the staff when the train had passed.

National Railway Museum

The passenger pilot, again facing 'downhill' probably in the course of 'tailing' a train. The wartime goods line to Moreton sidings can be seen here on the left, running behind the East Junction box. *National Railway Museum*

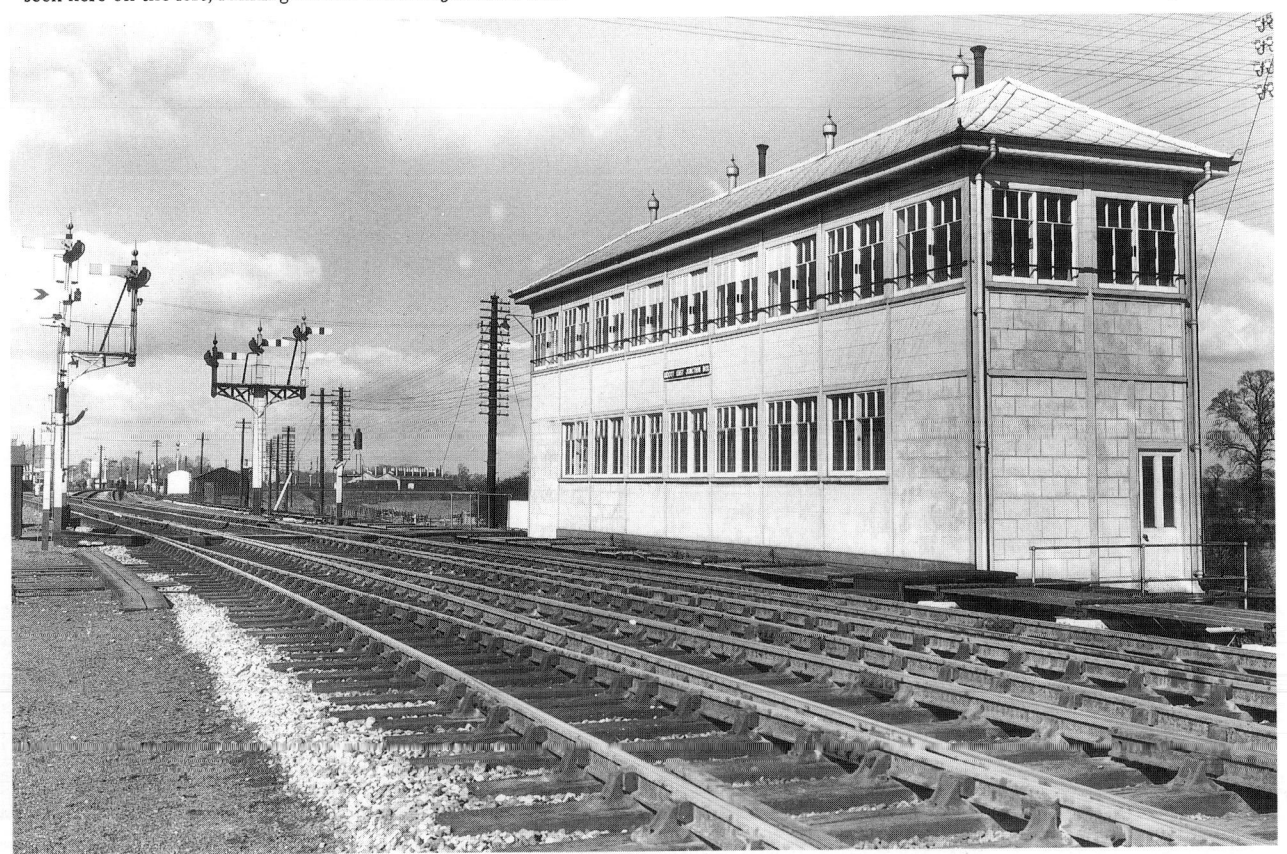

Didcot East Junction signal box when first built in the early 1930s. It was extensively supported on the side of the embankment, but more spoil was added behind when the goods line to Moreton was added during the war. The bracket alongside the up relief, on the right, read: up relief, up main, Newbury branch. Before the line was doubled, the single line staff for the branch was collected from the pick-up post on the right. In bad weather it could be difficult to spot the staff holder so thoughtful signalmen sometimes trapped or tied something white (like newspaper) to it to catch the fireman's attention. *National Railway Museum*

A railwayman's lot is not always easy. Concentrating on handling a train with problems at home called for a strong constitution.

In 1953 my eldest son, David, was born. I remember this very well, as poor Winnie had a very rough time and spent the last six weeks of her pregnancy in and out of hospital. Breast-feeding was out of the question because of an abscess, so I found myself bottle-feeding our 7½lb baby son every four hours, as Winnie was too ill. I was on duty at 2.25 a.m. so the baby usually started to cry about ten o'clock, just as we had settled down for the night. This continued until after midnight, when I found myself sitting on a stool in front of the bedroom fire, feeding David and nursing him until 2 a.m., with a blanket around my shoulders.

Rushing off to work, I had to tuck them both up in bed and trust in providence that they would be all right until I got home again at 11 o'clock. Fortunately, they were. This continued for a week more, until things eventually settled down.

Three years later, our second son, Kevin, was born, and I was determined not to encourage either of them to become railwaymen, as I could see little prospect of them getting very rich. We were never hard up, although there was little spare cash at times. An occasional holiday by the seaside was a much appreciated luxury.

All the years spent firing were a long and vital apprenticeship for becoming a driver so that by the time we were called to Swindon for examination, handling an engine in all weathers with all types of trains, experience of working practice, knowledge of the rules, etc., were ingrained.

We were prepared gradually over the years and gained no end of knowledge from the Didcot Mutual Improvement Class. This was a voluntary group run amongst locomen who instructed us in their free time — a traditional and effective way to train young staff. We used to meet every Thursday evening at 6 o'clock in a disused railway carriage, after we had drawn our weekly wages.

Rules and regulations were an important part of our training which included learning the mechanical parts of a loco: little ends, eccentric rods, quadrant blocks, valves and pistons, connecting rods, and side-rods. We also had to prove our knowledge of the boiler and handling skills, in fact all that was necessary for us to become good locomen.

When any of the men were given a date to attend the examination by the HQ Loco Inspector

Looking west along the down main on the approach to Didcot with the Newbury branch coming in from the left, on 13th June 1956. The allotments below were kept by railway employees.
National Railway Museum

at Swindon, the chief instructor of the class would invite him to his own home in order to 'prime him up' with the necessary knowledge to help him pass the exam the next day.

I was fortunate in having driver Bill Prior for my final revision, the day before going to Swindon. On arrival at Bill's house, the door was opened by his wife, who gave me a warm welcome and showed me into a room where Bill was sitting behind a large wooden table, with books and diagrams laid out in front of him. He was smoking a pipe, from which a feather of smoke was rising. When he smiled at me, I was reassured and began to feel completely at ease.

Knowing that we would be some time, his wife had arranged to go to the local cinema and leave us in peace to get on with our important work — a gesture I have never forgotten. She gave up an evening's companionship with her husband in order to help me and this was no isolated occasion, such was the understanding and co-operation of these unrecognised members of the railway world!

Bill's quiet, patient manner made him a natural tutor. His questions were clear, and he would lead me on or pull up the reins when I was racing along too fast. I was a bit hot-blooded in those days, and needed someone like Bill to slow me down!

The evening passed very quickly and I think we both enjoyed the experience. I felt very relieved when Bill said I would pass easily — a previous colleague had failed at Swindon and I was afraid of doing the same, but Bill's confidence was a great help.

Travelling to Swindon reminded me of my first medical in 1936-7. I still had exam nerves and was all keyed-up, but at least I now had several years preparation behind me. First of all I was asked to take an eyesight test, the first time I had experienced this, but luckily I had no problem in searching for numbers within a page full of coloured dots. These pages were flicked over very quickly, allowing little time to stop and think. The first number you called was the one taken as seen — an excellent way to test eye vision. Mine was fortunately still 20/20 - I was over the first hurdle!

Soon I was sitting opposite loco inspector Jenkins, a Welshman of portly stature, with a watch-chain fastened across his waistcoat. He sat, with his legs apart, facing sideways to his desk. His manner was far from reassuring — but perhaps he was having an 'off' day.

Bill Prior, my chief class instructor.

With no introduction, he went straight into his questions.

"Do you belong to the Improvement Class?", he asked, "and do you know Bill Prior?"

"Yes," I said, with some amazement.

"A good instructor," he replied, "Well, we'll soon find out what you know."

"Read the shaft across on a Stephenson link motion, with the right-hand big end on the top front."

I started off. "Right-hand big end at top front, left-hand big end on the top back, right-hand fore gear eccentric just over the bottom front, right-hand back gear eccentric just over the back, the left-hand fore gear eccentric just over the top front, the left-hand back gear eccentric just over the back, right-hand side rod on the bottom back, left-hand side rod on the bottom front."

I was trying to heed Biil's advice about not racing along.

"Correct," came the reply from a Welsh voice which was firm and sharp.

He continued, "Followed by right-hand big end on the front, lever in fore gear."

"Where do the first four beats come from?"

"Right-hand side steam at the front, exhaust at the back, left-hand side steam at the back, exhaust at the front, right-hand side lead steam at the back exhaust, at the front, left-hand side lead steam, exhaust at the back . . . "

"Correct," came the reply again.

By now I was feeling a lot easier, and I could sense that Inspector Jenkins was also friendlier. He turned around in his chair and faced me for the first time, putting his clenched hands on the table. His manner was easier, knowing I was not wasting his time.

"What's lead steam?" he asked.

"A cushion of steam when the piston is near the end of its stroke," I replied, "to assist the piston on its return journey."

"Correct," said Inspector Jenkins. "What is lap?"

"The amount the valve overlaps the steam port when the valve is central", I told him.

Once again his reply was "Correct".

The inspector carried on asking many questions and I was able to give a good account of myself. Occasionally he would assist me by raising an eyebrow if I was wrong, or used a facial expression a bit like Fred Jones had done. I knew he was telling me to think again, but he led me along without actually saying I was wrong. A correction was allowed, provided you satisfied his demand.

My last question was "Explain how a vacuum pump works".

This was not easy, as it involved the vacuum braking system, but I managed to satisfy him with my answer.

He told me that I had passed, but said he would want to know more about the vacuum pump the next time I attended.

Delighted that my ordeal had come to a successful conclusion, I hurried downstairs with the famous slip of white paper with the word 'Passed' written on it!

The mess room at Didcot loco, known as the 'Cabin', had a notice over the door — 'ENGINEMEN', a name which indicated the high esteem in which the GWR held their locomen. The title 'Driver' was never used, it was always engineman, a term which reflected our intimate knowledge of all the mechanical parts of a steam locomotive. The actual driving was the end product and the level of skill usually reflected how well the man in control knew his locomotive.

If walls could speak, the bricks in the Cabin could certainly tell some amazing stories. The room was situated inside the shed, next to the stores. It was the first mess room after the offices, which were arranged in order of importance, the shed master and running-foreman being the first in rank, the Cabin came next, followed by mechanical fitter foreman, boilersmith fitters mates, chargeman cleaner, shed staff and engine cleaners. Finally there were the toilets, where a special cubicle was reserved for the supervisors who held a key. Such were the grade distinctions in the GWR.

I recall my first entry into this sea of benches and scrubbed wooden table tops, with lockers surrounding the walls, all of them numbered. It was customary for No. 1 to be that of the senior engineman, known as 'Number One'.

My feelings as an innocent youth as I eyed the enginemen, was one of awe. Now the men who controlled the steam giants were accepting me as one of them. I was content just to sit and listen to their friendly rivalry, some keen to show off their skills in handling a locomotive. Sometimes, when a highly respected driver came in, his opinion was sought on a handling method. They soon gave me the impression of being a very close-knit bunch of men, always portraying the importance of their profession.

Nicknames were much in evidence, but if an engineman did not have one he was merely called by his surname. Collectively, they were a colourful bunch, with names like 'Gentleman Jim', 'The Vicar', 'Ike', 'Chick', 'Tipster', 'Paget', 'Kuffy', 'Desperate Dan' and 'Old Man River'.

As the years passed, it became evident that a fireman who had been many years with a driver, developed his handling and technical habits, good and bad. Drivers had a strong influence over some of their firemen, moulding them into almost a duplicate of themselves, and in many cases this was of great benefit to the railway.

A driver or 'engineman' and his fireman acted as one — a team which often had a father/son relationship, some bonds becoming very strong. After all, they shared hardships and triumphs and worked together very often every day for as long as five or six years. Working in unison on the footplate, they each knew what the other could do, and relied on each other accordingly.

A team who could tame a hundred tons of steel, at 70 or 80 mph, sometimes with 500 tons behind, and make it respond to any demand, in

Didcot enginemen during the 1955 strike. My father and myself are seated together in the front row, 9th and 10th from the left. Paget Brown is second from the left, kneeling, whilst my good friend Sam Essex is standing in front of the telegraph pole in the middle of the picture.

C & W examiner G. W. (Harry) Andrews, passenger shunter Dennis (Den) Betteridge, foreman shunter James (Jim) Smith, and engineman Arthur Goodall. Coming from a long line of railwaymen, he was a particularly good engineman with a pleasant personality reflected in the way he handled an engine.

whatever conditions, was a valuable asset to the railway company!

Discussions in the Cabin were not always serious, particularly on Grand National Day, when excitement gripped the occupants. Once a trusted, well-liked engineman had given them all a hot tip the day before, almost straight from the horse's mouth, as he had taken the head stable lad and his charge to Crewe and on to Liverpool the day before.

"Who won, Fred?" everyone asked in unison as he arrived at the Cabin door.

Fred had just heard the results on the wireless, before he left home, which was only a mile away, but by the time he got to the shed, he'd forgotten the names and was telling them "What is it?" was first, "Who is it?" came second, and "I can't remember what" was next! They weren't impressed.

Did it matter that Fred was not a 'racing' man, and couldn't retain this vital information? No, he was an engineman, his mind was on his work, and his next trip.

POSTWAR SERVICE

Fireman Ted Brown and engineman Bill Jones on the 12.42 Didcot–Southampton waiting for the up train to cross at Worthy Down. Note a spare shovel was always carried in case of loss or damage to the one in use.
T. B. Sands

Fireman Ted Brown and engineman Bill Baylis.

Fireman Charlie Wilcox (on the left) was a good friend and a fellow border canary fancier, and I was best man at his wedding. The engineman on the right was Stan Webb. The chalked 'boiler empty' warning on the tank side meant that the boiler had to be filled before this engine was lit up. *Barry Warr*

While I was a passed fireman (passed for driving but still serving as a fireman) various driving duties came my way, mostly on pilots in the local yards. The change in role gave me a fresh approach to life on the footplate, but although I changed sides in the cab, it was actually a bit of an anticlimax. I had been expecting a feeling of excitement, but as many drivers had allowed me to drive during my firing days, the changeover seemed natural — just as it should have been. I had been moulded into a steam locomotive engineman by the drivers I had fired to, although I hadn't realised this at the time. These good men had learnt the same way, and in proper tradition were passing on their skills — things that couldn't be found in books, knowledge that otherwise died with them.

The Milton disaster came at a very crucial time in my career, just before I was made up to driver. It was an enormous shock to us all and the greatest possible influence on my attitude to the footplate. It was a timely reminder of what could happen if I made an error of judgement as a driver.

It happened on Sunday, 20th November 1955, when the up main between Foxhall Junction and Milton signal box was closed for engineering works and all trains were being diverted onto the up goods line via a crossover which was subject to a 10 mph speed restriction. That day I had been on the early shift as fireman on a 63XX working a permanent way engineers train in connection with relaying the up main. After a peaceful morning typical of Sunday work, we were relieved at Milton by another crew who had walked out from Didcot Loco to take over at 1.00 p.m. We strolled back to the shed to book off duty at 1.45 p.m., only to be greeted with the news that a derailment had taken place at Milton just after we had left.

A loco was being dispatched to take the loco foreman to assess the severity of the incident. I collected a No. 2 First Aid cabinet from one of the guard's compartments of the empty carriage stock stabled in the carriage sidings and hastily joined the others on the engine. The scene which confronted us was horrific. The train was halfway down the embankment with coaches on their sides, some resting precariously on top of others. We felt so utterly helpless. Our resources were inadequate but we were united with a determination to press on regardless and get all the trapped people out of the wreckage. The local emergency services were there within minutes and with the help of personnel from RAF Milton, it didn't take long to get survivors and dead bodies out. Out of 293 passengers on board, 157 were injured and 11 lost their lives.

However, throughout this traumatic operation, my mind was on the unfortunate engine crew. The fireman, A. G. P. Marsh, had gallantly rescued his driver who was buried under a heap of coal, and immediately carried out protection in accordance with the rule book by laying detonators to warn approaching trains of the hazard. He then helped rescue the injured until he was persuaded to stop and come onto our engine for examination by a doctor. He complained of back pains and was suffering from severe shock, so I gave him my jacket and a cup of tea before he began his journey back to Swansea. The driver had been led away from the scene by early arrivals.

It seems that in reading the weekly notice, the driver had not noticed the entry concerning the closing of the up main at Didcot and was therefore not expecting to be switched into the up goods line. As with many disasters, there were other contributing factors including the suspicion that the ATC system on the loco concerned, a BR Standard 4-6-2 No. 70026, was not working as the warning siren was very weak. Also, situated on the left-hand side of the engine, instead of the more usual right-hand side of GWR types, the driver failed to notice that his train was signalled for the goods line. Furthermore, according to the MOT report, there should have been a hand signalman exhibiting red or green flags at the entry to the goods line.

Not expecting to be routed off the up main, the train was said to have been travelling at 40-50 mph as it went over the 10 mph crossover onto the up goods line, which was situated on the edge of a 20ft high embankment. At that speed the engine toppled over and crashed down the embankment, followed by much of its train.

When all the unauthorised helpers had been cleared from the site, I looked at the row of dead bodies laid in line on the edge of the field — a sight and experience I will never forget.

I had been on duty since 6.00 a.m. that morning and didn't arrive home until well after 7 p.m., by which time my wife was extremely worried. She had heard there had been an accident and that people had been killed, so she broke down in tears when I walked through the door. I collapsed onto the carpet in front of the fire, with the horrible scenes of the day swimming around in my head, and cried. Being so close to all that death left me feeling unclean inside and out — it had been hell. I was cold, miserable and felt drained of life. I was thankful to be home, but many sleepless nights were to follow, and that horrible scene continued to flash through my mind throughout the days ahead for what seemed an eternity before I finally overcame the emotional strain.

Disaster at Milton. The scene which I witnessed remained in my mind throughout all my years as an engineman. There were eleven corpses reverently laid in line in the field, to the right of this picture.
Mrs. W. Miles

No. 5026 on the up relief at Reading. I was so glad to climb aboard her after the failure of 5029 on the Rugby special.

Brian Wright

CHAPTER NINE

THE MOMENT OF TRUTH

ON my first main line trip as a driver, I felt like the proverbial 'duck taking to water', completely at ease with the footplate and my surroundings. I was in my element — my boyhood ambition had been realised at last. At the time, I was still a passenger fireman, and had signed the 'Knowledge of Road' book for the various routes I was working over in the passenger link at Didcot. Driver George Hill was rostered to work a Sunday freight train from Acton Yard to the Severn Tunnel Junction as far as Didcot, where he would be relieved, but his regular fireman, Fernley Dodd, told me that George wanted the weekend off, and asked if I would work his turn of duty.

Being only a passenger fireman, it was unheard of for someone like me to take charge of a train, especially in the London area. Some of the regular drivers became alarmed that a 28-year old like myself was taking over the ivory handle. The 'wets' were wringing their hands, no confidence in themselves, even less in us, the drivers of the future!

Seeing my name on the Sunday duty roster in place of George Hill was exhilarating; at last I was going back to Old Oak Common loco shed after twelve years, this time as a driver. The fact that I was actually 'weaned' at Old Oak Common was overlooked by the Didcot 'wets'!

The big day arrived, and I remember booking on duty at 11 o'clock in clean overalls, polished shoes, with no sign of nervous tension — just complete confidence! I examined the late notice board for any emergency notification of temporary speed restrictions, permanent way working, signal alterations, etc. I also obtained my copy of the weekly notice, a booklet detailing any pre-arranged alterations to signalling, etc.

Fernley, my cheerful fireman, had now arrived, greeting me with "Morning, mate" and a broad grin all over his face, mentioning a few personalities who had placed a 'flea in his ear' about my being big-headed and running before I could walk!

Collecting our quota of cotton waste from the stores, and tea can and pocket book from my locker, we were away back up the path leading from Didcot loco shed to the station. We travelled as passengers and, on arrival at Paddington, stayed in the train which was being taken empty stock to Old Oak Common carriage sidings, opposite the loco shed.

Jumping out of the coach as it finally came to a halt at our destination, I had a sudden light-headed feeling. For years I had groomed myself for this moment, and I was not going to allow anything to upset my great joy. I am sure Fernley sensed my feelings and was looking forward to our trip.

Engineman Harry Harris and fireman Fernley Dodd.
Cty. Mrs. Fernley Dodd

219

After a can of tea, we began to search the berths around the turntable in the far corner of the shed. It was here we found our loco, a '28XX' 2–8–0 that had been on boiler washout the previous day. Fitters had also carried out minor repairs, including the renewal of piston glands and brake blocks, and had left the footplate in a poor state.

We had plenty of time to make things shipshape, but had to search for many of the tools we needed, 'lifting' anything we were short of from a nearby loco. Ours had been stripped; there wasn't even a pricker or fire shovel, but it was not long before Fernley and I collected all we needed.

While I was oiling underneath, Fernley went to collect red flags and detonators from the stores. He placed a 'not to be moved' board on the front of the loco, facing the turntable, so that I would be safe during his absence.

On his way back, the running foreman asked him if I knew the road to Severn Tunnel Junction as I had only signed to Swindon. They returned together, and spoke to me while I was oiling underneath the loco. It was the Sunday following the England v. Wales International match at Twickenham and I was asked if I would work No. 5029 *Nunney Castle* to Swindon on a return rugby special for South Wales. We were told this train had no crew as the Cardiff men had not arrived.

As usual, I jumped in where angels fear to tread, and accepted what I thought was a better turn — a full passenger train and a 'Castle' Class loco, non-stop to Swindon. This made the adrenalin flow, especially as 5029 had already been prepared and was waiting outside the shed for us.

My mind was flooding with excitement. The feel of a 'Castle' Class under my feet, my hand on the regulator. Surely Dame Fortune was smiling on me, and what would the 'wets' at Didcot say now?

However, when I climbed into the cab of 5029 my high spirits were quenched. It was all an anti-climax as I sensed a coldness about her. There was no heat coming from the boiler cladding, the firebox doors were closed and a silence prevailed. I sensed something was wrong. As I opened the firebox doors, I saw that the fire was black, and the back end had been built up to the extent that it was impossible to see over the brick arch and inspect the tube plate.

I expressed my concern to Fernley over this state of affairs, but we both agreed to carry on regardless. He was very keen to 'have a go', and so was I. At Didcot there was seldom a chance to work an express passenger from Paddington, so we fell for it like innocent lambs. The trap was set, and we knew nothing of what lay in store for us!

I drove her gently through the yard and as I gave a couple of crows on the whistle, the departure signal from Old Oak Common engine shed box came off. I was outside the shed limits now, the point of no return, having informed the signalman that we were for the rugby special to South Wales.

During the trip we left the blower fully open and my mate pulled the fire-irons through the fire, trying to generate some heat. By this time, I was getting a bit concerned as there was no free steaming and the pressure seemed to be slow in coming to 'blow-off' point in spite of Fernley doing all he could and with both back dampers open to provide all the air possible through the fire grate. Needless to say, in these circumstances, the water level in the boiler was low.

As we passed over the bridge carrying the up and down carriage lines over the main line, I noticed that the signal at the bottom of the bank was green. These signals were smaller aspects than the colour lights on the main line.

We followed on until Ranelagh Bridge, where an aspect directed us to No. 1 platform, the 'Holy of Holies' where all the important trains left from. I had achieved my ambition but in far from ideal circumstances and there were problems in store for us.

After pressing the buffer springs up tightly, I waited for the shunter to drop the engine coupling on to the coach hook. I then released the engine brakes, a sudden jolt convincing me that the coupling was secure. Destroying the vacuum allowed the shunter to couple up the vacuum brake pipe between the engine and train. While he was doing that, I walked round to the back of the tender to satisfy myself that the coupling was sufficiently tight. There were four threads showing between the links, so I was happy. I then returned to the cab and blew off the brakes with the large ejector. The gauge showed 25in train pipe and 23in reservoir, which was correct, and it held steady, indicating there was no loss of vacuum. Then the guard did a brake test.

I wound the reverser to forward gear and left the small ejector open to maintain 'brakes off'. I wiped the spectacle glass to provide a clearer

THE MOMENT OF TRUTH

view of the signal underneath the verandah. The guard came up to advise the load of the train, which was 384 tons, twelve 8-wheeled coaches. First stop Swindon for relief.

He also asked for my name which, as always, had to be recorded in his log.

"Driver B. Barlow," I replied, "of Didcot".

At last I could add the prefix 'Driver' to my name. I was now in the senior ranks!

Meanwhile, Fernley, my mate, had managed to fill the boiler and now had a 'full head' of steam going. A gentle hiss could be heard from the safety valve, the steam gauge showing 225 lbs per square inch, with the needle on the red mark. The gauge frame lamp was showing the water level just below the top nut. The headlamps had been placed one over each front buffer, indicating 'A' head code. We both felt important, and intended to make anyone who spotted us aware of the fact!

By now darkness was descending over the grey January day, and signal lights began to flicker as flurries of snow scattered the landscape. A cold biting wind was getting up, from which there was little protection on the footplate. At last the 'RA' came up on the indicator, meaning 'right away'. I stood up and eased the regulator open just enough to set us in motion.

With the reverser set at 55% cut-off, I could feel the weight of the train as 5029 came to terms with her task. Under my feet I could feel the sensation of power coming from the wheels, and as we slowly gathered speed, the 'clickety-click' of the rail joints and the sway of the suspension began to combine with the sound of the exhaust blasting from the chimney.

I nicked the reverser up gradually as our speed increased. The ring of the Automatic Train Control bell was a great assurance as we passed over each of the 'whale-back' ramps between the rails. The bell indicated that we had a clear road ahead, a double check on my observance of the signals, which were green as far as visibility would allow.

As we proceeded towards Acton I began to feel uneasy as Fernley had been desperately trying to maintain steam pressure, but with no response. There was a moist smell coming from the exhaust

No. 5029 approaching Old Oak Common with an express on the down main.   R. C. Riley

which occasionally drifted into the cab — my earlier fears had been confirmed. We had taken over a 'crab'.

My mate was pulling out all the stops but the firebox was lifeless, despite his efforts. The boiler water was dropping fast, and the ring of water inside the boiler gauge glass was bobbing up and down like a yo-yo. A feeling of despair closed in on us. We were both experienced firemen and knew our job well, but the steam pressure had now fallen to 175, so I eased the regulator back to the first valve and Fernley shut off the steam heating valve to the coaches to conserve what steam we had.

My mate was doing an excellent job and was a super fireman. He had been swinging the shovel, sprinkling small amounts of coal carefully around the firebox and constantly pulling the fire through with the 12ft long poker. Each time he had finished, he put the injector on in an effort to maintain the water level in the boiler. Great credit was due to him, as he couldn't possibly have done more under these difficult conditions.

As we approached West Drayton, I gave two crows on the whistle, 'cock-a-doodle-doo, cock-a-doodle-doo', followed by two blasts, indicating to the signalman that I wanted to be switched to the relief line at Dolphin Junction.

By this time we had reduced speed to 30 mph, and steam pressure was 120. If it dropped any lower I would be unable to maintain the brakes.

The continual fall of pressure was now affecting our speed as we approached Slough on the down relief, so I decided to stop there for a 'blow-up' and wait until steam pressure had been built up and the boiler refilled. Between us we shovelled some better coal off the back of the tender. Instead of being a brilliant white, the fire showed a bluish-mauve colour, which was most depressing.

At last, after twenty-five minutes, we had a full head of steam, and a full boiler. I blew the whistle to let the signalman know that we were ready and the signal came off. I was overwhelmed with guilt. It was a shame and a disgrace, but in true railway tradition I did not show my frustration.

As we proceeded towards Reading, I suggested to Fernley that he did the driving and that I would fire. I didn't think I could do any better than him, which he understood, but I wanted to have a go and, after working so hard, he was quite content to let me take hold of the shovel.

I realised by now that I was going to have to ask for another engine at Reading and therefore began to run the fire down so that an inspection of the tubes could be carried out there. Easing the long poker out of the rack on the side of the tender, I pushed the back end of the fire all over the box. It was like stirring up a mass of treacle.

All this time the train heating had been off, and the coaches were freezing. The Welsh rugby supporters were no doubt cursing, quite unaware of the drama on the footplate.

Several times the water level disappeared below the bottom nut of the gauge frame and only bobbed up again when the blow-through cock was opened. I had no intention of allowing this to continue. By this time I had forgotten this was my very first main line trip, and I stopped at Ruscombe signal box to ask for another loco at Reading. The signalman informed me that this had already been arranged. Limping into Reading with 140 lbs of steam, I felt that our abilities had been thoroughly tested by arriving at all!

I felt a sense of relief when Fernley stopped on the down main platform, and we could see No. 5026 waiting for us on the through road. A Reading driver was waiting on the platform and he explained that 5026 had been on the station pilot duty, and was in good order. I was pleased to leave the sorry state of affairs on the footplate of 5029. The atmosphere was lethargic, and there was a feeling of great remorse. Hardly any energy was left inside the firebox or boiler, and the blower jet was merely whimpering steam from the chimney, even though the valve was wide open.

I stood on the platform while she was eased off the train to limp on to the loco shed. She looked a very sad spectacle. As I watched the back of her tender recede into the distance, the dangling steam heat pipe put me in mind of an animal with its tail between its legs. Only a gentle squeal, like a sigh of relief, could be heard as she negotiated the curve and passed out of sight.

Continuing from Reading with 5026 was like being in a different world. Immediately I stepped into the cab I could feel the heat of the firebox, the atmosphere was alive and there was a full head of steam. As the heat began to penetrate through my overalls, I knew we had a snip of a loco this time!

We had a perfect trip to Swindon, passing through Didcot on the down main and rushing

A 'Castle' heading away from Reading on the down main. The weather was not so kind the day we pulled out of Reading with 5026.
Maurice Earley

under Foxhall Bridge at 75 miles an hour. We arrived at Swindon just on the hour. We had experienced two extremes of locomotive!

On the Monday morning I was fireman on the 7.10 Didcot to Paddington. We then worked back to Old Oak Common where we had to turn the engine and take some empty stock to Paddington. I knew the Chief Mechanical Foreman at Old Oak vaguely from my days as engine cleaner there, and sought him out to ask about 5029. After telling him about our abysmal trip at the weekend, he made the necessary enquiries and discovered that 5029 had been in service for fifteen days, which was over the limit, and was ten days overdue for a wash-out. There was a lot of shale in her boiler and he was certain that she had not been given a really thorough wash-out. Someone now had to explain why 5029 was allowed to go into service when she should have been stopped.

Later that week, while I was on the same turn, an HQ boiler inspector came to see me and explained in detail the sorry history of 5029. It transpired that a set of enginemen, well aware of her condition, had refused to take her out on the Rugby Special. Being a Sunday, there was no crew available, so the loco foreman had 'pulled a fast one' on me – and I fell for it!

On reflection, this was probably the best thing that could have happened, as it made me fully aware of the pitfalls in my profession. From the loco foreman's point of view, once he had got the engine off his patch *he* had no worries!

Now I had developed a 'nose', and could smell a bad engine, boilerwise or mechanically, and this was to save me endless trouble in the future.

The south end of Oxford station in the early 1950s. The Southern Region loco had worked a service from the Bournemouth area into the station, and having turned at the shed, it is shown here waiting to take over the southbound train from Birkenhead. One SR locomotive could be seen every weekday at Oxford on the Bournemouth to Birkenhead (and return) service, but two or three more would work through onto the Western Region on summer Saturday extra trains.

R. H. G. Simpson

CHAPTER TEN

FADING PRIDE

IN 1956 we took our summer holidays at St. Ives in Cornwall where I met a driver, Jim Bennett, who had transferred there from Didcot during the war years. He had seen the appointment list that week and noticed that I'd been appointed a driver at Oxford. I could have been posted anywhere on the Western Region but Dame Fortune was smiling on me, Oxford was only a few miles from home. At last I had reached the other side of the footplate permanently, and our holiday seemed all the more wonderful!

When I reported at Oxford for the first time, the shedmaster asked if I would accept a position on the relief supervisors panel as I had been recommended by the Didcot shed foreman. I accepted but found it to be a 'snake pit' because of the attitude of the militant union activists. I was not successful in the appointment because I could not bring myself to 'suck up' to hard line personalities. Like my father, I was 'straight down the line' and never two-faced. I suppose it cost me a lot, but I've always had an easy conscience.

The time when I was booked to drive a pigeon special from Oxford to Westbury provides an example of the kind of sniping that went on. The shed foreman at Oxford gave me two days over the Westbury road to re-acquaint myself with the route so that I could qualify to sign the knowledge of road book and satisfy the railway inspectorate.

I booked on duty at Oxford at 2.00 a.m. with an excellent fireman, who had been selected to be my mate because this was my first trip. The pigeon special train, consisting of eight large parcels vans bound for Weymouth, arrived at Oxford at 2.15 a.m. and we relieved the Tyseley men on a 'Hall' class loco in very good nick at the South box. The signal on the gantry was already off, showing a green light, and after checking the vacuum gauge for any sign of leaks, we eased away. As we passed the signal box, the signalman gave me the 'hit 'em up' signal, waving his arm up and down in a frantic manner. Obviously the late night passenger was waiting to run into the station and we had to clear Didcot in front of it.

After an effortless trip to Didcot North, everything was in our favour, and the free-steaming loco was running quietly and responding to all our efforts. I was soon at ease with myself, but

No. 2826 heading south through Oxford with an 'F' freight on 22nd April 1953. *J. H. Moss*

at Didcot North we were turned into the up goods loop, which rather surprised me, and on arrival at the Didcot East Junction goods loop home signal, we rang the signalman, only to be told we were going to be relieved, as we were Oxford men who didn't know the road to Westbury!

The signalman's instructions were to keep us at the signal, so while I was waiting, I lit the flare lamp and oiled the bars and piston rods while I carried out a visual examination of the loco. When I climbed back onto the footplate, I was amazed to see a Didcot driver sitting in my seat. Innocently, he had been told to pilot me to Westbury. The situation was very tense until I assured him his services were not required, I was quite competent. In retrospect, he was obviously unaware of what was happening and very kindly returned to the loco shed. The signalman, now under the impression that the pilotman was on board, pulled off the signal for us to leave, and I promptly obliged. This was arranged to distress me and was just one example of the kind of thing that happened to me because of a vendetta between a loco supervisor, who shall remain nameless, and my father.

After an uneventful trip to Westbury, my Oxford fireman remarked that I was certainly in no need of a pilotman. Although he had kept out of the argument, he must have been concerned, and afterwards went on to say what a wonderful trip we'd had. I'm pleased to say we became good friends. I found that younger men seemed very adaptable to my footplate attitude.

The time soon came for me to return to Didcot as a vacancy had arisen, and on my last day at Oxford I was asked to take an urgently required light engine to Didcot Loco — just the job, on my way home. The loco foreman at Oxford gave me all my personal records to return to Didcot, including my knowledge of the road record. Glancing through the paperwork, I noticed that it showed my signature for Westbury, the date and the Oxford foreman's initials as confirmation. Then to my delight and infinite pleasure, when I arrived on shed at Didcot, who should be waiting for the engine I was delivering but the foreman who tried to embarrass me by telling Reading Relief Control that I had not signed the road to Westbury! It was pleasure sublime when I threw all my papers down at his feet and told him that if he picked them up and read them, he would be a wiser man. Was I really a rebel? I leave the reader to judge.

Before the war, enginemen were dedicated and took real pride in their work, but things were never quite the same after the war with the rapid promotion of new recruits. By the time I became a driver, the turnover of footplate staff was surprisingly fast, no doubt due to the growth of the unions and other changes in industry. Those who would never make enginemen soon left for easier pickings whilst those that remained developed into dedicated steam men.

Amid all these comings and goings, it was heartwarming to come across youngsters with real promise and one that sticks in my mind from that time was Dai Evans, a 16½ year old lad fresh from mid-Wales. Short and sturdy looking, he wore a cloth cap tilted at a slight angle. The first time I saw him he was striding along the walkway to book on duty, and I remember how when he stopped to light up, his satchel slipped off his shoulder while his hands were cupped round his cigarette. He turned away from the wind to draw on the cigarette, then tossed his head with an air of confidence and strode off to the lobby. Little did I know then that he was to be my mate for several years in No. 2 link. He was intelligent and hard-working and, in his early years at Didcot, soon developed into one of the best firemen I ever had the pleasure to work with. His attitude to hard work was a quality by then rarely found on the footplate and he had a sixth sense that all good enginemen had.

He could always manage to produce a full head of steam where it was needed most. For instance, in anticipation of going up Savernake incline he would have prepared his fire miles beforehand and only had to lift up the bed with the long bar to release all the heat.

I will always recall the scene on the footplate while working the 10.00 p.m. Banbury one night with a 28XX. The glow from the firebox lit up the inside of the cab as I watched Dai put the bar in the fire and lift the white-hot mass, then with a serious expression of concentration, peer through the firehole, making a mental note of every area of the grate. As the blast from the exhaust grew stronger, the fire drew into an even whiter heat and the occasional spark flew out from over the flap, which itself was becoming red hot. The fire was at its hottest and, as we reached the steepest part of the incline, the safety valves began to blow. Dai never had to shovel any coal onto the fire while the engine was working at its hardest — he planned it all well beforehand. As we approached the top of the bank with 460 tons of freight behind us, he lowered the flap, and with mutual satisfaction we enjoyed an easy drift down the falling gradient. The moon was high in the sky and we were left sailing along on a beautiful starlit night. Dai sat on his seat with one leg on the fly valve handle of the exhaust injector and took out his tobacco tin, rolled a cigarette and lit it on the gauge frame lamp. "Well done, Spud", was all I said, and he sat there with a contented look on his face and a twinkle in his eyes.

Teamwork was vital and the two of us blended together like ducks taking to water. The chemistry was right and we were so compatible that we each knew what the other would be doing at any particular time. There were other firemen as skilled as Dai, but we didn't necessarily get on together; some had a flippant approach whilst others were over-anxious. To get the best out of a fireman, he had to be treated as an equal to a point, although I always made a careful study of whoever I allowed to drive, and not until I was satisfied that they could fire an engine would I trust them with the regulator.

A conscientious, careful, capable engineman, familiar with his charge, would climb upon the footplate of any engine with confidence and maintain a cool nerve under adverse and sometimes very difficult conditions. Conversely, an inexperienced man with a happy-go-lucky or 'couldn't-care-less' attitude, asked to take over a train unexpectedly, would shrink for lack of confidence, with fear striking like cold steel

The changing scene — in the mid-1950s Southern men had started working over the DN&S right through to Didcot. This picture of a Southern 'T9' in No. 7 platform with the 3.40 p.m. train for Southampton, was taken on 21st April 1956. No. 2209, in the background, was on the Oxford avoiding line with an oil train which had come from Fawley via the Newbury branch. *R. C. Riley*

through the nerves of his body. The wrong attitude could lead to serious trouble in an emergency.

After a satisfactory medical, the initial training for an engineman started with a period of engine cleaning, and this early stage gave me as a prospective engineman invaluable familiarisation with the boiler and numerous mechanical parts of a steam engine.

When I became a fireman, I soon learned that I needed both intelligence and stamina to cope with the physical demands of the job. Keeping the needle of the pressure gauge on the red mark enabled the driver to maintain speed and run to time, and experience was the only way to learn. No written word could give the fireman the feel for the job, the circumstances of which constantly varied with differing engines, types of coal, loads, gradients, weather conditions, etc. Some engines burned more coal at the front of the firebox whilst others burned more at the sides or in the back corners. An intelligent fireman would soon have this all weighed up and fire accordingly.

Driving a passenger train or express goods on a dark foggy night, peering out for signals ahead left little time to instruct a novice fireman, and in these circumstances falling steam pressure made extra demands on concentration. As a driver, I would see the fire was in good shape before starting out with a novice fireman, and make sure we had a full boiler and sufficient coal brought forward onto the shovelling plate of the tender. I would tell him the best shape of fire for the type of engine we had, but really this was all I could do prior to starting away. If the engine was free steaming, all was well and I could relax in the smell of burning coal from a properly shaped and efficient fire. If things were not right, tension rose and I could feel extra adrenalin pumping round my nervous system. Shovelling coal on a moving footplate, which was rolling and tossing at speed, was a skill of its own and could be frightening to an inexperienced fireman. Some took to it all surprisingly well and made natural firemen, whilst others, through no fault of their own, didn't even know how to operate an injector properly because in the earlier years the shed foreman hadn't allowed youngsters on the footplate, and they received little training even weeks prior to tackling a large engine in traffic.

Those who'd received instructions on the theory of firing and had been familiarised with

A down freight, probably for Severn Tunnel or Bristol, passing Swindon East signal box on 14th August 1956. In later years Didcot crews worked these trains. *Photographer unknown*

This picture of me driving the 11.10 Didcot–Westbury 'F' class freight, was taken by the signalman at Marston West signal box. My fireman was Ron Lear. The photo was given to me the following week.

the working of various parts through models and diagrams, made better footplate men, but, before the war, cleaners relied on picking things up from watching the crews and asking questions. Of course, poor advice was often difficult to eradicate and many young firemen carried bad practices throughout their careers. It was one thing to instruct someone on the theory of it all but if you asked a driver whereabouts on a journey he shut off steam or where he applied the brakes to stop at a certain point, he wouldn't be able to tell you despite the fact that he'd been doing it for twenty years or more – it was all done by instinct and feel. A trip on the footplate wouldn't necessarily leave a novice much wiser and he certainly wouldn't even be aware of the finer points of train running. In order to become a first class driver, a man had to live on the footplate until he became part of it and run over routes until he knew them in every detail. Even in the worst fog (our worst enemy) I always knew exactly where I was, and that's how it should be.

There was seldom any conversation between the driver and fireman of an express as both were engaged in their own duties and the noise made conversation difficult anyway. Both men became a part of the locomotive and a glance at each other with a 'thumbs up' sign confirmed all was well. Both fingers held horizontally indicated a signal was on, and pointing downwards indicated it was off. A wave from the driver with an open hand held downwards indicated he wanted more coal on, and flapping his hand meant open the firebox door. Pointing at the damper controls meant alteration, and a glance at the fire-irons was all that was needed for the fireman to realise he was expected to make use of them. Communication between some men was uncanny and reflected in efficient running.

The footplate could be a lonely place, especially at night when both men could spend hour upon hour with eyes and ears strained while peering through the spectacle glasses as the signals passed by. This was particularly demanding at busy junctions when any misreading of signals could all too easily result in tragedy. Winter often brought loathsome conditions with fog and falling snow and temperatures well below freezing. In a real pea-souper, distances were difficult to judge and often the ticking sound of the vacuum pump was the only real indication of speed. An exploding detonator beneath the wheels would indicate a distant at caution, an amber light being displayed by a fog signalman holding a hand lamp at the foot of the signal post.

Stopping at a red signal could also be a problem as the spectacle was sometimes blanked out by snow or misted with condensation. Sometimes the post was too high for visibility in the fog and I have had to climb the ladder to see if the arm was at danger. When a delay was expected, I took the bucket up the post and hung it over the signal arm with a couple of spanners inside, then when the arm was lowered, the sound of the bucket crashing to the ground was enough to alert us.

In dense fogs, freight and some passenger trains were cancelled under what was known as the 'Black scheme', otherwise the railways would have come to a complete standstill. Fewer trains were cancelled under the 'Grey scheme', whilst the 'White scheme' meant running was back to normal.

Gale-force winds often whipped across the footplate, blowing small coal off the shovel before it reached the firebox. It was not as cosy inside the cab as it appeared, and there were no windscreen wipers to remove snow from the spectacle glasses. We just had to open the windows every so often and wipe them clear with cotton waste. In those conditions, leaning our heads outside the cab to catch the signals, unavoidably resulted in eyes full of ice-cold snow, taut facial skin and bronchial pains from breathing in the cold air. The cab was a cold draughty place and I remember how some of the older drivers used to pack their overalls with newspapers to keep warm. Preparation, often in a bitter wind, was gruelling too. The fire-irons could be so cold that your fingers stung with pain, and trying to hold an oil feeder in a frozen hand while removing corks from a side rod oil well with the other could be extremely miserable. Injectors, to fill the boiler, frequently became frozen and had to be thawed out by dowsing a bundle of cotton waste in paraffin, setting light to it on a shovel and holding it under the body of the injector until the water ran. Alternatively, we sometimes took a shovel of hot coal from the firebox.

Working a freight train in these conditions could be like a game of Russian roulette as many of the water columns would freeze up. It was important to know that there was water at the next station, and I remember one occasion during the bad winter of 1962-3 confidently leaving Didcot with a 63XX in the knowledge that the water columns at Newbury were still working. However, in the time it took to get there, they had all frozen and we still had half a tank of water, so with the assurance of the Whitchurch signalman that water was available there, I took the chance and set off again. As we descended the bank to Whitchurch, the injector blew out — the tank was empty. Relieved, we stopped at the column with half a boiler of water showing in the gauge glass, and I struggled off through the snow to the water column, only to find the valve had seized and the column itself was frozen solid. There was nothing left but to uncouple the engine, berth it inside the goods shed and throw out the fire. This was a lousy job but at least the signalman had a tender full of coal to rob for his stove!

During the early 1960s, the most prestigious job at Didcot Loco was still the 7.10 a.m. to Paddington, so I felt some degree of pride and achievement when I first had the opportunity of working this train as a driver. I was in No. 2 link at the time but Jim Burridge in No. 1 link had exchanged turns with me and was working my No. 2 link turn, the 9.15 a.m. Moreton Cutting to Taplow.

I booked on duty at 5.50 a.m. to prepare No. 5935 *Norton Hall*, which, as one of the earlier 59XXs, was free-running and steamed like a kettle. Nos. 6983 or 6910 were also used on this turn sometimes. My fireman prepared the bed of the fire using small lumps, the size of coconuts, to a depth of about 18-24 inches, in good time to allow it to burn through gently to a bright red glow. The secret of a good run with the maximum heat when it was needed was to have the fire correct prior to departure.

While the fireman was preparing the fire, I oiled the valve gear, axleboxes, slidebars, piston rods, side rods, etc., and finally filled the lubricator in the cab.

Sadly, it was very noticeable that all the fuss and special treatment given to the loco working the early morning passenger in pre-war years had declined markedly. It was certainly not cleaned or serviced to such a high standard. Having learned my trade from proud enginemen, these things were always at the back of my mind, but we had

No. 4936 running into Paddington on 30th December 1962. This was a particularly bad winter. Everything looked, felt and smelt different, even the track made an unfamiliar sound, all of which gave a different feel to handling an engine. In these conditions we were glad to get in the corner of the cab to shelter from the cold winds. Even so, only a handful of crews wore gloves, but they didn't seem right on the footplate, so those that did were regarded as pansies. Some readers might like to think of their favourite engine in picturesque surroundings on a warm summer's day, but it was all very different working through antisocial hours during the long winter months.

National Railway Museum

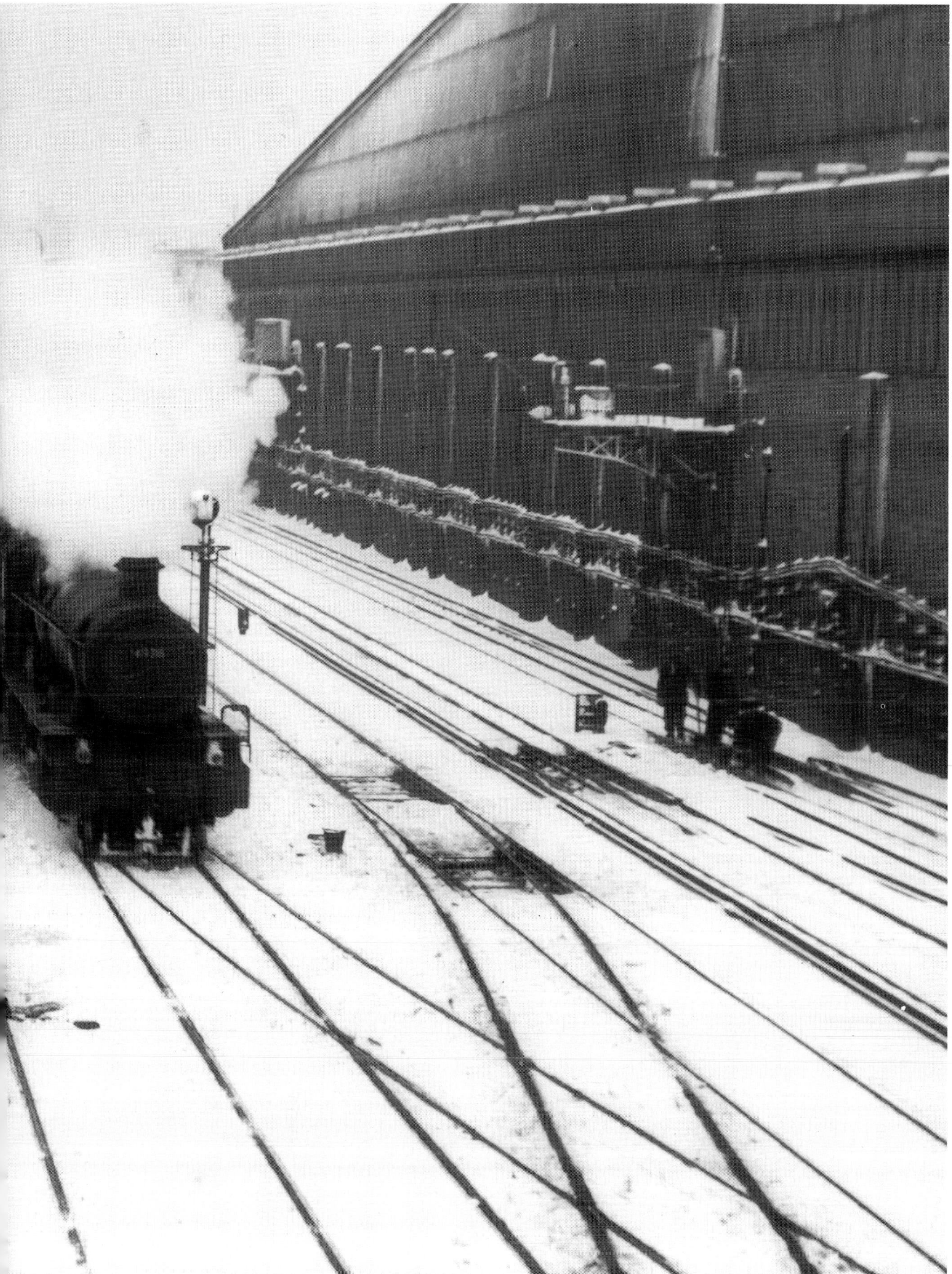

to take the deteriorating standards in our stride and accept them as normal. It was hopeless to try and work against the system and rekindle the old pride in the job.

Some things didn't change, however, and halfway through the preparation of a loco, the footplate came alive. The sound of the blower becoming stronger, hissing safety valves, the purr of an injector filling the boiler, and the coal watering pipe spraying cascades of water over the coal in the tender, even the snap of the brass lids on the oil wells, all contributed to the building anticipation as the time to leave shed, 6.50 a.m., drew nearer. This was all accompanied by the sound of the fireman cracking up lumps of coal with his pick, and sliding his shovel along the platework of the tender floor as he scooped up coal, followed by the sound of the heel of the shovel hitting the ring as each load was skilfully directed through the firehole door.

In a final check, I cast my eyes around 5935 to satisfy myself that all was well. The fireman was happy with his fire and, with the most essential can of fresh tea on the dish over the firebox doors, we were ready to leave. After taking the tender handbrake off, the fireman looked up the shed yard and confirmed we were 'all clear', and, as I gave a sharp tug on the whistle chain over my head, a shrill whistle pierced the calm air. With the reverser in full forward gear and cylinder cocks closed, I lifted the handle of the regulator and we moved off gently towards the shed signal. The purist will say the cylinder cocks should have been open, but this obscured vision so I always kept them closed when coming off shed.

As we rolled up the yard, I opened the nipple of the sight feed lubricator controlling the flow of oil to the regulator valve, then I opened and closed the regulator quickly several times to persuade extra oil towards the valve — a habit I learned to give the regulator easier movement.

When we reached the shed signal, the arm was lowered, the signalman had expected our arrival. We were sent over to the up relief line and I gave two short blasts to indicate that we were clear of the points. When the middle of the three circular discs was pulled off, directing us back onto our train in Platform 7, I eased the engine back towards the station and buffered up onto the coaches. It was 7.00 a.m. after my mate had coupled up, and we had ten minutes before departure to square everything on the footplate, stowing the oil jugs in the toolbox and tightening the nut on one of the injector steam valves that was weeping steam, then sipping tea while the guard did a vacuum brake test. We had ten 8-wheeled coaches totalling 340 tons.

At 7.10 the signal was off, the brakes were off, the last passengers had jumped into the rear coach and slammed the door, and the guard waved his green flag in a cheerful action.

I acknowledged with a short tug on the whistle and, with the reverser in full forward gear, eased the regulator open just enough to start us moving. I could soon feel the weight of the train in tow, and looking ahead through the cab window all the East Junction signals were off as I nicked up the reverser to 45% and opened the regulator further. The sound from the chimney was reassuring, a crisp sharp beat contrasting with the gentle continuing hiss from the safety valves. There was a gentle lurch as the engine took the points near East Junction signal box where we joined the up relief and I nicked the reverser up to 30% and nudged the regulator across into the main valve. By the time we left the outskirts of Didcot, we were travelling at about 35-40 mph and I could tell 5935 was performing well and the momentum of the train allowed me to nick up the reverser to 20% cut-off. We soon reached the 60 mph maximum allowed on the up relief and when we got near to Cholsey, our first stop, I shut off steam, but left the regulator on the jockey valve to keep the oil feeding the valves and pistons. We maintained 60 mph until we passed under the farm bridge some 300 yards from the station, then I made a full brake application, the train pipe needle dropping to zero with the rush of air being sucked into the system, accompanied by the reassuring sound of the brake blocks biting on the wheels of the coaches, turning to a squeal as our speed reduced. I kept a close eye on the vacuum gauge and the train speed, and when our speed dropped to about 30 mph, I opened the large ejector to release the brakes which began to ease as the single line of the Wallingford branch came alongside us, our speed still reducing as we ran through the platform until we came to a stand with the brakes off and the engine just off the ramp at the far end. I had done it — I had successfully employed Paget's technique which I'd admired so much during my time as a fireman in the passenger link.

This pattern was repeated at all the stations to Reading, by which time we had a full load of passengers.

Our next stop was Twyford, then Maidenhead, where we crossed to the up main and ran fast to Paddington. All our skills were necessary now to arrive on time to please our commuter friends, who were on my mind as we sped through Slough at 75-80 mph and saw the time was 8.10 by the Horlicks clock, leaving us 25 minutes to get to Paddington. The usual running time was 21 minutes, the extra four being recovery time in case of lateness, so we were doing alright.

I checked the Scotch Cod Liver Oil clock between West Drayton and Hayes, then the Acton station clock, which became the most important one after the clock in Old Oak Common yard became unreliable. If we had less than four minutes left at Acton, we'd be late arriving at Paddington, whereas six minutes in hand passing Old Oak Common signal box meant the regulator could be shut and we could freewheel to Portobello Junction box where we had to reduce speed to negotiate the scissors crossover by Ranelagh Bridge at 20 mph. If our speed was handled correctly, the signals would change to green and give a clear run to the platform indicator signal at Paddington arrival box. As we rolled into Platform 8, the favourite for the 7.10 a.m., we both felt a glow of pride – the clock over the lawn showed 8.35 a.m. As our satisfied passengers passed by on their way to the underground, we were given cheerful smiles, a nod, the odd 'Well done', and the usual newspapers tossed into the cab. We hadn't let anyone down.

This scene is reminiscent of our arrival at Platform 8 at Paddington with the 7.10 Didcot. The steps in the background led to the Metropolitan line and Platform 13 which I used to reach Ladbrook Grove as a lad on my journey from Didcot to take up lodgings at Barlby Gardens.
National Railway Museum

Half-coffin shaped creatures with no elegance were now creeping in, to replace the dignified steam locomotives. The romance of steam was giving way to remote control, and sickly diesel fumes. Instead of the freshness of an open cab, there was the stuffy atmosphere of the closed diesel 'footplate'.

On one occasion, a 70XX diesel hydraulic was booked to me on the 7.10 a.m. Didcot to Paddington, in place of 4–6–0 No. 6910 which failed due to vacuum brake deficiency. I had only been passed out on diesel traction the previous week so it was fortunate that I was able to handle her.

The trip was uneventful but the 70XX was certainly not capable of hauling 375 tons on a stopping train to Reading, and then fast to Paddington in the same way as the steam loco could have done. When returning to Didcot at the end of my shift, I was asked my opinion of diesels, and had no hesitation in saying that 6910 would have done a far better job, and I would have much preferred her!

Of course diesels improved, but, despite that, the remaining years convinced me that driving them was like driving a tram. There was no personal reaction from a human hand – no real contact. I found automation dull and still believe it kills initiative. The skills that went into handling a steam locomotive were evaporating, and robots were taking their place – load regulators, field diverts, traction motors, and super chargers.

The changes came in too fast for me and the traction and the new staff structure was reason enough to accept redundancy. My own discipline, instilled by strict schooling and accepted railway training, was being hard pressed. I was unable to accept the lack of respect for senior drivers shown by junior grades, which was becoming all too common, and would not have been tolerated in my younger days when we were classed as 'railway servants', but the unions did not like this, so it was changed to railway*men*.

It was inevitable that sooner or later all new recruits to the railway would be approached by a trades union official and asked to join. A young lad, anxious to please and without enough confidence to risk being unpopular with his workmates by refusing, would often be talked into becoming a 'brother' whether he believed in it or not. It was a terrible stigma not to conform.

After being canvassed by a local union activist, I became a member of the Associated Society of Locomotive Enginemen and Firemen, and I even became a member of the Labour Party. Innocence was my failing. I believed in the preachings of older men, but was soon to learn that Didcot Loco Depot had a particularly militant union branch which was dominated by a close group of activists who had been at school together. My father referred to them as 'the kidney'. If anyone had the courage to disagree with them, life could become very difficult. It was a sort of 'Mafia'.

There were national agreements between the HQ of the union and the management which we had very little influence over at local level, but local agreements became such a maze of do's and dont's that sometimes it could be difficult to know what to do for the best. The shedmaster tended to let the activists have their own way for the sake of peace and quiet, and eventually, in the 1940s, the union representatives drafted out the rosters for each driver's and fireman's duty instead of the management. A union rep once told me he had 'more power than the management'. If any local agreement was broken by the men, there was no redress from the union, but if the management broke an agreement, there was always a fuss.

Such attitudes caused divisions and the simplest of tasks could become an issue. One example which lingers in my mind was an agreement that all footplate crews would collect engine tools and take them to the stores, because headlamps, shovels, smokeplates, etc., tended to become scattered all over the site and led to a shortage of tools on the engines. One Sunday morning, when the loco foreman asked a young fireman to collect the headlamps scattered around, he objected and insisted it was not a duty for his grade, an attitude encouraged by the activists who had been provoking the young lad. In the end, he went to the foreman with tears streaming down his cheeks. The situation was too much for him; who should he obey, the loco foreman or his colleagues with whom he had to associate so closely? Realising the lad's awkward situation, the foreman gave in and told him to await further orders. It was the 'in thing' to be anti-management at that time, even when a local agreement was in place. However, the matter didn't rest there, for the activists contacted the local shop steward and

Didcot station in the 1960s.
National Railway Museum

a letter of complaint was forwarded to the Loco Superintendent about the bullying behaviour of the loco foreman towards the young fireman. It was completely untrue, but, regardless of denials, the damage had been done.

It was easier to go with the tide and it was a brave man who stood up for what he felt was right. One driver I particularly recall was a well-liked and respected union branch official who for years had collected weekly contributions from union members towards sickness allowance. Led by his conscience, he refused to join one strike and took the brave step of crossing the picket line on his own. When the strike was over, he was 'sent to Coventry' by his mates and expelled from the union which he'd been in all his working life. Everyone was afraid to be seen speaking to him, even though they wanted to, afraid the union would make life awkward for them. Shortly afterwards he was taken ill and I found him collapsed in a toilet. It was all too much for him and within months he died.

Union officials were elected by the local branch at Annual General Meetings. These were always poorly attended, left-wing agitators greatly outnumbering the few moderates who troubled to attend. Eventually, only the agitators remained to make vital decisions on behalf of the branch. I feel certain that the agitators did much harm to the industry during the postwar years with the introduction of restrictive practices and falling standards of work.

One of the most chaotic areas were agreements on manning, particularly who did what? A staunch union man would only carry out the work he was expected to do and no more — it never occurred to him to be flexible. It was almost considered a crime for engine crews to coal an engine, drop a fire or light up, and, when no maintenance staff were available, train crews couldn't help because the work was outside their grade. Strictly speaking, they were correct, of course, but following this to the letter was of little help to the smooth running of a railway.

I could go on at length about stupidity, inflexibility and just plain stubbornness of the militants within the union, but I think I've made my point. At times they made life thoroughly unpleasant and that is the one and only aspect of my railway career which has left a bad taste in my mouth.

With the unions becoming stronger, it is doubtful if the youngsters coming on would have put up with the 'thump around the ears' that we accepted as a matter of course when we stepped out of line!

There were also changes on the footplate, with the single manning of locos, and guards having no van of their own. Militant unions demanded that redundant firemen should be carried as a second man, and also given the chance to drive.

The pride and skill in handling a steam loco was no longer there. We could transform a cold, useless lump of steel into a creature of pulsating life, at her core a white-hot glowing mass of

Foxhall bridge over the main line at Didcot. This is where it all began while engine spotting from school, and appropriately also where my story ends. *Cty. Brian Lingham*

energy, capable of hauling a 450 ton passenger train, with 700 on board, at speeds of up to 100 miles an hour. That was some achievement, compared with today's trains, which, although faster, carry less passengers and aren't so demanding on their crew. I had a sense of belonging, feeling relaxed and confident, completely at home, whether I was on the footplate or just near to a steam engine. This affinity was something quite personal, and had nothing to do with any 'conditioning' I may have received during the years I had seen my father come home with coal dust still ringing his eyes, grimy hands, and bringing with him that old familiar smell of oily, work-stained overalls.

On 2nd May 1977, when I was fifty-five years old, I left the railway. It was a sad moment, but looking back, I have no regrets, and I know that I did the right thing.

There was one moment which gave me great pleasure, when I handed over my keys to Clive Rooker, a very able young second man. I left an old GWR button on the keyring — it was one from my uniform when I was a messenger lad. Clive had great promise and the right qualities to succeed. He had a quiet confident manner, and the sense of dedication and tradition which was becoming all too rare. He became a driver himself and it was nice to think that a part of me was still going to travel the old familiar routes, but since then he has been appointed train crew supervisor, which came as no surprise to me. I had recognised his abilities and wish him every success.

Today I still think back to a scene I experienced when walking back from Appleford one dusky winter's evening during the last months of steam. I wasn't thinking of anything in particular, but when I reached Foxhall Bridge, there was a shrill, ear-piercing whistle as a 'Castle'-hauled express sped beneath on its way towards London. The orange glow from the open firebox doors flashed across the surroundings, illuminating the heavy billowing exhaust which hung over the roofs of the coaches as they rattled by and disappeared into the enveloping darkness ahead, leaving a silence in their wake. Unexpectedly, my emotions were aroused, but while the smoke still lingered over the station canopies, it wasn't the problems of restrictive union practices, falling standards or fading pride which flashed through my mind, but fond boyhood memories of the 'Cheltenham Flyer', and the bond and cameraderie among real railwaymen who'd shown such kindness to me as a raw recruit. It struck me that what I had just witnessed was symbolic — a sunset of steam. The emptiness that followed still hurts.

BRITISH RAILWAYS WESTERN REGION

𝕭ernard 𝕷uke 𝕭arlow

This CERTIFICATE records that on the occasion of your retirement the British Railways Western Region Management desire to congratulate you upon the completion of **40** years' employment, and wish you happiness in your retirement.

They also wish to place on record their high appreciation of the service which you have rendered to the railways and to the public during that period.

Divisional Manager

2nd 𝕸ay 19 **77**

General Manager

West Curve Yard

Foxhall Junction Signal Box

APPENDIX 1
TRACK PLAN OF DIDCOT STATION

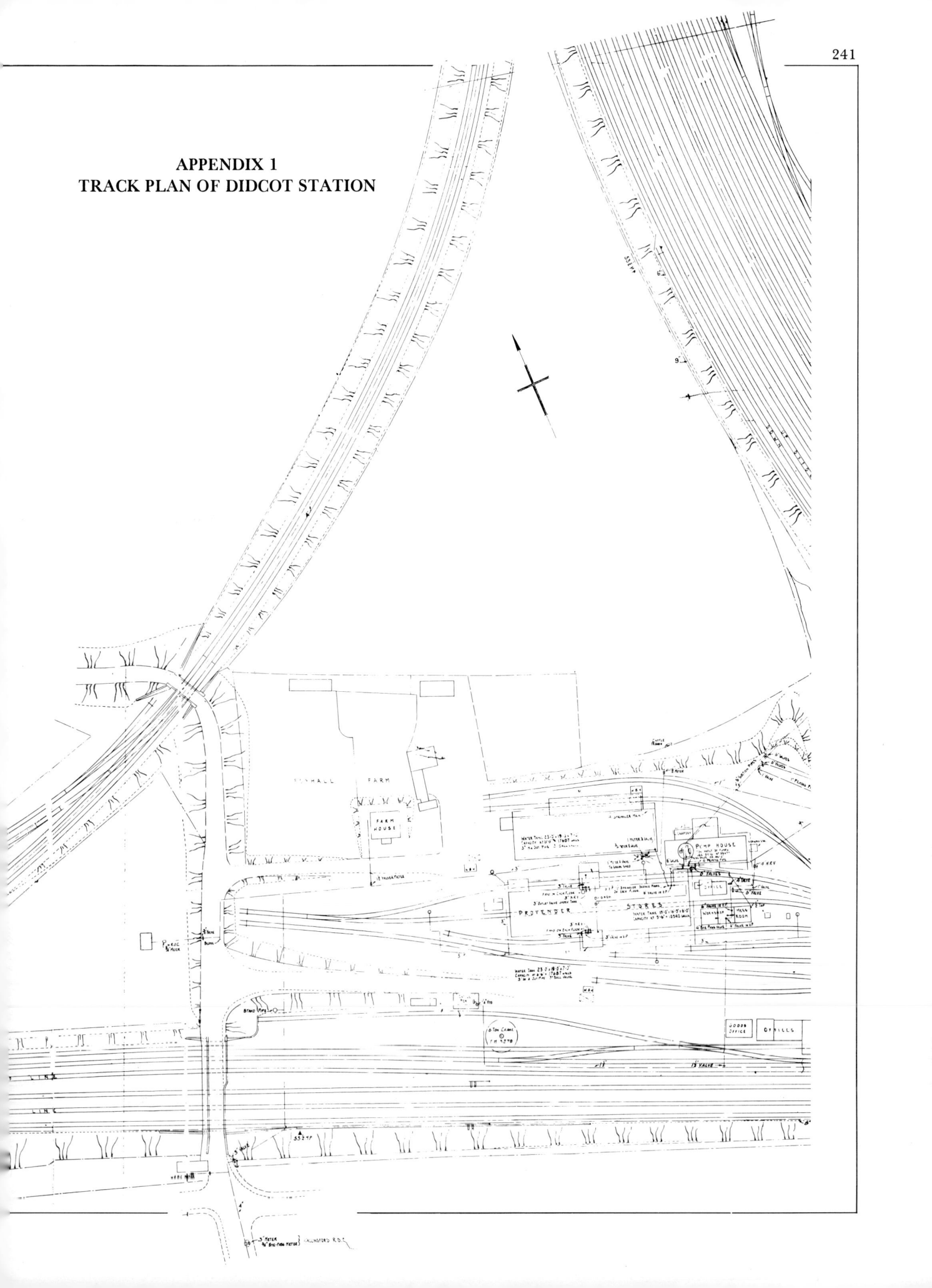

Dardanelles Sidings

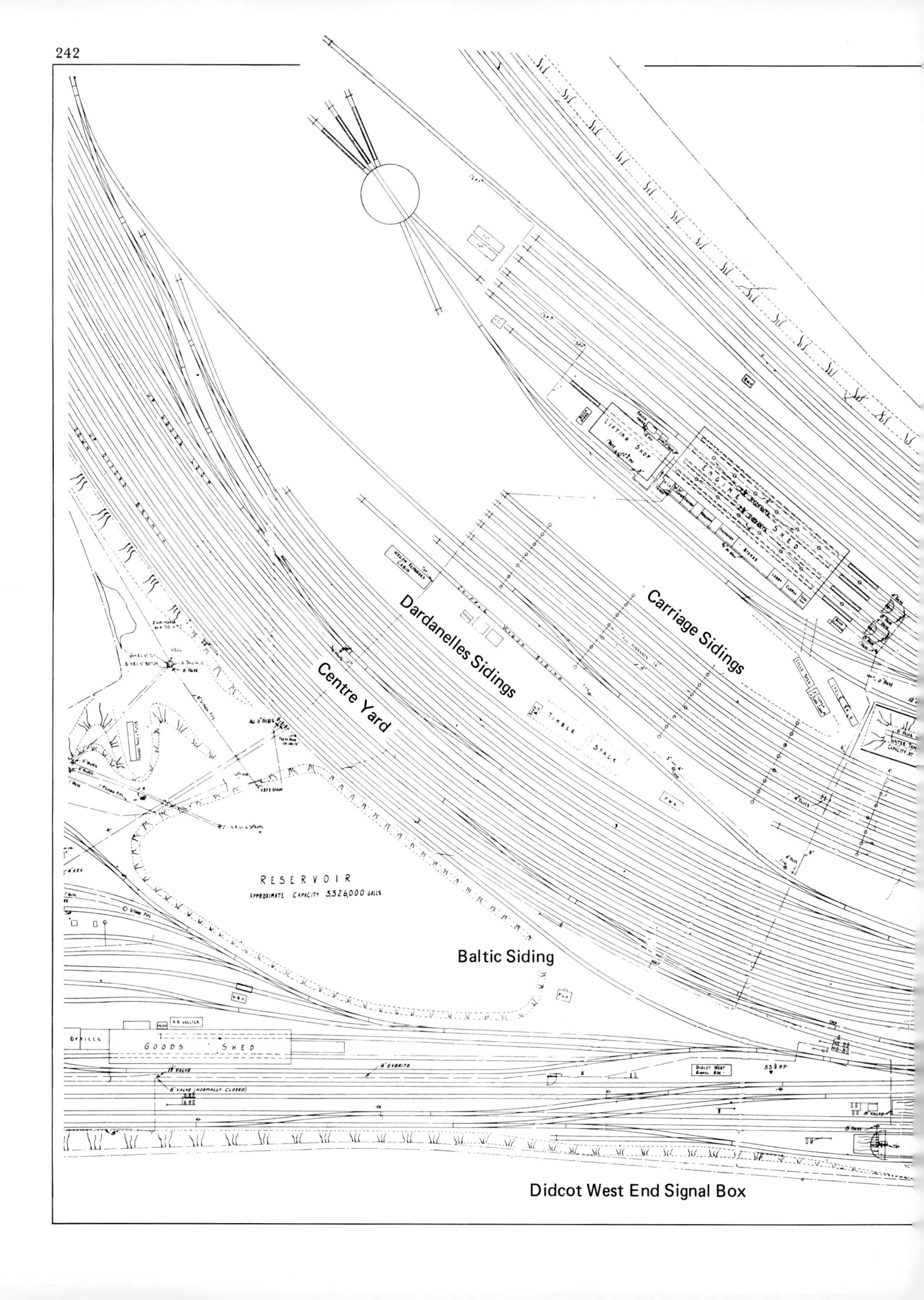

Carriage Sidings

Centre Yard

RESERVOIR
APPROXIMATE CAPACITY 3,326,000 GALLS.

Baltic Siding

GOODS SHED

Didcot West End Signal Box

B. R. W. R.
DIDCOT

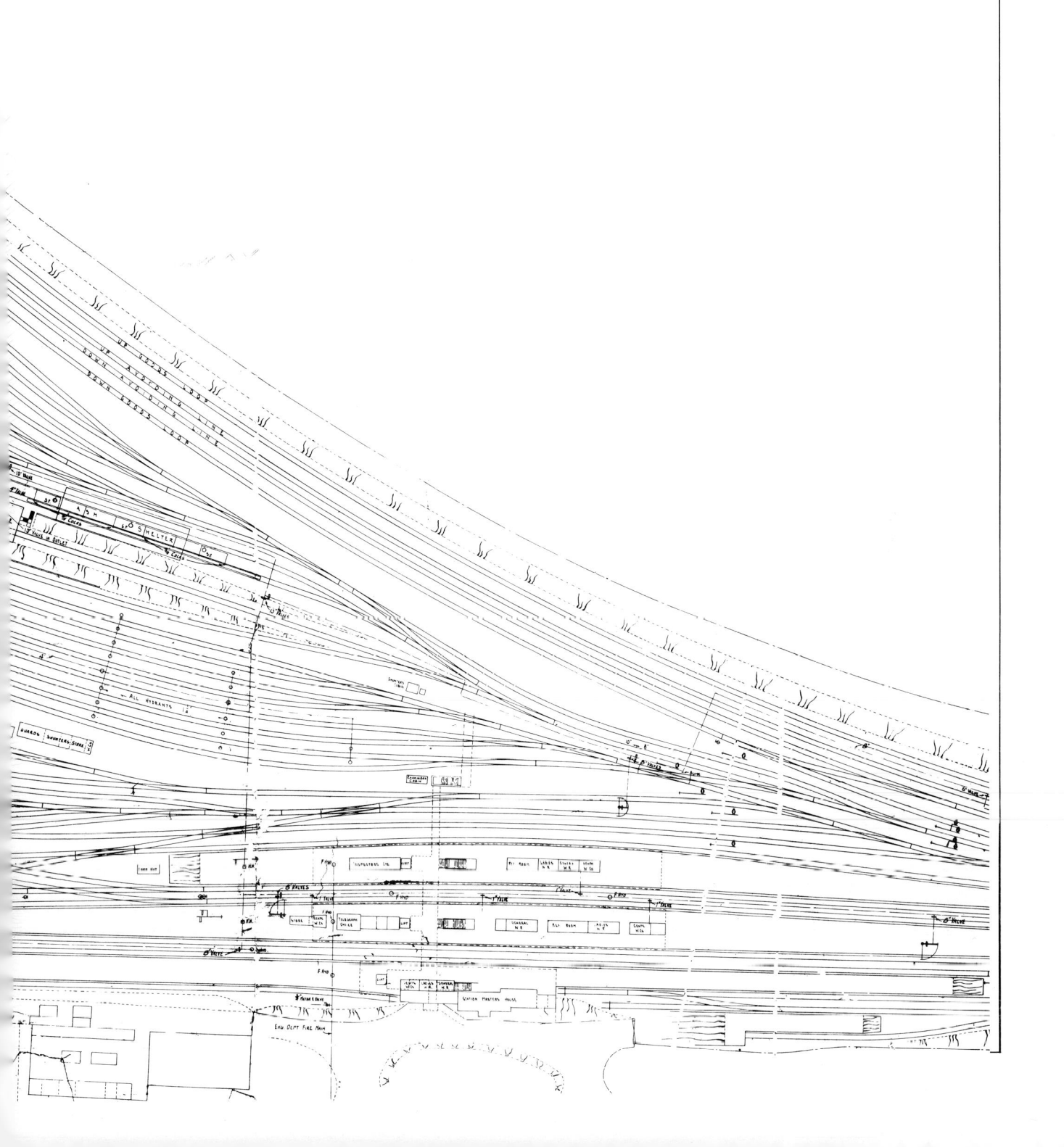

Didcot East Junction Signal Box

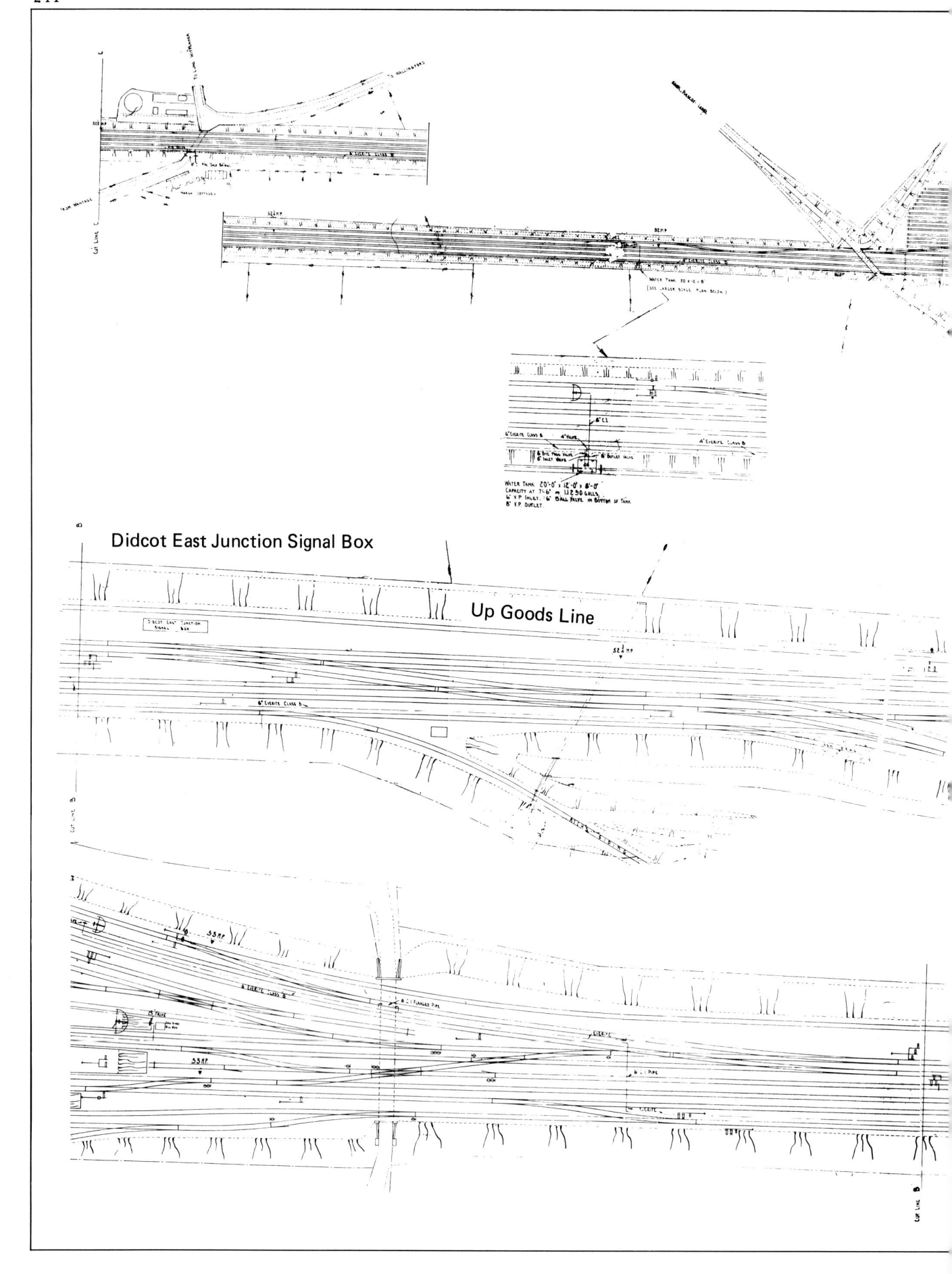

Up Goods Line

MORETON SIDINGS

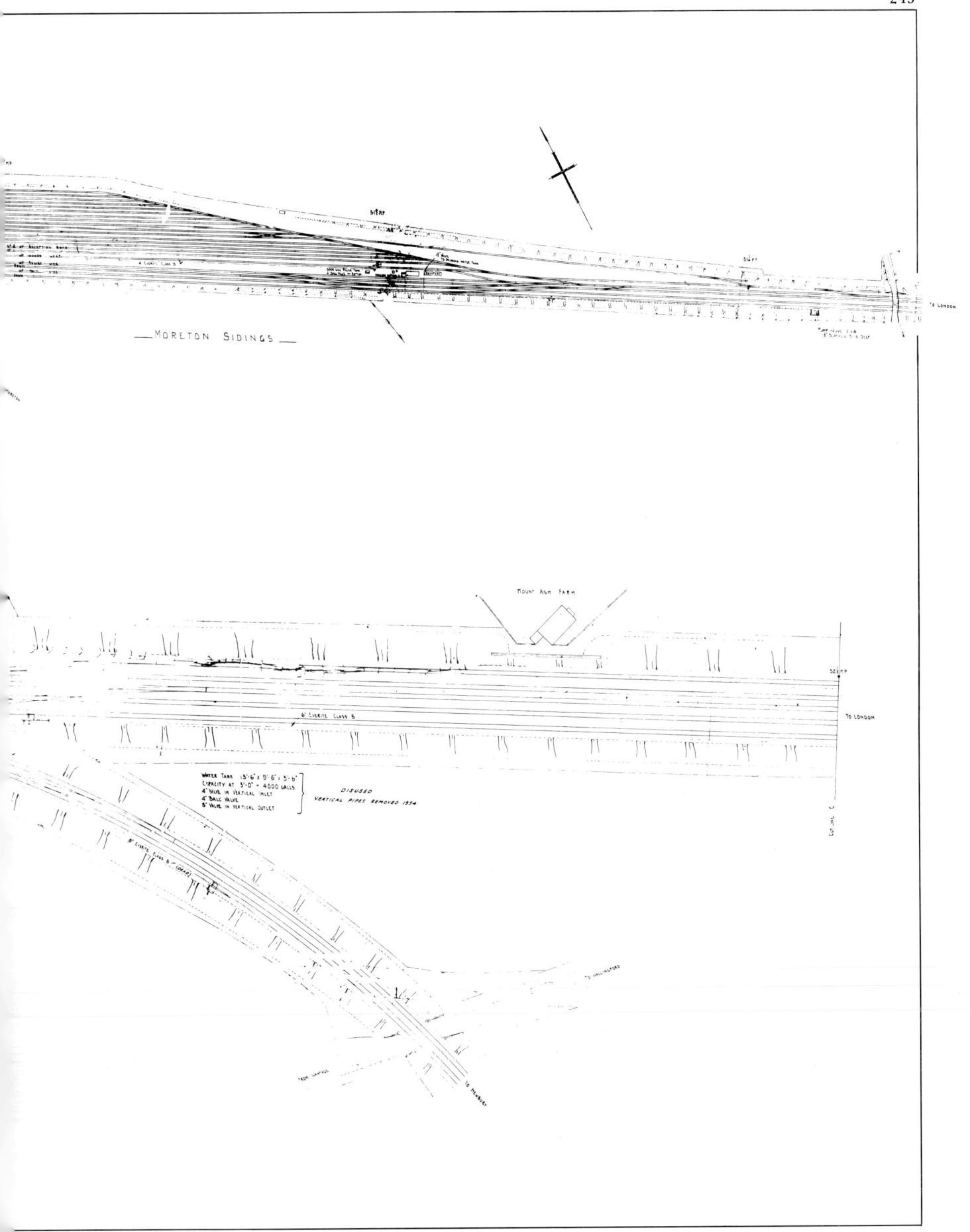

MOUNT ASH FARM

TO LONDON

WATER TANK 13'-6" x 9'-6" x 5'-6"
CAPACITY AT 5'-0" = 4000 GALLS
4" VALVE IN VERTICAL INLET
4" BALL VALVE
5" VALVE IN VERTICAL OUTLET

DISUSED
VERTICAL PIPES REMOVED 1954

TO NEWBURY

NOS. 1 TO 12 ARE VEHICLE SHEDS

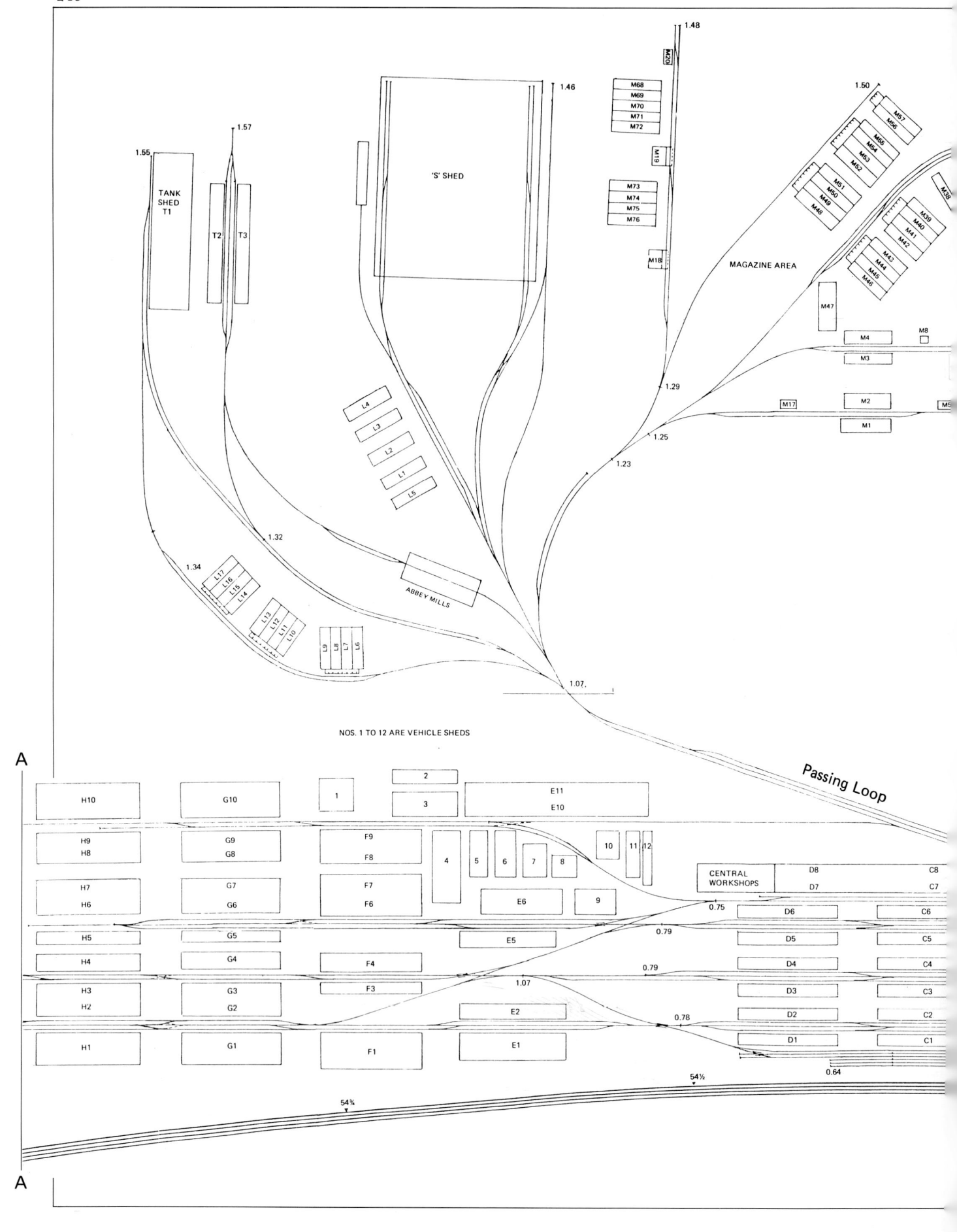

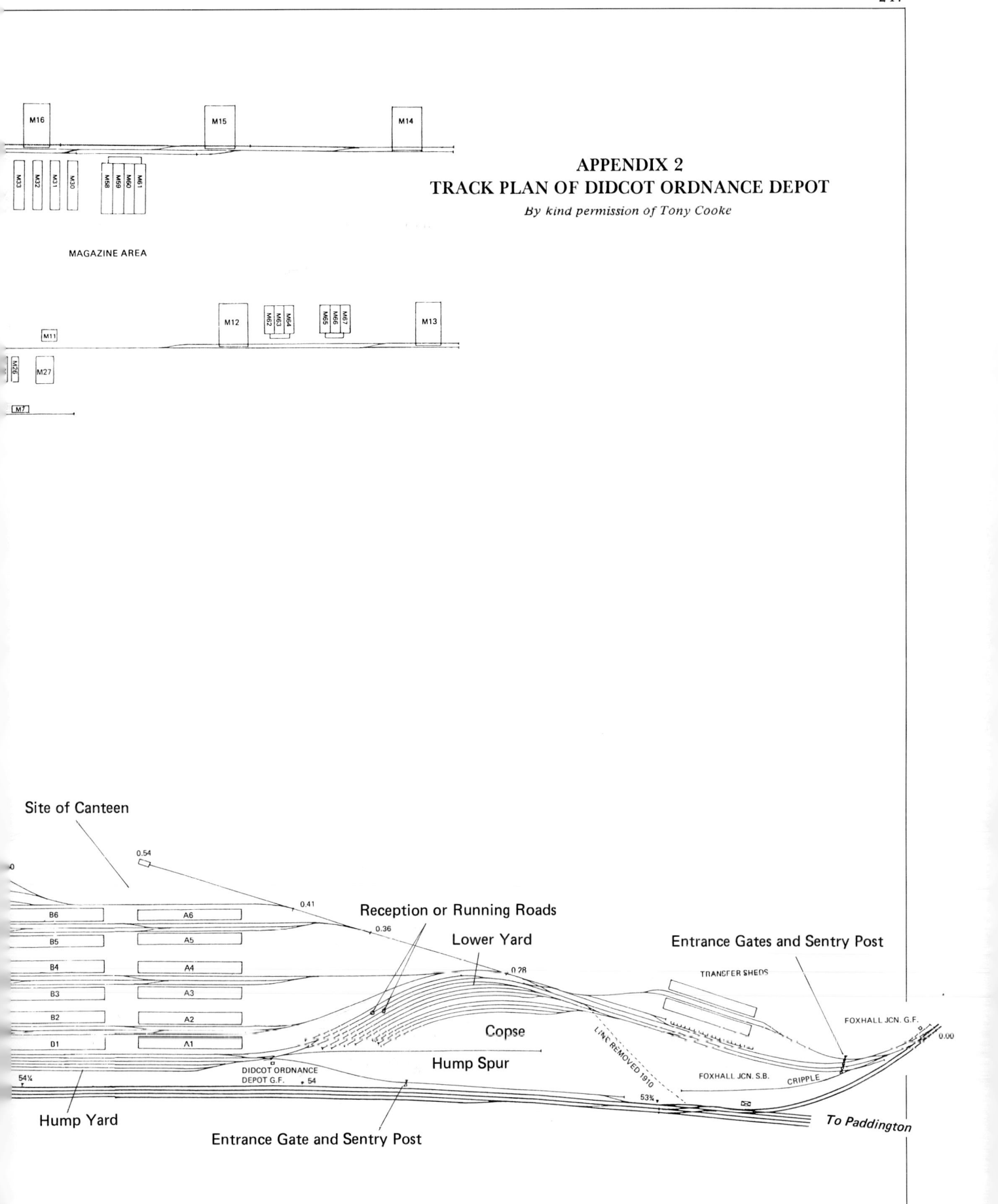

APPENDIX 2
TRACK PLAN OF DIDCOT ORDNANCE DEPOT
By kind permission of Tony Cooke

MAGAZINE AREA

Site of Canteen
Reception or Running Roads
Lower Yard
Entrance Gates and Sentry Post
TRANSFER SHEDS
Copse
Hump Spur
LINE REMOVED 1910
FOXHALL JCN. G.F.
DIDCOT ORDNANCE DEPOT G.F.
FOXHALL JCN. S.B.
CRIPPLE
Hump Yard
Entrance Gate and Sentry Post
To Paddington

R.A.F. M.U. MILTON

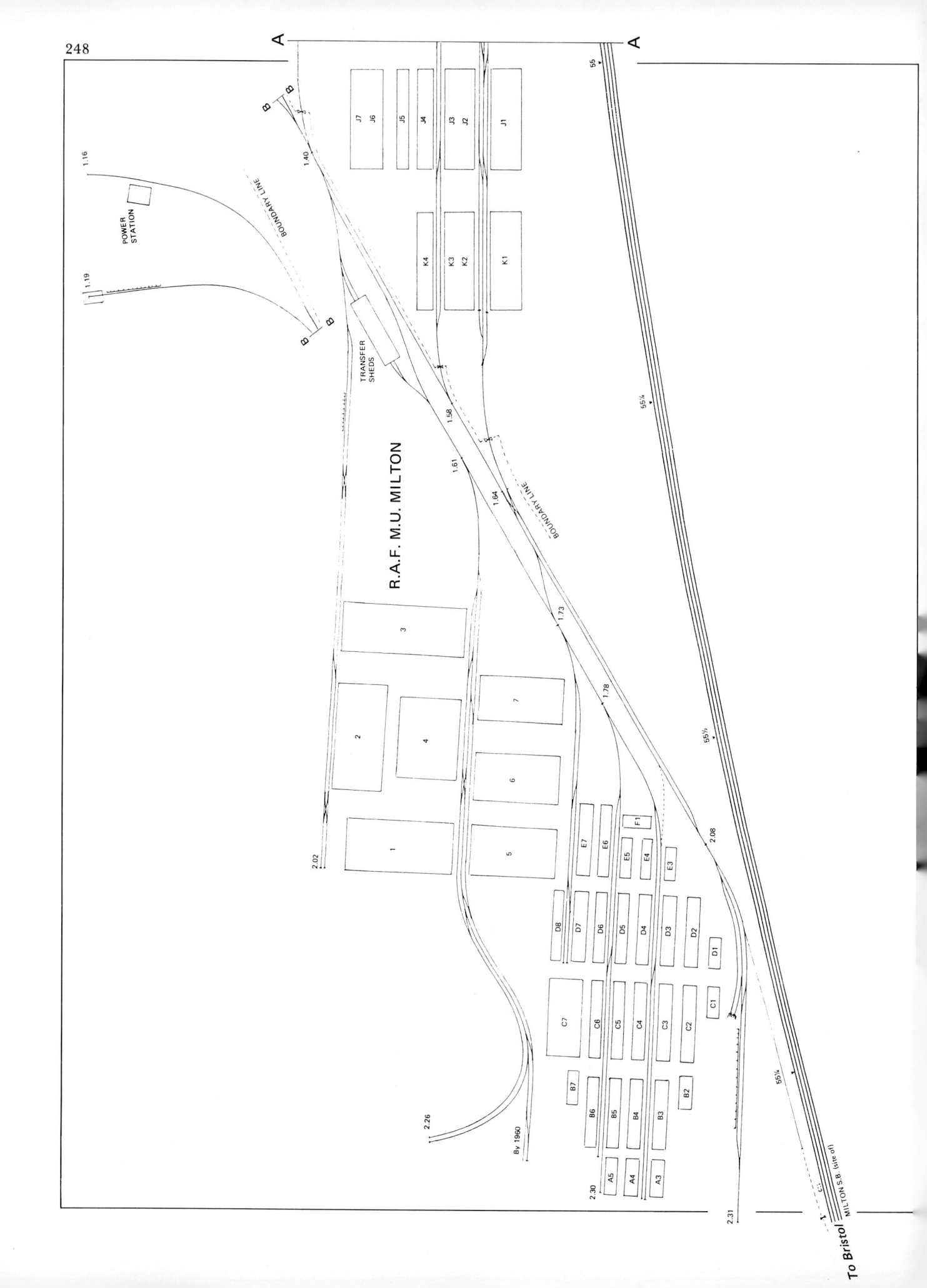

To Bristol

MILTON S.B. (site of)

APPENDIX 3
ENGINE & ENGINEMEN'S TURNS
Weekdays, Winter Service 1951/2

Details of the turns carried out by Didcot shed were issued on printed sheets, largely for the use of supervisory staff. These contained the times and the points between which each train was worked by men and/or locomotives from the shed, together with an indication of the class of train being conveyed. As can be seen, the turn numbers contain a number of gaps, many of which would be allocated to extra engines and staff in the summer season, or when additional work was allocated to Didcot by the diagramming section.

The passenger turns for engines were allocated numbers up to 39, whilst those men whose work was entirely or mainly on the one Didcot engine were given the same number. Other men's turns on passenger duties were numbered from 40 to 64. Sunday duties for engines and men were numbered between 65 and 79.

Freight engine and men's turns were allocated numbers between 80 and 131, men only up to 162, and inter-divisional men's turns onwards from 601.

PASSENGER ENGINE TURNS

TURN No.1   **One Hall Class**
L.E.	D	6.0	Shed	Didcot	6.10
Passr		7.4	Didcot	Birmingham	9.42
Passr		10.10	Birmingham	Wolverhampton	10.42
Prcls		2/0	Wolverhampton	Didcot	7/27
L.E.		7/35	Didcot	Shed	7/45

TURN No.2   **One Hall Class**
L.E.	D	9.15	Shed	Didcot	9.20
Passr		9.48	Didcot	Oxford	10.5
Passr		11.15	Oxford	Didcot	11.38
L.E.		11.45	Didcot	Shed	11.50
L.E.		12/30	Shed	Didcot	12/35
Passr		1/15	Didcot	Swindon	2/14
Passr		5/45	Swindon	Didcot	6/39
Shtg		8/0	Didcot Passenger Pilot		11/15
L.E.		11/20	Didcot	Shed	11/30

TURN No.3   **One Hall Class**
L.E.	D	7.15	Shed	Didcot	7.20
Passr		8.0	Didcot	Paddington	9.30
E.C.	SX	10.25	Paddington	Old Oak Yard	11.10
		(Coaches, 7.0 Weston-super-Mare)			
E.C.	SO	10.0	Paddington	Old Oak Yard	11.0
		(Coaches, 8.48 Henley-on-Thames)			
E.C.	D	12/30	Old Oak Yard	Paddington	1/0
		(Coaches, 1/30 Paddington)			
Passr		2/28	Paddington	Didcot	5/44
L.E.		5/50	Didcot	Shed	6/0

TURNS Nos. 4 to 9
Not used

TURN No.10   **One 43XX Class**
L.E.	D	5/20	Shed	Didcot	5/25
Passr		5/55	Didcot	Winchester	8/16
L.E.		8/30	Winchester	Shed	8/45
L.E.		6.50	Shed	Winchester	6.55
Passr		7.15	Winchester	Reading	9.8
L.E.		9.20	Reading	RDG Shed	9.30
L.E.		5/0	Shed	Reading	5/10
Passr		5/35	Reading	Didcot	6/16
L.E.		6/35	Didcot	Shed	6/40

TURN No.11   **One 43XX Class**
L.E.	Sun	7/50	Shed	Didcot	7/55
Shtg		8/0	Didcot Passenger Pilot		5/0
Passr	MO	5/20	Didcot	Reading	5/55
Passr		7/25	Reading	Didcot	8/0
L.E.		8/10	Didcot	Shed	8/15
L.E.	SX	4/15	Shed	Didcot	4/20
Shtg		4/20	Didcot Passenger Pilot (N/D)		5/0
Passr	MSX	5/20	Didcot	Reading	5/55
Passr		7/25	Reading	Didcot	8/0
L.E.		8/10	Didcot	Shed	8/15
Shtg	SO	5/0	Didcot Passenger Pilot		4.20
L.E.	Sun	4.25	Didcot	Shed	4.30

TURNS Nos. 12 to 14
Not used

TURN No.15   **One 57XX Class**
L.E.	D	4.0	Shed	Didcot	4.10
Asst		4.20	Didcot	Newbury	5.9
Shtg		6.0	Newbury Passenger Pilot		9.30
Shtg		9.30	Newbury Town Yard Pilot (N/D)		6.0
Passr		6.45	Newbury	Didcot	7.28
L.E.		7.40	Didcot	Shed	7.45

TURNS Nos. 16 to 19
Not used

TURN No.20   **One Hall Class**
L.E.	D	6.0	Shed	Didcot	6.10
Passr		7.10	Didcot	Paddington	8.35
Attd		9.45	Paddington	Didcot	10.59
		(9.45 Paddington	Hereford)		
Passr		12/5	Didcot	Oxford	12/32
L.E.		12/35	Oxford	OXF Shed	12/40
L.E.	SX	3/30	OXF Shed	Oxford	3/35
E.C.		3/50	Oxford	Morris Cowley	4/2
Passr	MO	5/27	Morris Cowley	Banbury	6/27
Passr	MSX	5/12	Morris Cowley	Banbury	6/12
Fish	SX	8/15	Banbury	Swindon	10/1
		(1/10 Hull	Swindon)		
L.E.		10/20	Swindon	DID Shed	11/0
L.E.	SO	5/0	OXF Shed	Oxford	5/10
Passr		5/25	Oxford	Banbury	6/12
L.E.		6/15	Banbury	BAN Shed	6/25
L.E.	Sun	2.30	BAN Shed	Banbury	2.40
Frt		3.0	Banbury	Didcot W. Curve	4.23
L.E.		4.30	Didcot W. Crve	Shed	5.0

NOTES

The times are portrayed in the traditional CME's format, with 0.00 indicating a.m., and 0/00 indicating p.m. The suffix 'n' denotes noon, and 'm' midnight.

L.E.	Light Engine	D	Daily
Passr	Passenger Train	M	Monday
Pcls	Parcels Train	T	Tuesday
Frt	Freight Train	W	Wednesday
Fish	Fish Train	Th	Thursday
F.Es	Empty Fish Train	F	Friday
E & V	Engine & Van	S	Saturday
Attd	Attached to an Engine and Train	Sun	Sunday
E.C.	Empty Coach Stock	O	(day) only
Shtng	Shunting	X	(day) excepted
A.P.	Travel as Passengers	RR	Runs when Required

250

TURN No.21		One Hall Class		
L.E.	SO	12/30 Shed	Didcot	12/35
Passr		1/15 Didcot	Reading	1/50
Passr		2/35 Reading	Paddington	3/54
L.E.		4/15 Paddington	Ranelagh Bridge	4/20
L.E.		5/10 Ranelagh Br.	Paddington	5/15
Passr		5/35 Paddington	Didcot	7/8
L.E.		7/20 Didcot	Shed	7/25
L.E.		7/55 Shed	Didcot	8/0
Passr		8/27 Didcot	Reading	9/5
Passr		10/50 Reading	Didcot	11/24
L.E.		11/50 Didcot	Shed	11/55

TURNS Nos. 22 to 29
Not used

TURN No. 30		One 22XX Class		
L.E.	D	7.15 Shed	Didcot	7.20
Passr		7.39 Didcot	Southampton	10.48
Passr		11.45 Southampton	Didcot	2/38
L.E.		2/45 Didcot	Shed	2/50

TURN No. 31		One 22XX Class		
L.E.	D	8.30 Shed	Didcot	8.35
Shtng		8.35 West End Pilot		12/5
Passr		12/42 Didcot	Southampton	3/45
Passr		4/56 Southampton	Didcot	8/0
L.E.		8/20 Didcot	Shed	8/25

TURN No. 32		One 22XX Class		
L.E.	D	10.20 Shed	Didcot	10.25
Passr		10.50 Didcot	Eastleigh	1/41
Passr		2/22 Eastleigh	Didcot	5/4
L.E.		5/10 Didcot	Shed	5/15

TURNS Nos. 33 and 34
Not used

TURN No. 35		One 61XX Class		
L.E.	SO	1/30 Shed	Didcot	1/40
Passr		2/0 Didcot	Newbury	2/45
Passr		5/35 Newbury	Didcot	6/15
L.E.		6/30 Didcot	Shed	6/35

TURNS Nos. 36 to 39
Not used

PASSENGER ENGINEMEN'S TURNS

TURN No. 20
On Duty 5.0
Prepare Engine (Turn No.20) and work:

L.E.	D	6.0 Shed	Didcot	6.10
Passr		7.10 Didcot	Paddington	8.35
Attd		9.45 Paddington	Didcot	10.59

Relieved by DID Turn No.54 at 11.0; Off duty 1/0 - Hours 8.0

TURN No. 21
On Duty 11.30
Prepare Engine (Turn No. 21) and work:

L.E.	SO	12/30 Shed	Didcot	12/35
Passr		1/15 Didcot	Reading	1/50
Passr		2/35 Reading	Paddington	3/54
L.E.		4/15 Paddington	Ranelagh Bridge	4/20
L.E.		5/10 Ranelagh Br.	Paddington	5/15
Passr		5/35 Paddington	Didcot	7/8

Relieved by DID Turn No. 21A at 7/10; Off Duty 7/35 - Hours 8.5

TURN No. 21A
On Duty 5/30
Prepare engine for 7/55 Parcels
Relieve DID Turn No.21 at 7/10, turn engine at shed, and work:

Passr	SO	8/27 Didcot	Reading	9/5
Passr		10/50 Reading	Didcot	11/24
L.E.		11/50 Didcot	Shed	11/55

Off Duty 1.30 - Hours 8.0

TURN No. 30
On Duty 7.0
Take to engine prepared by DID Turn No.31 (Engine Turn No.30) and work:

L.E.	D	7.15 Shed	Didcot	7.20
Passr		7.39 Didcot	Southampton	10.48
Passr		11.45 Southampton	Didcot	2/38
L.E.		2/45 Didcot	Shed	2/50

Off Duty 3/5 - Hours 8.5

TURN No. 31
On Duty 5.30
Prepare Engine (Turn No. 30) for DID Turn No. 30
Prepare Engine (Turn No.31) and work:

L.E.	D	8.30 Shed	Didcot	8.35
Shtng		8.35 West End Pilot		12/5

Relieved by DID Turn No. 31A at 12/35. Off Duty 1/30 - Hours 8.0

TURN No. 31A
On Duty 12/20
Relieve DID Turn No. 31 at 12/35 and work:

Passr	D	12/42 Didcot	Southampton	3/45
Passr		4/56 Southampton	Didcot	8/0
L.E.		8/20 Didcot	Shed	8/25

Off Duty 8/40 - Hours 8.20

TURN No. 32
On Duty 9.35
Prepare Engine (Turn No.32) and work:

L.E.	D	10.20 Shed	Didcot	10.25
Passr		10.50 Didcot	Eastleigh	1/41
Passr		2/22 Eastleigh	Didcot	5/4
L.E.		5/10 Didcot	Shed	5/15

Off Duty 5/35 - Hours 8.0

TURN No. 35
On Duty 12/45
Prepare Engine (Turn No. 35) and work:

L.E.	SO	1/30 Shed	Didcot	1/40
Passr		2/0 Didcot	Newbury	2/45
Passr		5/35 Newbury	Didcot	6/15
L.E.		6/30 Didcot	Shed	6/35

Off Duty 8/45 - Hours 8.0

TURN No. 40
On Duty 3.15
Prepare Engine (Turn No. 15) and work:

L.E.	D	4.0 Shed	Didcot	4.5
Asst		4.20 Didcot	Newbury	5.9

Change footplates with Newbury Turn No. 1A (MO) at 6.30 and No. 1C (MX) at 5.30 , and work:

Passr		6.45 Newbury		7.28

Relieved by DID Turn No. 146 at 7.30
Prepare Engine (Turn No. 2) and work:

L.E.		9.15 Shed	Didcot	9.20
Passr		9.48 Didcot	Oxford	10.5

Relieved by DID Turn No. 48 at 10.5; travel as passengers

A.P.		10.35 Oxford	Didcot	11.0

Off Duty 11.15 - Hours 8.0

TURN No. 41
Not used

251

TURN No.42
On duty 6.15
Prepare Engine (Turn No. 3) and work:
| L.E. | D | 7.15 Shed | Didcot | 7.20 |
| Passr | | 8.0 Didcot | Reading | 8.38 |

Relieved by RDG Turn No. 109 at 8.40
Relieve WES Turn No.101 on 7.15 Trowbridge and work:
L.E.		9.25 Reading	RDG Shed	9.35
L.E.		10.30 RDG Shed	Reading	10.40
Passr		10.50 Reading	Didcot	11.25
L.E.		11.30 Didcot	Shed	11.35

Off duty 2/15 - Hours 8.0

TURN NO. 43
On Duty 1.25
Relieve DID Turn No. 70 at 1.40 and work:
| Shtng | MO | 1.40 Didcot Passenger Pilot | | 4.45 |

Relieved by DID Turn No.44 at 4.45
Off Duty 9.25 - Hours 8.0

TURN No. 44
On Duty 4.30
Relieve DID Turn No.43 at 4.45 (MO), Turn No.47 at 4.50 (MX) and work:
| Shtng | D | 4.0 Didcot Passenger Pilot | | 12/20 |

Relieved by DID Turn No. 45 at 12/20
Off Duty 12/40 - Hours 8.10

TURN No. 45
On Duty 12/5
Relieve DID Turn No.44 at 12/20 and work:
Shtng	D	12/20 Didcot Passenger Pilot		5/0
Passr	SX	5/20 Didcot	Reading	5/55
Passr		7/25 Reading	Didcot	8/0
L.E.		8/10 Didcot	Shed	8/15
Shtng	SO	5/0 Didcot Passenger Pilot		8/45

Relieved by DID Turn No. 47 at 8/45
Off Duty 8/30 (SX) - Hours 8.25; 9/0 (SO) - Hours 8.55

TURN No. 46
On Duty 3/30
Prepare Engine (Turn No.11) and work:
| L.E. | SX | 4/15 Shed | Didcot | 4/20 |
| Shtng | | 4/20 Didcot Passenger Pilot | | 8/55 |

Relieved by DID Turn No. 47 at 8/55
Relieve DID Turn No.101B at 9/5 and work:
| Shtng | | 9/5 Didcot Centre Yard | | 11/5 |

Relieved by DID Turn No. 101C at 11/5
Off Duty 11/30 - Hours 8.0

TURN No. 47
On Duty 8/40 (SX), 8/30 (SO)
Relieve DID Turn No. 46 at 8/55 (SX), Turn No. 45 at 8/45 (SO), and work:
| Shtng | SX | 8/55 Didcot Passenger Pilot | | 4.50 |

Relieved by DID Turn No 44 at 4.50 (MX)
| Shtng | SO | 8/45 Didcot Passenger Pilot | | 4.20 |
| L.E. | Sun | 4.25 Didcot | Shed | 4.30 |

Off Duty 5.5 (MX) - Hours 8.25; 4.45 (Sun) - Hours 8.15

TURN No. 48
On Duty 5.0
Prepare Engine (Turn No.1) and work:
| L.E. | D | 6.0 Shed | Didcot | 6.10 |
| Passr | | 7.4 Didcot | Banbury | 8.23 |

Relieved by BAN Turn No. 51 at 8.25
Relieve BAN Spare Set at 8.45 at Banbury station and work:
| Passr | | 9.5 Banbury | Oxford | 9.51 |

Relieved by RDG Turn No. 105 at 9.55
Relieve DID Turn No.40 at 10.5 and work:
| Passr | | 11.15 Oxford | Didcot | 11.38 |
| L.E. | | 11.45 Didcot | Shed | 11.50 |

Off Duty 1/0 - Hours 8.0

TURN No. 49
On Duty 7/55
Prepare BAN engine off 6/25 Oxford and work:
L.E.	D	8/55 Shed	Didcot	9/0
Pcls		9/40 Didcot	Banbury	11/20
L.E.		11/30 Banbury	BAN Shed	11/40

Relieve WPN Turn No. 178 on 11/45 Birmingham to Paddington Parcels (MSX), and work:
| Pcls | MX | 1.35 Banbury | Didcot | 2.47 |

Relieved by DID Turn No.53 at 2.47

Prepare engine at Banbury shed (Suns) and work
L.E.	Sun	2.40 BAN Shed	Banbury	2.50
Frt		3.0 Banbury	Didcot W. Curve	4.23
L.E,		4.30 Didcot W. Crv.	Shed	4.40

Off Duty 3.55 (Tu - Sat) - Hours 8.0; 4.55 (Sun) - Hours 9.0

TURN No. 50
On Duty 12/0 noon
Take to engine off 11.15 Oxford (Turn No.2) and work:
L.E.	D	12/30 Shed	Didcot	12/35
Passr		1/15 Didcot	Swindon	2/14
Passr		5/45 Swindon	Didcot	6/39

Relieved by DID Turn No.55 at 6/40
Off Duty 8/0 - Hours 8.0

TURN No. 51
On Duty 3.15
Prepare Engine (Turn No. 90) and work:
L.E.	D	4.0 Shed	Didcot	4.5
Frt		4.20 Didcot	Newbury	5.9
Frt		7.52 Newbury	Woodhay	8.4

Change footplates with Winchester Turn No. 2 on 7.15 Winchester, and work:
| Passr | | 8.16 Woodhay | Reading | 9.8 |
| L.E. | | 9.20 Reading | RDG Shed | 9.30 |

Then travel as passengers
| A.P. | | 10.6 Reading | Didcot | 10.27 |

Off Duty 11.15 - Hours 8.0

TURN No. 52
On Duty 2/10
Prepare engine (ex-Winchester) and work:
L.E.	D	2/55 Shed	Didcot	3/0
Passr		3/35 Didcot	Winchester	5/31
L.E.		5/50 Winchester	Win. Shed	5/55

Travel as passengers
| A.P. | | 6/31 Winchester Cty | Reading | 8/9 |
| A.P. | | 8/26 Reading | Didcot | 8/49 |

Off Duty 10/10 - Hours 8.0

TURN No. 53
On Duty 6.30 (MO), 2.35 (MX)
Travel as passengers (MO)
| A.P. | MO | 8.0 Didcot | Reading | 8.38 |

Relieve RDG turn No.131 at 9.30 and work as below

Relieve DID turn No. 49 at 2.47 (MX) and work:
| Pcls | MX | 3.0 Didcot | Paddington | 4.50 |
| L.E. | | 5.20 Paddington | OOC Shed | 5.50 |

Travel as passengers
| A.P. | | 7.50 Paddington | Reading | 9.30 |

Relieve OOC Turn No. 103 at 9.40 and work
| Passr | D | 9.45 Reading | Didcot | 10.22 |
| L.E. | MO | 10.30 Didcot | Shed | 10.35 |

Relieved by DID Turn No. 54 (MX) at 10.22
Off Duty 2/30 (MO) - Hours 8.0; 10.45 (MX) - Hours 8.10

TURN No. 54
On Duty 7.30
Relieve OOC Turn No. 352 on 5.33 Paddington Parcels at 7.45
and work:
Passr	D	7.50 Didcot	Oxford	8.23
L.E.		8.40 Oxford	OXF Shed	8.50

Travel as passengers
A.P.		9.13 Oxford	Didcot	9.28

Relieve DID Turn No. 53 (MX) at 10.22 and work:
L.E.	MX	10.35 Didcot	Shed	10.40

Relieve DID Turn No. 20 at 11.0 and work:
Passr	D	12/5 Didcot	Oxford	12/32
L.E.		12/35 Oxford	OXF Shed	12/40

Travel as passengers
A.P.		1/25 Oxford	Didcot	1/49

Off Duty 3/30 - Hours 8.0

TURN No. 55
On Duty 2/0
Prepare Reading engine and work:
L.E.	D	3/0 Shed	Didcot	3/5
Shtg		3/5 Didcot Station Pilot		6/30

Relieved by RDG Turn No. 112 at 6/30
Relieve DID Turn No.50 at 6/40 and work
Shtg		6/40 Didcot Passenger Pilot		9/40

Relieved by DID Turn No. 56 at 9/40
Off Duty 10/0 - Hours 8.0

TURN No. 56
On Duty 4/35
Prepare engine and work:
L.E.	D	5/20 Shed	Didcot	5/25
Passr	SX	5/55 Didcot	Upton	6/1
Passr	SO	5/55 Didcot	Compton	6/12

Change footplates with Winchester (SR) Turn No.3 on the 12/45
Winchester freight and work:
Frt	SX	6/4 Upton	Didcot	6/15
L.E.		6/35 Didcot	Shed	6/40
Frt	SO	6/12 Compton	Didcot	6/35
L.E.		7/10 Didcot	Shed	7/15

Relieve DID turn No. 55 at 9/40 at station and work:
Shtg	D	9/40 Didcot Passenger Pilot		11/15
L.E.		11/20 Didcot	Shed	11/30

Off Duty 12.35 - Hours 8.0

TURN No. 57
On Duty 7.59
Relieve OOC Turn No. 369 at 8.14 and work:
Passr	D	8.45 Didcot	Oxford	9.11
L.E.		9.20 Oxford	OXF Shed	9.25

Prepare engine for 12/52 Oxford to Wolverhampton
Relieve OXF Turn No. 106 on 8.18 Wolverhampton at 12/37
and work:
Passr		1/25 Oxford	Reading	2/41
L.E.		2/45 Reading	RDG Shed	3/0

Take to engine prepared by RDG Turn No.71A and work:
L.E.		3/25 RDG Shed	Reading	3/35
Passr		3/45 Reading	Didcot	4/22
L.E.		4/30 Didcot	Shed	4/35

Off Duty 4/50 - Hours 8.31

TURN No. 58
On Duty 8.19
Travel as passengers
A.P.	SX	8.34 Didcot	Paddington	9.48

Prepare engine at Old Oak shed for Neyland fish empties and
work:
L.E.		12/30 OOC Shed	Old Oak Yard	12/38
F.Es.		12/45 Old Oak	Swindon	2/48

Relieved by SDN Turn No. 141. Travel as passengers
A.P.		4/20 Swindon	Didcot	4/52

Off Duty 5/12 - Hours 8.53

TURN No. 59
On Duty 10.35
Travel as passengers
A.P.	SO	10.54 Didcot	Paddington	12/21

Prepare engine at Old Oak shed for Neyland fish empties and
work:
L.E.		1/45 OOC Shed	Old Oak Yard	1/50
F.Es.		2/2 Old Oak Yard	Swindon	4/10

Relieved by Swindon Turn No. 141. Travel as passengers
A.P.		4/20 Swindon	Didcot	4/52

Off Duty 6/35 - Hours 8.0

TURNS Nos. 60 to 64
Not used

FREIGHT ENGINE TURNS

TURN No. 80   Two 43XX Class
L.E.	MO	1.55 Shed	Didcot	2.10
Frt		2.25 Didcot	Oxley Sdgs	11.56
L.E.		0/00 Oxley Sdgs	STB Shed	0/00
L.E.	M	1.55 Shed	Didcot	2.10
Frt		2.25 Didcot	Kingswinford Jct	7.50
L.E.		0/00 Kingswinford Jc	STB Shed	0/00
L.E.	D	7/15 STB Shed	Lye	7/30
Frt	SX	8/0 Lye	Moreton Cutting	4.33
L.E.		4.45 Moreton Cttg	DID Shed	5.0
Frt	SO	8/0 Lye	Banbury	3.9
L.E.	Sun	3.15 Banbury	BAN Shed	3.25
L.E.	MO	2.45 BAN Shed	Banbury	2.55
Frt		3.0 Banbury	Moreton Cutting	4.27
L.E.		4.40 Moreton Cutting	DID Shed	4.55

TURN No. 81   One Grange Class
(Alternates with TYS 224/1)
L.E.	MWF	11/10 Shed	Didcot W. Curve	11/20
Frt		11/45 Didcot W.Crv	Yarnton	12.20
L.E.	TThS	2.20 Yarnton	Hinksey	2.50
Frt		3.55 Hinksey	Bordesley Jct	7.12
L.E.		7.30 Bordesley Jct	TYS Shed	7.45
L.E.		11/5 TYS Shed	Bordesley Jct	11/15
Frt		11/30 Bordesley Jct	Moreton Cutting	4.28
L.E.	WFSun	4.45 Moreton Cttng	DID Shed	5.15

TURNS Nos. 82 to 85
Not used

TURN No. 86   One 61XX Class
L.E.	D	8.0 Shed	Didcot	8.15
Frt	SX	8.30 Didcot	Swindon	1/0
Frt		2/30 Swindon	Didcot W. Curve	6/15
L.E.		6/30 Didcot W. Crv	Shed	6/40
Frt	SO	8.30 Didcot	Swindon	1/34
Frt		2/30 Swindon H'wrth	Didcot W. Curve	7/39
L.E.		7/50 Didcot W. Crv	Shed	8/0

TURNS Nos. 87 to 89
Not used

TURN No. 90   **One 22XX Class**
L.E.	D	4.0 Shed	Didcot	4.5
Frt		4.20 Didcot	Newbury	5.9
Frt		7.52 Newbury	Winchester	11.45
L.E.		11.50 Winchester	Win. Shed	11.55
L.E.		12/25 Win. Shed	Winchester	12/30
Frt	SX	12/35 Winchester	Didcot	6/15
L.E.		6/35 Didcot	Shed	6/40
Frt	SO	12/35 Winchester	Didcot	6/35
L.E.		7/10 Didcot	Shed	7/15

TURNS Nos. 91 and 92
Not used

TURN No. 93   **One 43XX Class**
L.E.	D	8.0 Shed	Didcot	8.5
Frt		8.25 Didcot	Newbury	10.50
Frt		11.40 Newbury	Didcot	2/25
L.E.		2/30 Didcot	Shed	2/40

TURN No. 94
Not used

TURN No. 95   **One 61XX Class**
L.E.	D	9.0 Shed	Didcot	9.5
Frt		9.15 Didcot	Moreton Cutting	9.21
Frt		10.15 Moreton Cttng	Taplow	11.48
L.E.	SO	12/0n Taplow	DID Shed	2/0
L.E.	SX	12/0n Taplow	SLO Shed	12/30
L.E.		7/0 SLO Shed	Slough	7/5
Frt		7/30 Slough	Reading	8/57
L.E.		9/15 Reading	DID Shed	10/15

TURN No. 96   **One 61XX Class**
L.E.	D	10/45 Shed	Didcot	10/50
E&V		10/55 Didcot	Moreton Cutting	11/5
Frt		11.30 Moreton Cttng	Reading W. Jct	12.0
Frt		12.20 Reading W. Jct	Moreton Cutting	12.50
Frt.		3.45 Moreton Cttng	Reading H. Level	4.45
L.E.		5.0 Reading H. Lvl	DID Shed	5.30

TURNS Nos. 97 to 99
Not used

TURN No. 100   **One 94XX Class**
L.E.	MO	5.45 Shed	Moreton Cutting	6.0
Shtg		6.0 Moreton Cutting No.2 Pilot		11/0
L.E.	D	10/45 Shed	Moreton Cutting	11/0
Shtg		11/0 Moreton Cutting No.2 Pilot (24hr)		11/0
L.E.	M-S	11/0 Moreton Cttng	Shed	11/15
L.E.	Sun	6/0 Moreton Cttng	Shed	6/15

TURN No. 101   **One 57XX Class**
L.E.	MO	1.0 Shed	Didcot	1.10
Shtg		1.10 No.2 Centre Yard Pilot		2/0
L.E.	M-F	2/0 Shed	Didcot	2/10
Shtg		2/10 No.2 Centre Yard Pilot (24hrs)		2/0
L.E.	M-F	2/0 Didcot	Shed	2/10
L.E.	SO	9/55 Didcot	Shed	10/0

TURN No. 102   **One 57XX Class**
L.E.	MO	6.0 Shed	Didcot	6.10
Shtg		6.10 No.1 Up Yard Pilot		10/0
L.E.	D	10/0 Shed	Didcot	10/10
Shtg	M-F	10/10 No.1 Up Yard Pilot (24hrs)		10/0
L.E.		10/0 Didcot	Shed	10/5
Shtg	SO	10/10 No.1 Up Yard Pilot		5.55
L.E.	Sun	5.55 Didcot	Shed	6.0

TURN NO. 103   **One 57XX Class**
L.E.	SX	6.45 Shed	Didcot Depot	6.50
Shtg		6.50 Ordnance Pilot		7/20
Frt		7/30 No.1 Gully	Didcot Yard	7/35
Shtg		7/35 Didcot Yard		8/0
L.E.		8/0 Didcot Yard	Shed	8/15
L.E.	SO	6.15 Shed	Didcot Yard	6.30
Shtg		6.30 Didcot Yard		11.25
L.E.		11.30 Didcot Yard	Didcot Depot	11.40
Frt		12/0n Didcot Depot	Didcot Yard	12/10
L.E.		12/20 Didcot Yard	Shed	12/30

TURN No. 104   **One 57XX Class**
L.E.	SX	7.15 Shed	Didcot Depot	7.30
Shtg		7.30 No.3 Gully Pilot		5/0
L.E.		5/5 Didcot Depot	Shed	5/20

TURNS Nos. 105 to 109
Not used

TURN No. 110   **One 94XX Class**
L.E.	D	5.45 Shed	Moreton Cutting	6.0
Shtg		6.0 No.1 Pilot (24hrs)		6.0
L.E.		6.0 Moreton Cttng	Shed	6.15

TURNS Nos. 111 to 114
Not used

TURN No.115   **One 15XX Class**
L.E.	D	2/50 Shed	Didcot	3/0
Frt		3/20 Didcot	Hinksey	3/45
Frt		4/50 Hinksey	Oxford South	4/55
L.E.		5/25 Oxford South	Oxford Exchange	5/35
Frt		6/0 Oxford Exchange	Oxford Lower Yd	6/10
Frt		6/30 Oxford Lower Yd	Hinksey	6/35
Frt		7/5 Hinksey	Didcot	7/30
Frt	RR	8/0 Didcot	Moreton Cutting	8/7
Frt.	RR	8/15 Moreton Cttng	Didcot	8/30
L.E.		8/30 Didcot	Shed	8/40

TURNS Nos. 116 to 119
Not used

TURN No. 120   **One 22XX Class**
L.E.	D	11.15 Shed	Didcot	11.20
Frt		11.30 Didcot	Reading	1/45
Frt		3/50 Reading	Didcot North Jct	5/35
L.E.		5/50 Didcot N. Jct	Shed	6/0

TURNS Nos. 121 to 124
Not used

TURN No.125   **One 2301 Class**
L.E.	D	7.15 Shed		
		To work Ballast Specials as ordered		

TURNS Nos. 126 to 131
Not used

FREIGHT ENGINEMEN'S TURNS

TURN No. 93
On Duty 7.15
Prepare Engine (Turn No. 93) and work:
L.E.	D	8.0	Shed	Didcot	8.5
Frt		8.25	Didcot	Newbury	10.50
Frt		11.40	Newbury	Didcot	2/25
L.E.		2/30	Didcot	Shed	2/40

Off Duty 3/15 - Hours 8.0

TURN No. 95
On Duty 8.15
Prepare Engine (Turn No.95) and work:
L.E.	D	9.0	Shed	Didcot	9.5
Frt		9.15	Didcot	Moreton Cutting	9.21
Frt		10.15	Moreton Cttng	Taplow	11.48
L.E.	SX	12/0n	Taplow	SLO Shed	12/30
L.E.	SO	12/0n	Taplow	DID Shed	2/0

Off Duty 4/15 - Hours 8.0

TURN No. 95A
On Duty 4/40 (SX)
Travel as passengers
A.P.		5/2	Didcot	Slough	5/54

Prepare Engine (Turn No. 95) and work:
L.E.		7/0	SLO Shed	Slough	7/5
Frt		7/30	Slough	Reading	8/57
L.E.		9/15	Reading	DID Shed	10/15

Off Duty 12.40 - Hours 8.0

TURN No. 96
On Duty 10/0
Prepare Engine (Turn No.96) and work:
L.E.	D	10/45	Shed	Didcot	10/50
E&V		10/55	Didcot	Moreton Cutting	11/5
Frt		11/30	Moreton Cttng	Reading W. Jct	12.0m
Frt		12.20	Reading W. Jct	Moreton Cutting	12.50
Frt		3.45	Moreton Cttng	Reading High Lvl	4.45
L.E.		5.0	Reading H.L.	DID Shed	5.30

Off Duty 6.0 - Hours 8.0

TURN No. 100
On Duty 5.0 (MO), 5.30 (MX)
Prepare Engine (Turn No.100, MO), or Relieve DID Turn No.100B at 6.15 (MX), and work:
L.E.	MO	5.45	Shed	Moreton Cutting	6.0
Shtg		6.0	Moreton Cutting No.2 Pilot		12/40
Shtg	MX	6.15	Moreton Cutting No. 2 Pilot		12/40

Relieved by DID Turn No. 135 at 12/40
Off Duty 1/30 - Hours 8.30 (MO), 8.0 (MX)

TURN No. 100A
On Duty 3/20
Relieve DID Turn No.135 at 4/15 and work:
Shtg	D	4/15	Moreton Cutting No.2 Pilot		11/0
L.E.		11/0	Moreton Cttng	Shed	11/15

Off Duty 11/30 (SX) - Hours 8.10; 12.0mn (SO) - Hours 8.40

TURN No. 100B
On Duty 10/0
Prepare Engine (Turn No.100) and work:
L.E.	D	10/45	Shed	Moreton Cuttng	11/0
Shtg		11/0	Moreton Cutting No.2 Pilot		6.15

Relieved by DID Turn No.100 (MX) or 100C (Sun) at 6.15
Off Duty 7/0 - Hours 9.0

TURN No.101
On Duty 12.15 (MO)
Prepare Engine (Turn No.101) and work:
L.E.	MO	1.0	Shed	Didcot	1.10
Shtg		1.10	No.2 Centre Yard Pilot		6.40

Relieved by DID Turn No.101A at 6.40
Off Duty 8.15 - Hours 8.0

TURN No.101A
On Duty 6.25
Relieve DID Turn No.101 (MO) or 101C (MX) and work:
Shtg	SX	6.40	No.2 Centre Yard Pilot		2/0
L.E.		2/0	Didcot	Shed	2/10
Shtg	SO	6.40	No.2 Centre Yard Pilot		1/30

Relieved by DID Turn No.101B at 1/30 (SO)
Off Duty 2/25 - Hours 8.0

TURN No.101B
On Duty 1/15
Prepare Engine (Turn No.101, SX), or Relieve DID Turn No.101A (SO) at 1/30, and work:
L.E.	SX	2/0	Shed	Didcot	2/10
Shtg		2/10	No.2 Centre Yard Pilot		9/5
Shtg	SO	1/30	No.2 Centre Yard Pilot		9/55
L.E.		9/55	Didcot	Shed	10/0

Relieved by DID Turn No.46 at 9/5 (SX)
Off Duty 9/15 (SX) - Hours 8.0; 10/15 (SO) - Hours 9.0

TURN No. 101C
On Duty 10/50 (SX)
Relieve DID Turn No. 46 at 11/5 and work:
Shtg	SX	11/5	No.2 Centre Yard Pilot		6.40

Relieved by DID Turn No.101A (MX) at 6.40
Off Duty 6.50 - Hours 8.0

TURN No. 102
On Duty 5.15 (MO), 4.50 (MX)
Prepare Engine (Turn No.102, MO), or Relieve DID Turn No.102B (MX) at 5.10, and work:
L.E.	MO	6.0	Shed	Didcot	6.10
Shtg		6.10	No.1 Up Yard Pilot		1/0
Shtg	MX	5.10	No.1 Up Yard Pilot		12/45

Relieved by DID Turn No.134 at 1/0 (MO) or 12/45 (MX)
Off Duty 1/15 (MO) - Hours 8.0; 1/0 (MX) - Hours 8.10

TURN No.102A
On Duty 2/15
Relieve DID Turn No.134 at 2/30 and work:
Shtg	D	2/30	No.1 Up Yard Pilot		10/0
L.E.		10/0	Didcot	Shed	10/5

Off Duty 10/20 - Hours 8.5

TURN No. 102B
On Duty 9/15
Prepare Engine (Turn No.102) and work:
L.E.	D	10/0	Shed	Didcot	10/10
Shtg	SX	10/10	No.1 Up Yard Pilot		5.10
Shtg	SO	10/10	No.1 Up Yard Pilot		5.55
L.E.	Sun	5.55	Didcot	Shed	6.0

Relieved by DID Turn No.102 (MX) at 5.10
Off Duty 5.25 (MX) - Hours 8.10; 6.15 (Sun) - Hours 9.0

TURN No. 103
On Duty 6.0 (SX), 5.30 (SO)
Prepare Engine (Turn No.103) and work:
L.E.	SX	6.45	Shed	Didcot Depot	6.50
Shtg		6.50	Ordnance Pilot		1/30
L.E.	SO	6.15	Shed	Didcot Yard	6.30
Shtg		6.30	Didcot Yard		11.25
L.E.		11.30	Didcot Yard	Didcot Depot	11.40
Frt		12/0n	Didcot Depot	Didcot Yard	12/10
L.E.		12/20	Didcot Yard	Shed	12/30

Relieved by DID Turn No.103A at 1/30 (SX)
Off Duty 2/0 (SX) - Hours 8.0; 1/30 (SO) - Hours 8.0

TURN No. 103A
On Duty 1/0 (SX)
Relieve DID Turn No.103 at 1/30 and work:
Shtg	SX	1/30	Ordnance Pilot		7/20
Frt		7/30	No.1 Gully	Didcot Yard	7/35
Shtg		7/35	Didcot Yard		8/0
L.E.		8/0	Didcot Yard	Shed	8/15

Off Duty 9/0 - Hours 8.0

TURN No.104
On Duty 6.30 (SX)
Prepare Engine (Turn No.104) and work:
L.E.	SX	7.15	Shed	Didcot Depot	7.30
Shtg		7.30	No.3 Gully Pilot		1/35

Relieved by DID Turn No.104A at 1/35
Off Duty 2/30 - Hours 8.0

TURN No.104A
On Duty 1/0
Relieve DID Turn No.104 at 1/35 and work:
Shtg	SX	1/55	No.3 Gully Pilot		5/0
L.E.		5/5	Didcot Depot	Shed	5/20

Off Duty 9/0 - Hours 8.0

TURN No.110
On Duty 5.0
Prepare Engine (Turn No.110) and work:
L.E.	D	5.45	Shed	Moreton Cutting	6.0
Shtg		6.0	Moreton Cutting No.1 Pilot		12/10

Relieved by DID Turn No.136 at 12/10
Off duty 1/10 - Hours 8.10

TURN No. 110A
On Duty 3/20
Relieve DID Turn No.136 at 4/15 and work:
Shtg	D	4/15	Moreton Cutting No.1 Pilot		11/15

Relieved by DID Turn No.110B at 11/15
Off Duty 11/55 - Hours 8.35

TURN No.110B
On Duty 10/30
Travel on 10/45 engine from shed for Moreton Cutting,
Relieve DID Turn No.110A at 11/15, and work:
Shtg	D	11/15	Moreton Cutting No.1 Pilot		6.0
L.E.	MX	6.0	Moreton Cttng	Shed	6.15

Off Duty 6/30 - Hours 8.0

TURN No.110E
On Duty 1.0 (MO)
Relieve DID Turn No.110D (Sun) at 1.55 (MO) and work:
Shtg	MO	1.55	Moreton Cutting No.1 Pilot		6.0
L.E.		6.0	Moreton Cttng	Shed	6.15

Off Duty 9.0 - Hours 8.0

TURN No.115
On Duty 7.45
Prepare Engine (Turn No.115) and work:
L.E.	D	8.30	Shed	Didcot Yard	8 40
Frt		9.0	Didcot Yard	Culham	9.10
Frt		11.20	Culham	Didcot	11.30
			Trips as required to Didcot Depot		
L.E.		12/50	Didcot	Shed	1/0

Prepare the engine for DID Turn No.134
Off Duty 3/45 - Hours 8.0

TURN No.120
On Duty 10.30
Prepare Engine (Turn No.120) and work:
L.E.	D	11.15	Shed	Didcot	11.20
Frt		11.30	Didcot	Reading	1/15
Frt		3/50	Reading	Didcot N. Jct	5/35
L.E.		5/50	Didcot N. Jct	Shed	6/0

Off Duty 6/30 - Hours 8.0

TURN No.125
On Duty 6.30
Prepare Engine (Turn No.125) and work:
L.E.	D		7.15	Shed (for Ballast Specials)	

Off Duty 2/30 - Hours 8.0

TURN No.132
On Duty 7.10 (MO), 7.55 (MX)
Prepare Engine (MO) , Relieve SHL Turn No.71 at 8.15 (MX,
on SHL engine), and work:
L.E.	MO	8.10	Shed	Didcot	8.15
L.E.	D	8.15	Didcot	Moreton Cutting	8.30
Frt		8.55	Moreton Cttng	Slough	10.55
L.E.	SX	11.20	Slough	SHL Shed	11.50
L.E.	SO	11.20	Slough	OOC Shed	12/0n

Return as ordered by Control
Off Duty 3/10 (MO) - Hours 8.0; 3/55 (MX) - Hours 8.0

TURN No.133
On Duty 7.45 (MO)
Prepare engine off 10/0 Severn Tunnel Jct to Didcot (SO)
and work:
L.E.	MO	8.45	Shed	Moreton Cutting	9.0
Fr		9.15	Moreton Cttng	Reading New Jct	10.10
L.E.		10.30	Reading New Jct	RDG Shed	10.45

Return as ordered by Control
Off Duty 3/45 - Hours 8.0

TURN No.134
On Duty 12/50 (MO), 12/25 (MX)
Relieve DID Turn No.102 at 1/0 (MO) or 12/45 (MX) and work:
Shtg	MO	1/0	No.1 Up Yard Pilot		2/30
Shtg	MX	12/45	No.1 Up Yard Pilot		2/30

Relieved by DID Turn No.102A at 2/30
Take to Engine (Turn No.115) prepared by DID Turn No.115 and work:
L.E.	D	2/50	Shed	Didcot	3/0
Frt		3/20	Didcot	Hinksey	3/45
Frt		4/50	Hinksey	Oxford South	4/55
L.E.		5/25	Oxford South	Oxford Exchange	5/35
Frt		6/0	Oxford Exchange	Oxford Lower Yd	6/10
Frt		6/30	Oxford Lwr Yd	Hinksey	6/35
Frt		7/5	Hinksey	Didcot	7/30
Frt	RR	8/0	Didcot	Moreton Cutting	8/7
L.E.	RR	8/30	Moreton Cttng	Shed	8/40

Off Duty 8/50 (MO) - Hours 8.0; 8/25 (MX) - Hours 8.0

TURN No.135
On Duty 11.45
Relieve DID Turn No.100 at 12/40 and work:
Shtg	D	12/40	Moreton Cutting No.2 Pilot		4/15

Relieved by DID Turn No.100A at 4/15
Relieve RDG Turn No.112 at 6/16 and work:
L.E.	D	6/25	Didcot	Shed	6/30

Off Duty 7/45 - Hours 8.0

TURN No.136
On Duty 10.15
Relieve Winchester Turn No.1 at 10.30 and work:
L.E.	D	10.30	Didcot	Shed	10.35

Relieve DID Turn No.110 at 12/10 and work:
Shtg	D	12/10	Moreton Cutting No.1 Pilot		4/15

Relieved by DID Turn No.110A at 4/15
Prepare engine for 7/55 Didcot
Off Duty 6/15 - Hours 8.0

TURN No. 137
On Duty 4/45
Prepare engine off 6.25 Cardiff to Moreton Cutting and work:
L.E.	D	5/30	Shed	Moreton Cutting	5/45
Frt		6/15	Moreton Cttng	Southall	8/48
L.E.		9/0	Southall	OOC Shed	9/30

Return as ordered by Control
Off Duty 12.45 - Hours 8.0

255

TURN No.138
DRIVER ONLY - On Duty 7.30
Shtg   SO   7.45 Provender Stores   4/0
Off Duty 4/25 - Hours 8.55

TURN No. 139
On Duty 4/30
Work daily as ordered by HQ Engine Control
Off Duty 12.30 - Hours 8.0

TURNS Nos.140 to 144
Not used

SHED TURNS
No.145 On Duty 6.0   } Shed duties. Syringe
No.146 On Duty 7.15 } axleboxes. Relieve DID
No.147 On Duty 2/0   } Turn No.40 at 7.30 and
No.148 On Duty 10/0 } bring engine to Shed

No.149 On Duty 7.0   }
No.150 On Duty 3/0   } Shed assisting
No.151 On Duty 11/0 }

CONTROL RELIEF TURNS
No.152 On Duty 2.15   Control Turn 2.30
No.153 On Duty 5.15   Control Turn 5.30
No.154 On Duty 7.15   Control Turn 7.30
No.155 On Duty 8.15   Control Turn 8.30
No.156 On Duty 10.15 Control Turn 10.30
No.157 On Duty 1/15   Control Turn 1/30
No.158 On Duty 2/30   Control Turn 2/45
No.159 On Duty 3/15   Control Turn 3/30
No.160 On Duty 4/45   Control Turn 5/0
No.161 On Duty 7/45   Control Turn 8/0
No.162 On Duty 10/45 Control Turn 11/0

TURNS Nos.162 to 600
Not used

INTER-DIVISIONAL FREIGHT ENGINEMEN'S WORKINGS

TURN No.601
On Duty 5.5
Relieve GLO Turn No.601 and work:
Frt   MX   5.37 Didcot   Old Oak Common   9.8
                (11/30 Newport AD Jct)
L.E.   9.30 Old Oak Cmmn   SHL Shed   10.0
Return as ordered by Control
Off Duty 1/5 - Hours 8.0

TURN No.602
On Duty 6.30
Relieve SDN Turn No.610 at 6.50 and work:
Frt   MX   7.12 Didcot Foxhall Old Oak Common   9.57
                (11/0 Rogerstone)
L.E.   10.10 Old Oak Cmmn   OOC Shed   10.20
Return as ordered by Control
Off Duty 2/30 - Hours 8.0

TURN No.603
On Duty 6/10
Relieve BAN Turn No.629 and work:
Frt   SX   6/35 Didcot   Sutton Scotney   9/3
                (3/30 Banbury to Eastleigh)
Change footplates with Eastleigh SR men at Sutton Scotney (or meeting point) and work:
Frt   SX   9/10 Sutton Scotney Didcot N. Jct   11/35
                (8/10 Eastleigh to Banbury)
Relieved by BAN Turn No.633
Off duty 2.40 (MX) - Hours 8.0

TURN No.604
On Duty 5/49
Travel as passengers
A.P.   D   6/4 Didcot   Swindon   6/55
Relieve STJ Turn No.629 and work:
Frt   D   7/50 Swindon   Didcot   8/57
                (2/45 Severn Tunnel Jct)
L.E.   9/5 Didcot   OXF Shed   10/0
Return as ordered by Control
Off Duty 1.49 - Hours 8.0

TURN No.605
On Duty 12.55
Prepare Engine (Turn No.80) and work:
L.E.   MX   1.55 Shed   Didcot   2.10
Frt   2.25 Didcot   Hinksey   2.50
                                     (to Kingswinford)
Relieved by WOS Turn No.613
Prepare engine and work:
L.E.   MX   0.00 OXF Shed   Hinksey   0.00
Frt   5.0 Hinksey   Moreton Cutting   6.15
Then as ordered by Control

L.E.   MO   1.55 Shed   Didcot   2.10
Frt   2.25 Didcot   Banbury   4.21
                                     (to Oxley)
Relieved by BAN Relief Set at 4.31; return as ordered by Control
Off duty 8.55 - Hours 8.0

TURN No.606
On Duty 8.14 (MO), 6.30 (MX)
Travel as passengers (MO)
A.P.   MO   8.29 Didcot   Banbury   9.26

Relieve WES Turn No.613 (MX) and work:
Frt   MX   6.57 Didcot N. Jct   Banbury   7.56
                (1.15 Taunton to Oxley)
Relieved by BAN Turn No.607 (MX)
Prepare engine and work:
L.E.   D   0/00 BAN Shed   Banbury   0/00
Frt   12/15 Banbury   Didcot   2/5
                                     (to Moreton Cutting)
Relieved by DID Turn No.615
Off Duty 4/14 (MO) - Hours 8.0; 2/30 (MX) - Hours 8.0

TURNS Nos. 607 to 609
Not used

TURN No. 610
On Duty 11/40
Relieve BAN Turn No.633 and work:
Frt   D   12.3 Didcot E. Jct   Westbury   2.58
            (10/0 Banbury to Hackney)
Relieved by WES Turn No. 602
Return as ordered by Control
Off Duty 7.40 - Hours 8.0

TURNS Nos. 611 and 612
Not used

TURN No. 613
On Duty 2/10
Prepare engine and work:
L.E.   D   3/10 Shed   Moreton Cutting 3/25
Frt   3/55 Moreton Cttng   Hayes   6/55
L.E.   7/10 Hayes   SHL Shed   7/20
Travel as passengers
A.P.   7/52 Southall   Didcot   10/5
Off Duty 10/25 - Hours 8.15

TURN No.614
On Duty 2/0
Relieve OOC Turn No.603 and work:
Frt   D   2/24 Didcot   Swindon   4/15
            (11.5 Old Oak Common to Rogerstone)
Relieved by SDN Turn No.615
Relieve STJ Turn No.626 and work:
Frt   6/20 Swindon H. Jct   Yarnton   9/5
            (2/25 Severn Tunnel Jct)
L.E.   9/10 Yarnton   OXF Shed   9/30
Travel as passengers
A.P.   10/25 Oxford   Didcot   10/50
Off Duty 11/10 - Hours 9.10

TURN No.615
On Duty 1/45
Relieve DID Turn No.606 and work:
Frt   D   2/3   Didcot   Moreton Cutting 2/10
            (12/15 Banbury)
Frt   4/5   Moreton Cttng   Reading W. Jct   4/45
Return as ordered by Control
Off duty 9/45 - Hours 8.0

TURN No.616
Not used

TURN No.617
On Duty 10/15
Prepare engine and work:
L.E.   D   11/15 Shed   Didcot   11/25
Frt   11/45 Didcot   Yarnton   12.20
Remain with engine, and work:
Frt   3.35 Hinksey   Oxford North   4.0
Relieved by TYS Turn No.625
Return as ordered by Control
Off Duty 6.15 - Hours 8.0

TURN No.618
On Duty 7.15
Prepare engine and work :
L.E.   D   8.0   Shed   Didcot   8.15
Frt   SX   8.30 Didcot   Swindon   1/0
Frt   SO   8.30 Didcot   Swindon   1/34
Relieved by SDN turn No.616
Return as ordered by Control
Off Duty 3/15 - Hours 8.0

TURN No.619
On Duty 5.50 (MX)
Prepare engine off 3/20 Severn Tunnel Jct and work:
L.E.   MX   6.50 Shed   Didcot Yd   7.0
Frt   7.10 Didcot Yd   Old Oak Common   10.3
L.E.   10.8 Old Oak Cmmn   OOC Shed   10.20
Return as ordered by Control
Off Duty 1/50 - Hours 8.0

TURN No.620
On Duty 6/46
Relieve OOC Turn No.362 at 7/6 and work:
L.E.   SX   7/30 Didcot   RDG Shed   8/0
            (Engine for 12.5 Reading to Tyseley Frt)
Relieve RDG Turn No.102 at station at 6/50 (SO) and work:
L.E.   SO   7/0   Didcot   RDG Shed   7/30
            (Engine for 2.40 Reading to Bordesley Frt)
Relieve SLO Turn No.63 (SX) or 68 (SO) at Reading station
at 10/27 and work:
E.C.S. D   10/32 Reading   Triangle Sdgs   10/37
L.E.   10/55 Triangle Sdgs   OXF Shed   11/30
            (Engine off 9/15 Paddington to Oxford)
Return as ordered by Control
Off Duty 2.46 - Hours 8.0

Details kindly supplied by John Copsey

During the war our work was classed as a reserved occupation, so we were issued with National Service identity cards which we carried with us, particularly at establishments like the Ordnance Depot.

APPENDIX 4
ALLOCATION OF LOCOMOTIVES - DIDCOT, 1939 to 1956

JANUARY 1939

4-6-0
Hall   5935 *Norton Hall*

4-4-0
Earl   3206, 3215
Duke   3254 *Cornubia*   3256 *Guinevere*
        3280 *Tregenna*   3283 *Comet*
Bulldog 3377   3408 *Bombay*
        3419   3430 *Inchcape*
        3448 *Kingfisher*

2-4-0
M & SW 1334

0-6-0
2251   2276, 2285
2301   2393, 2395, 2423, 2532, 2533, 2549, 2573

2-6-2T
61XX   6106

0-6-0T
655   1743
850   1925, 2007
2021   2076
2721   2765, 2783, 2787

JANUARY 1940

4-6-0
Hall   5935 *Norton Hall*

4-4-0
Earl   3206, 3215
Duke   3283 *Comet*
Bulldog 3376 *River Plym*   3408 *Bombay*
        3430 *Inchcape*   3448 *Kingfisher*

2-6-0
43XX   6379

2-4-0
M & SW 1334

0-6-0
2251   2202, 2276, 2282, 2289
2301   2532
LMS 2F 3108

2-6-2T
61XX   6106

0-6-0T
655   1742
850   907, 1861
2021   2076
2721   1925, 2007
1854   2765, 2783, 2784, 2787
57XX   3622, 5710, 5735, 5744, 7709

JANUARY 1941

4-6-0
Hall   5935 *Norton Hall*

4-4-0
Earl   3206, 3215
Duke   3283 *Comet*
Bulldog 3376 *River Plym*   3408 *Bombay*
        3448 *Kingfisher*

2-6-0
43XX   4318, 4326, 5397, 6302, 6379

2-4-0
M & SW 1334

0-6-0
2251   2202, 2221, 2227, 2289
2301   2573
LMS 2F 3108, 3485, 3564

2-6-2T
61XX   6106

0-6-0T
655   1742
850   2007
1854   907, 1861
2021   2076
2721   2765, 2783, 2784, 2787, 2790
57XX   3622, 3677, 4601, 5710, 5735, 5744, 7709

JANUARY 1942

4-6-0
Hall   4914 *Cranmore Hall*   5935 *Norton Hall*
        6923 *Croxteth Hall*

4-4-0
Earl   3206, 3215
Duke   3283 *Comet*
Bulldog 3376 *River Plym*   3408 *Bombay*
        3448 *Kingfisher*

2-6-0
43XX   4318, 4326, 5397, 6379

2-4-0
M & SW 1334

0-6-0
2251   2202, 2222, 2276, 2282, 2289
2301   2573
LMS 2F 3108, 3121, 3485, 3564

2-6-2T
61XX   6106

0-6-0T
655   1742
850   2007
1854   907, 1861
2021   2076
2721   2783, 2784, 2787, 2790
57XX   3622, 3677, 4601, 5710, 5735, 5744, 5752, 7709, 7710, 9781

JANUARY 1943

4-6-0
Hall   5935 *Norton Hall*   6923 *Croxteth Hall*

4-4-0
Earl   3206, 3215
Duke   3283 *Comet*
Bulldog 3376 *River Plym*   3408 *Bombay*
        3419   3448 *Kingfisher*

2-6-0
43XX   4318, 4326, 5380, 5397, 6379

2-4-0
M & SW 1334

0-6-0
2251   2202, 2221, 2222, 2227, 2252, 2289
LMS 2F 3108, 3119, 3121, 3485, 3564

2-6-2T
61XX   6106

0-6-0T
655   1742
1854   907, 1861
2721   2783, 2784, 2787, 2790
57XX   3622, 3677, 4601, 5710, 5735, 5744, 5752, 7709, 7710, 9781

JANUARY 1944

4-6-0
Hall   5935 *Norton Hall*   6923 *Croxteth Hall*
        6952 *Kimberley Hall*

4-4-0
Earl   3206, 3215, 3216
Duke   3283 *Comet*
Bulldog 3376 *River Plym*   3396 *Natal Colony*
        3408 *Bombay*   3419
        3448 *Kingfisher*

2-8-0
LMS 8F 8404, 8405, 8406
USA   1689, 1915, 2352, 2377, 2430

2-6-0
43XX   4318, 4326, 5380, 5397, 6359, 6379

2-4-0
M & SW 1334

0-6-0
2251   2226, 2227, 2252
2301   2532
LMS 2F 3108, 3119, 3121, 3485, 3564

0-6-0T
655   1742
1854   907, 1861
2721   2783, 2784, 2787, 2790
57XX   3622, 3677, 4601, 4661, 5710, 5735, 5744, 5752, 7709, 7710, 8738, 9781

JANUARY 1945

4-6-0
Hall   5935 *Norton Hall*   6923 *Croxteth Hall*
        6952 *Kimberley Hall*

4-4-0
Earl   3206, 3215, 3216
Duke   3283 *Comet*
Bulldog 3376 *River Plym*   3396 *Natal Colony*
        3408 *Bombay*   3419
        3448 *Kingfisher*

2-8-0
LMS 8F 8406, 8445
WD   7219

2-6-0
43XX   4318, 4326, 5322, 5330, 5380, 5381, 5397, 6329, 6334, 6359, 6369, 6379

2-4-0
M & SW 1334

0-6-0
2251   2202, 2221, 2222, 2226, 2252
2301   2532
LMS 2F 3108, 3119, 3121, 3564

0-6-0T
655   1742
1854   907, 1861
2721   2783, 2784, 2790
57XX   3622, 3677, 3721, 4601, 4661, 4670, 5710, 5735, 5744, 5752, 7710, 8738, 9722, 9781

JANUARY 1946

4-6-0
Hall   5903 *Keele Hall*   5935 *Norton Hall*
        6923 *Croxteth Hall*   6952 *Kimberley Hall*

4-4-0
Earl   3215, 3216
Duke   3283 *Comet*
Bulldog 3376 *River Plym*   3396 *Natal Colony*
        3408 *Bombay*   3419
        3448 *Kingfisher*

2-8-0
LMS 8F 8406, 8445

2-6-0
43XX   4318, 4326, 5330, 5380, 5381, 5397, 6329, 6359, 6379

2-4-0
M & SW 1334

0-6-0
2251   2202, 2221, 2226, 2227, 2240, 2252

0-6-0T
655   1742
1854   907, 1861
2721   2783, 2784
57XX   3622, 3721, 4601, 4698, 4699, 5710, 5735, 5744, 5752, 7710, 8738, 9722

JANUARY 1947

4-6-0
Hall	5903	*Keele Hall*	5935	*Norton Hall*
	6923	*Croxteth Hall*	6952	*Kimberley Hall*

4-4-0
Earl	9006, 9015		
Duke	9083 *Comet*		
Bulldog	3376 *River Plym*	3396	*Natal Colony*
	3408 *Bombay*	3419	
	3448 *Kingfisher*		

2-8-0
LMS 8F   8445

2-6-0
43XX   4318, 4326, 5330, 5380, 5381, 5397, 6329, 6359, 6379

2-4-0
M & SW   1334

0-6-0
2251   2221, 2227, 2252, 2289
2301   2532

2-8-2T
72XX   7214, 7228, 7252

0-6-0T
1854   907, 1861
2721   2783, 2784
57XX   3622, 3721, 4601, 5710, 5735, 5744, 5752, 7710

JANUARY 1948

4-6-0
Hall	5903	*Keele Hall*	5935	*Norton Hall*
	6923	*Croxteth Hall*	6952	*Kimberley Hall*

4-4-0
Earl	9006, 9015		
Duke	9083 *Comet*		
Bulldog	3376 *River Plym*	3396	*Natal Colony*
	3408 *Bombay*	3448	*Kingfisher*

2-8-0
WD   70843, 79303

2-6-0
43XX   4318, 4326, 5330, 5380, 5381, 5397, 6329, 6359, 6379

2-4-0
M & SW   1334

0-6-0
2251   2202, 2221, 2226, 2240, 2289, 3210, 3211, 3212
2301   2532

2-8-2T
72XX   7214, 7228, 7252

0-6-0T
1854   907, 1861
57XX   3622, 3721, 4601, 5710, 5735, 5744, 5752, 7710

JANUARY 1949

4-6-0
Hall	5903	*Keele Hall*	5935	*Norton Hall*
	6923	*Croxteth Hall*	6952	*Kimberley Hall*

4-4-0
Earl   9015
Bulldog   3419

2-8-0
WD   70843

2-6-0
43XX   4318, 5330, 5380, 5381, 5397, 6359

2-4-0
M & SW   1334

0-6-0
2251   2202, 2221, 2222, 2226, 2240, 2252, 2289, 3210, 3211, 3212
2301   2532, 2579

2-6-2T
61XX   6111, 6112, 6118, 6168

0-6-0T
1854   907, 1861
57XX   3622, 3709, 3721, 4601, 5710, 5735, 5744, 5752, 7710, 7713

JANUARY 1950

4-6-0
Hall	4935	*Ketley Hall*	5903	*Keele Hall*
	5935	*Norton Hall*	6923	*Croxteth Hall*
	6952	*Kimberley Hall*		

4-4-0
Earl   9015

2-8-0
30XX   3024
WD   70843

2-6-0
43XX   4318, 4326, 5330, 5380, 5381, 5397, 6329, 6340, 6359

2-4-0
M & SW   1334

0-6-0
2251   2202, 2221, 2222, 2226, 2240, 2252, 2289, 3210, 3211, 3212
2301   2532, 2579

2-6-2T
61XX   6112, 6118, 6132, 6134

0-6-0T
1854   907, 1861
57XX   3622, 3709, 3721, 4649, 5710, 5735, 5744, 5752, 7710, 7713

JANUARY 1951

4-6-0
Hall	4935 *Ketley Hall*	5903 *Keele Hall*	
	5935 *Norton Hall*	6910 *Gossington Hall*	
	6952 *Kimberley Hall*		

4-4-0
Earl   9015

2-8-0
30XX   3024

2-6-0
43XX   4318, 4326, 5330, 5380, 5381, 5397, 6329, 6340, 6359

2-4-0
M & SW   1334

0-6-0
2251   2202, 2221, 2222, 2226, 2240, 2252, 2289, 3210, 3211, 3212
2301   2532, 2579

2-6-2T
61XX   6112, 6118, 6132, 6134

0-6-0T
1854   907, 1861
57XX   3622, 3709, 3721, 4649, 5735, 5744, 5752, 7710
15XX   1502
94XX   9413, 9417

JANUARY 1952

4-6-0
Hall	4935 *Ketley Hall*	5903 *Keele Hall*	
	5935 *Norton Hall*	6910 *Gossington Hall*	
	6952 *Kimberley Hall*		

4-4-0
Earl   9015

2-8-0
30XX   3024

2-6-0
43XX   4318, 4326, 5330, 5380, 5381, 5397, 6329, 6340, 6359

2-4-0
M & SW   1334

0-6-0
2251   2202, 2221, 2222, 2226, 2240, 2252, 2289, 3210, 3211, 3212
2301   2532

2-6-2T
61XX   6116, 6118, 6134, 6166

0-6-0T
57XX   3622, 3709, 3721, 4649, 5735, 5744, 5752, 7710
15XX   1502
94XX   9413, 9417

JANUARY 1953

4-6-0
Hall	4935 *Ketley Hall*	5903 *Keele Hall*	
	5935 *Norton Hall*	6910 *Gossington Hall*	
	6952 *Kimberley Hall*		

4-4-0
Earl   9015

2-6-0
43XX   4326, 5330, 5380, 5381, 5397, 6329, 6340, 6359

0-6-0
2251   2226, 2240, 2252, 2289, 3210, 3211, 3212
2301   2532

2-6-2T
61XX   6109, 6116, 6118, 6134, 6166

0-6-0T
57XX   3622, 3709, 3721, 4649, 5735, 5744, 5752, 5783, 7710
15XX   1502
94XX   9413, 9417

JANUARY 1954

4-6-0
Hall	4935 *Ketley Hall*	4945 *Milligan Hall*	
	4994 *Downton Hall*	5903 *Keele Hall*	
	5935 *Norton Hall*	6910 *Gossington Hall*	
	6952 *Kimberley Hall*	6983 *Otterington Hall*	

2-8-0
28XX   2819, 3837, 3845

2-6-0
43XX   5380, 5397, 6313, 6329, 6340

0-6-0
2251   2240, 2252, 2289, 3210, 3211, 3212
2301   2532

2-6-2T
61XX   6166

0-6-2T
56XX   5626, 5639, 5697, 6654

0-6-0T
57XX   3622, 3653, 3709, 3721, 4649, 5735, 5744, 5752, 5783, 7710
15XX   1502
94XX   8435, 9413, 9417

JANUARY 1955					JANUARY 1956			
4-6-0					**4-6-0**			
Hall	4935	*Ketley Hall*	4945	*Milligan Hall*	Hall	4933	*Himley Hall*	4935	*Ketley Hall*
	4954	*Plaish Hall*	4994	*Downton Hall*		4945	*Milligan Hall*	4954	*Plaish Hall*
	5935	*Norton Hall*	6910	*Gossington Hall*		4979	*Wootton Hall*	4994	*Downton Hall*
	6952	*Kimberley Hall*	6983	*Otterington Hall*		5935	*Norton Hall*	6910	*Gossington Hall*
						6952	*Kimberley Hall*	6983	*Otterington Hall*

2-8-0		
28XX	3837, 3845	
2-6-0		
43XX	5380, 5397, 6304, 6313, 6340	
0-6-0		
2251	2214, 2221, 2240, 2252, 3206, 3210, 3211, 3212	
0-6-2T		
56XX	5629, 5639, 5697, 6630	
0-6-0T		
57XX	3622, 3653, 3709, 3721, 4649, 5735, 5744, 5752, 5783, 7710	
15XX	1502	
94XX	8435, 9413, 9417	

2-6-0		
43XX	5330, 5380, 5397, 6304, 6313, 6340	
0-6-0		
2251	2214, 2221, 2240, 2252, 3206, 3210, 3211, 3212	
0-6-2T		
56XX	5629, 5639, 5675, 5697	
0-6-0T		
57XX	3622, 3653, 3709, 3721, 3751, 4649, 5735, 5744, 5752, 5783, 7710	
15XX	1502	
94XX	8435, 9407, 9409	

Details kindly supplied by John Copsey

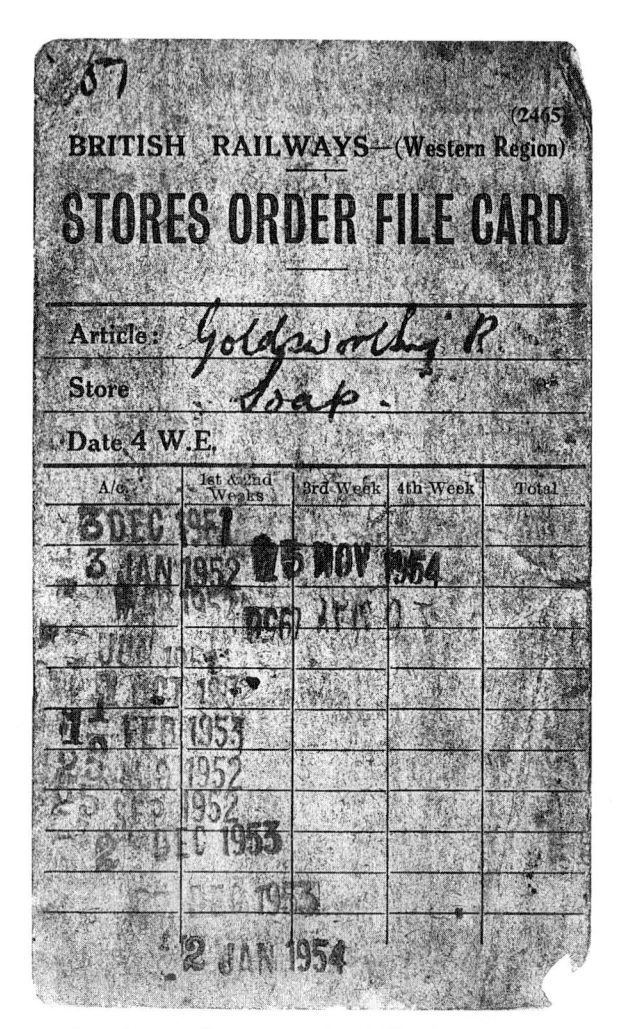

Footplate work was an unavoidably dirty job, and although the railway didn't provide baths or showers, we were eventually (in the 1940s) issued with Swarfega Soft Soap ladled onto a sheet of brown paper. We used to take old cocoa tins to collect it from the stores. This stores order card belonged to one of my colleagues, Bob Goldsworthy.

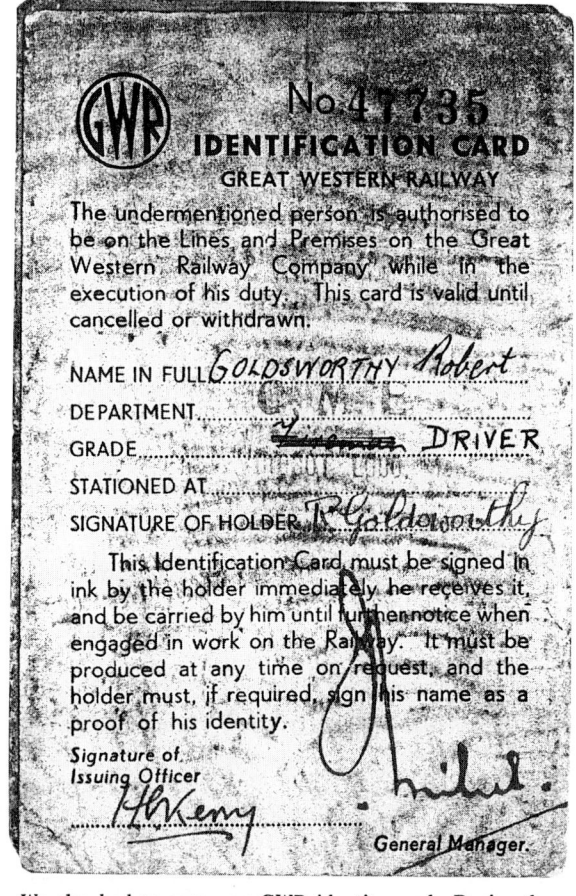

We also had to carry our GWR identity cards. During the war we were continually reminded of the possibility of sabotage, spies, etc.

This group, taken at Moreton yard, shows from left to right (seated) ?, Ron Jones, ?, Jock Lindsey, Mervyn Houseman, Bert Webster; (standing on footboard) Bill Clarke, Bill Membury, Bob Barefoot; (standing on ground) Reg Warr and Walter Rowe.

Johnny Beale.

Bert Webster, Reg Warr and Bill Membury.

The back of Moreton Cutting box, with the newer brickwork of the wartime extension at the far end.

Signalman Alec Membury at Moreton Cutting Signal Box.

Photos courtesy of Reg Warr and Bill Membury.

Signalman Pat Ware at Didcot West End box.   Jack Drew in Didcot East Junction box.

ACKNOWLEDGEMENTS

After reading a few other reminiscences, I was left with the feeling that I would like to be able to convey something of the life I experienced as a Didcot engineman, but I lacked the confidence and was too inhibited to attempt anything so ambitious myself. I never thought I'd do anything about it until I met Vanadia Humpnries who was researching an article on my uncle, a woodman and hurdle maker at Little Wittenham. After mentioning my thoughts, she insisted I should at least make rough notes in an exercise book, and that is how it all started.

Having made a start, my publisher, Paul Karau, spent many hours with me coaxing all sorts of information from the deepest corners of my memory, inspiring and stretching me to produce a detailed account well beyond my expectations.

Whenever I was uncertain of something, my colleagues came up with the answers and when we finally got the manuscript together, John Copsey kindly checked what timings he could against official service timetables. I would particularly like to thank Sam Essex for his time and support, and all of the following: Michael Baker, the late H. L. Boston, British Rail Archives, Hilda Brown, Teddy Brown, A. R. Carpenter, R. M. Casserley, C. R. L. Coles, Mrs. Fernley Dodd, Dai Evans, Donald Farmborough, the late Jim Gardner, T. J. Harvey, Mrs. Ken Haycroft, James Hewett, Philip Hopkins, Mervyn Johns, Brian Lingham, Joe Membury, Richard Miles, Mrs. W. Miles, Dennis Peedle, R. C. Riley, R. F. Roberts, Phillip Smart, A. E. Smith, Peter Swift, Chris Turner, the late Patrick Ware, Barry Warr, Reginald Warr, Mrs. W. Warr, Edward Watts, Johnny Weston, Brian Wright, J. H. Venn, and many of my railway colleagues who joined discussions, triggering off thoughts that helped to stimulate my recall and complete this book.